W9-ARF-293

THE SCHOOLHOUSE IN THE CITY

The Schoolhouse in the City

Edited and with an Introduction by

ALVIN TOFFLER

Published in cooperation with
Educational Facilities Laboratories by

FREDERICK A. PRAEGER, *Publishers*
New York · Washington · London

FREDERICK A. PRAEGER, *Publishers*
111 Fourth Avenue, New York, N.Y. 10003, U.S.A.
5, Cromwell Place, London S.W.7, England

Published in the United States of America in 1968
by Frederick A. Praeger, Inc., Publishers

Library of Congress Catalog Card Number: 68-23358

Printed in the United States of America

Foreword

Conferences sometimes produce new ideas. More often, they generate new applications of established ideas. At the very least, a well-planned conference concentrates some of the best expertise that can be brought to bear on a problem. Even when it does, however, that expertise seldom reaches a very wide public. This book is designed to insure that at least one conference will have broader than usual impact.

The conference held at Stanford University, July 10–14, 1967, had as its objective the development of a new approach to the problem of urban decay in America. It had its origins at the School Planning Laboratory of Stanford's School of Education. The Laboratory's staff, which doubles in brass as the Western Regional Center of Educational Facilities Laboratories (EFL), believed that the most pressing problems both in education and in schoolhouse planning were to be found in the central cities. The schoolhouse, in fact, appeared to have become a focal point in the battle to reverse the process of decay in the cities.

The Laboratory turned to EFL, a Ford Foundation offspring devoted to helping the schools and colleges with their physical problems, for assistance in planning and financing a nationally significant meeting on "The Schoolhouse in the City." EFL assigned James J. Morisseau, Editorial Associate, to help in the planning effort and agreed to help underwrite conference expenses.

At about the same time, the newly formed Office of Construction Services of the United States Office of Education learned of the conference plans and offered its support. Among other things, the federal assistance made possible the design and construction of an exhibit of imaginative urban school designs. The exhibit had its debut at the Stanford conference, is now touring major American cities, and is reflected in the illustrations employed in this book.

Recruited to speak at the conference were leading authorities in local, state, and federal government, civil rights, sociology, psychology, and urban planning, as well as education and architecture. The speakers analyzed the social, political, economic, physical, and educational problems facing the cities; offered solutions to these problems; traced developments in three cities, in case-study fashion; and projected the possible future of the schoolhouse in the city.

Much of this volume, which also is sponsored by Educational Facilities Laboratories, is freely adapted from the transcripts of that meeting, although it was not possible to include the contributions of every speaker. The conference had the benefit of highly valuable presentations from thirty-nine speakers. But because of the somewhat different objectives of the conference and of this book and because conferences do not easily translate into books, the contributions of only seventeen speakers appear in these pages. On the other hand, a number of contributions not offered at the conference but pertinent to a discussion of this topic have been added to the text. (A full list of conference speakers and of other contributors appears on pages 253–255.)

It is worth noting at the outset, therefore, that the title of this book refers not to the school but to the schoolhouse. This emphasis helps explain what is *not* in these pages. Thus, this book does not contain detailed proposals for curriculum reform, although it strongly implies the need for such changes. It does not evaluate the latest technological innovations in education or the latest advances in learning theory or pedagogical methods. A large and rapidly growing literature is properly devoted to these matters. The focus of this book is different. It emphasizes not merely the social ties between school and city and the need for administrative overhaul but also physical facilities and their impact on educational programs, a factor the public seldom takes into account.

It is hoped that the resultant book will help the cities, their governments, their educators, planners, architects, and citizens to come to grips with one of their most urgent problems and one of their most promising opportunities. The case, as stated in an earlier EFL report of the same name, is this: "The schoolhouse in the city cannot by itself become the dominant element in urban social planning. But the schools, as reflected by the buildings in which they operate, can be a magnet to hold or attract those who have the choice. Or, they can speed the exodus and compound the urban social issues with which the nation is grappling."

—Educational Facilities Laboratories

Contents

A sixteen-page section of illustrations follows page 88.

THE SCHOOLHOUSE IN THE CITY

Introduction

by Alvin Toffler

Alvin Toffler, former associate editor of *Fortune*, is an author, lecturer, and consultant. His book, *The Culture Consumers*, aroused wide controversy and became a Literary Guild Selection. He has contributed to such publications as the *Annals of the Academy of Political and Social Science*, *Horizon*, and *Life*. His new book, *Future Shock*, about the psychological and educational implications of high-speed social change, is in preparation. A member of the faculty of the New School for Social Research, he has served as a consultant to the Rockefeller Brothers Fund and to various corporations and educational institutions.

Night after night, in a thousand American cities and towns, television viewers flick on the tube and see idyllic scenes of the countryside. Cigarette commercials depict smokers puffing away in verdant glens, in waterfall grottoes, or out there in "Marlboro country." Airline commercials promise to sweep us away from our urban environment into a dream world of clean beaches, palm trees, or ski slopes. Nor are the dreams of our anti-establishment youth much different from those of our ad men. Hippies and avant garde artists will no doubt bridle at the comparison, but their films, newspapers, literary magazines, and paintings are filled with much the same pastoral imagery that the Madison Avenue men employ. We live in cities, but we dream of escape.

It is easy to explain this away by cataloguing the ills of the contemporary city. Yet it is worth remembering that Americans mistrusted the city long before air pollution was invented or garbage men went on strike. Morton and Lucia White, in their admirable study *The Intellectual Versus the City*, state that "enthusiasm for the American city has not been typical or predominant to our intellectual history." Indeed, they show how, from Jefferson to Thoreau, from Melville to Henry James, American writers, artists, and philosophers have produced a continuing barrage of subtle anti-urban propaganda.

Even John Dewey, in so many ways a spokesman for the urban

age, wrote nostalgically about the time when large families lived and worked together in rural households. A childhood spent under such circumstances, Dewey declared, provided a child with "continual training of observation, of ingenuity, constructive imagination, of logical thought, and of the sense of reality acquired through first-hand contact with actualities."

Today, at last, the anti-urban streak in our culture is being countered by a rising affirmation of the city. The urban crisis cannot be denied. The ghetto riots—or rebellions, as some would call them—are merely the ugliest and most dangerous symptom of the pathology of the city. Paralyzing transit strikes, power failures, pollution, crime, and violence in the streets only begin the list of urban ills. Yet even as these troubles multiply, more and more Americans are coming to the long-overdue conclusion that the city is too precious to lose, that it must be saved.

The city is nothing less than the most complex, versatile, and powerful tool ever devised by man. The rate of technological change today is so swift that all our tools, whether social, mechanical, or conceptual, must be either sharpened or discarded. Thus, that supertool we call the city is undergoing transformation. Its component subsystems, and especially those having to do with education, are creaking and groaning with change. What needs to be recognized is that all this wracking change in the structure and composition of our urban centers is only part of a much larger phenomenon—the transition of our entire society from industrialism to a new stage of eco-technological development. This new stage, which might properly be called "superindustrialism," brings with it entirely new imperatives. Among these is the demand for a more highly educated population.

It is in this context that the problems of the city and its schools must be seen.

Thus, the voices that speak to us from these pages are partisans of urban life. Robert C. Wood, Under Secretary of Housing and Urban Development, has said: "The need is to develop a metropolitan conscience which demands something more than a rural shopkeeper's values." The contributions in this volume are an answer to this call. Oriented toward the future, rather than the past, they speak for an end to that moral lesion called racism. They speak for the improvement of education for all children. They speak for great cities in which great schools contribute to a thoroughly humane and cosmopolitan civilization.

They do not always agree with one another. Kenneth Clark, for example, contends that our urban public schools are doing so poor a job that they must be energized by outside competition. Why, he asks, should we not have schools run by corporations, trade unions, even military agencies? John Fischer challenges this view, demanding evidence that nonpublic schools have done—or would do—a better job. Similarly, while Mario Fantini and Richard Magat present the case for school decentralization, Bayard Rustin questions the wisdom of this policy. Some of the contributors take it for a fact that our present urban school systems are doomed to fail. Robert Havighurst attacks irresponsible critics who demand too much of the schools.

Yet, a single common premise transcends these differences, for all of the writers view the school as a crucial weapon in the battle to reconstruct city life. They all insist that the school be seen as part of a larger context, and that educational policies be linked to broader social policies. Moreover, the contributors are unified by a proud refusal to despair. For, while the urgency of crisis pervades their comments, they offer constructive proposals rather than simple rhetorical denunciations. Indeed, few books on the city and its schools are so filled with stimulating ideas for action. Not all of these ideas are necessarily practical; not all of them are universally applicable. Nevertheless, many are. And if the book suggests a single fresh idea to partisans of the city or of public education, if it helps create the sense of urgency that is a prerequisite to effective action, it will have served a more than useful purpose.

For we can no longer afford the luxury of sentimentalizing the past. If our society is to complete the transition to superindustrialism, the city must become a place in which each of our children, of whatever ethnic or economic background, is offered precisely what John Dewey thought important: "continual training of observation, of ingenuity, constructive imagination, of logical thought, and of the sense of reality acquired through first-hand contact with actualities."

PART I

THE CITY

We begin with the context: the city. We used to believe that a school was a self-contained system, a walled enclave set apart from the outside world. In this protected environment, young minds would be formed without distraction. Knowledge, certain and unchanging, could be transmitted. Rationality and humane values could be inculcated. Men outside might invent new engines of technology. They might create empires, enslave whole populations, or fight bloody and pointless wars. For the most part, however, the educator regarded all this as transient and unimportant. What were important were the eternal and universal verities.

Today this model of the school is simply no longer tenable. Knowledge itself is changing at an accelerating pace. We are faced with evidence that few, if any, verities are either eternal or universal. And powerful outside forces are working on the minds of our children long before they arrive at the schoolhouse door. The decline of the extended family, the rising pervasiveness of the mass media, the collapse of traditional authority—all these have not so much torn down the walls of the enclave as rendered them porous. The walls are simply no longer relevant. It is no longer possible to keep the outside world at bay. In fact, the attempt to do so is now destructive of the very purposes of education itself.

Thus, Commissioner of Education Harold Howe describes the breakdown of the boundaries between school and city, the new ways in which they interpenetrate. And Bayard Rustin, a major figure in the movement for civil rights, carries the argument one step further: The school must now be seen not merely as part of a city, but of a nation. Unless that nation can come to terms with race—its most bitter and seemingly intractable domestic problem—the schools themselves will shake under the impact of violence and hate.

It is at this point that the other contributors in this section pick up the story, describing some of the demographic, financial, political, and social changes that are now remaking our cities. Probing behind the generalities, Brain, Havighurst, and Graves provide a detailed, data-filled picture of the present state of urban affairs. Brubaker then extends this picture into the future, by projecting some of the ways in which cities may change—and our schools with them.

1. The City as Teacher

by Harold Howe II

As U.S. Commissioner of Education, Harold Howe II directs a federal agency with an annual budget of $4 billion and responsibility for approximately eighty programs concerned with American education from preschool to postdoctoral. He has been a classroom teacher, a principal, a superintendent, and the director of the Learning Institute of North Carolina, a nonprofit organization set up to encourage research into the problems of education, especially those related to poverty. He has served as a trustee of the College Entrance Examination Board, chairman of the Mayor's Committee on Juvenile Delinquency in Cincinnati, and member of the Commission on the Humanities of the American Council of Learned Societies. He is a trustee of Yale and a former trustee of Vassar. This chapter is adapted from remarks made by Commissioner Howe before the "Schoolhouse in the City" conference and from addresses made to other groups.

The city is a teacher, Plutarch said, and everyone who has lived in a city knows why. Within its few square miles of glass, steel, and concrete are concentrated the greatest works of commerce, art, government, and entertainment. Its boundaries—particularly in the case of the American city, with its roots in a hundred different nations—encircle the cultures of an astonishing variety of national, religious, and ethnic groups.

Each of these facets of a city offers its own lesson. But the kind of lesson you learn depends on where you sit in the classroom.

To some, the metropolis represents excitement, a sense of being where the action is. For others—our ghetto millions—the city is a prison. The bars of this prison must be removed. For until they are, the nation's urban schools, once its pride, will continue to disintegrate, with grievous costs for the entire society—costs we simply cannot afford.

Before we probe some of the issues confronting our city schools today, it is necessary to grasp the simple, but often overlooked, fact that the problems of the schools cannot be separated from those of the city. We cannot have good schools in bad cities. And we cannot have good cities unless we have good schools. Any attempts to improve the schools solely from within—no matter how well intentioned these efforts may be—are doomed to failure. For the problems of the schools are intricately connected with larger economic and political questions, with such seemingly "noneducational" matters as land-use policies, taxation formulas, metropolitan government, and racial segregation.

The problems of the city's schools, therefore, must be seen in a larger context. The central fact is that both our cities and their schools are saddled with disproportionate responsibilities for what are really state and national problems. At the same time, the power of the cities and their schools to solve these problems—or even ameliorate the underlying conditions—has decreased. The sources of these opposing pressures—escalating responsibilities and decreasing power to act—are to be found in a crushing combination of circumstances.

The most publicized of these has been the spread of urbanization in the country, meaning that a higher proportion of Americans now live in metropolitan areas than ever before. However, it is not the simple growth of urban population that is to blame for our difficulties. Rather, it is the striking shift of populations that has played havoc with our cities.

Chicago offers a good illustration. Between 1940 and 1965, the Chicago *metropolitan* area's population increased about 44 per cent, from 4.5 million to 6.5 million. Only 3 per cent of that growth, however, occurred *within the city limits*. Normally, a major city would have little difficulty accommodating 3 per cent population growth over a 25-year period. But in that same period, within the city limits, Chicago's white population declined by 600,000, while its Negro population increased by nearly 700,000. Indeed, Chicago now has within it more Mississippi Negroes than Mississippi does. But because of racial discrimination in employment, in education, in housing, or in other fields, a high proportion of Negro families are also poor families. What this has meant for Chicago is simple and devastating: Money and education have moved out of the city, while poverty and ignorance have moved in.

Such massive shifts have placed great strains on all the city's services—not only its schools but its welfare agencies, its recreation department, its police, fire, health, and employment systems. And Chicago's experience has been duplicated, to greater or lesser extent, in every major American city.

The facts of urban blight, of large racially isolated minorities, angry ghettos, inadequate services—all these are by now drearily familiar. Depressing as the statistics may be, however, they compel us to take a fresh look at the relationship of the city to its people, and especially its schools. They force us to examine that shabby symbol of our time, the ghetto school.

What are some of the characteristics of the ghetto school? Why is it failing in its mission to create free, responsible, capable adults out of children who have the normal statistical potential for brilliance, mediocrity, or failure?

To begin with, the ghetto school is underfinanced in comparison to schools serving suburbs and even in comparison to those schools serving the more fortunate people of the city. This shortchanging of schools for poor people has several causes. Most important is the fact that it costs more per child to give the educationally deprived pupil a chance to develop his full potential. The school must have added resources to make up for the lack of advantages at home and in the neighborhood. Until the federal government started in late 1965 to provide additional funds for this purpose, ghetto children were getting little of the special attention they require. They are still not getting enough of it.

The children who attend ghetto schools walk in the door suffering from handicaps that do not hinder their counterparts in suburban schools. They typically come from homes that do not send them to first grade with the same readiness for success in reading as their counterparts in the suburbs. Although many of them share the universal culture provided by television, there is more than a little question of its value, in both content and stimulation.

The educator's jargon for these children is "disadvantaged." The term means that they will make a slower start than children from middle-class homes and that they will not run as fast. It implies that they will, in all likelihood, not pursue their educational journey as far, unless they receive special help. In some cases the designation of "disadvantaged" may be in itself a further handicap to a child—for it may subtly suggest to the teacher or the principal that, since such a child has good reason for not succeeding, the school should expect and require less of him than of other children.

Further, the ghetto schools usually have the least experienced teachers. The reason for this situation is not necessarily planned discrimination by the school board. Often it is simply understandable human preference. As a teacher gains tenure through years of service, he frequently gains the right to ask for another assignment. And it is entirely to be expected that a teacher with this choice would want to serve in the more attractive neighborhoods. Hence, year after year, the ghetto schools must replace vacancies on their staffs with brand-new graduates from the schools of education. It is fortunate indeed that a hard core of able, experienced teachers have made these schools their life work. We need more of them.

One of the conclusions that looms up inescapably from such facts is that urban education today must break with the sort of education American schools have traditionally offered. We have come to understand the impact of a deprived home environment on scholastic achievement. We have come to understand something that educators have been telling us for years—that the home does much more educating, for better or worse, than the school can do in six hours a day, five days a week—with three months off for a vacation spent in the summer school of the streets.

Traditionally, American schools evolved from white, middle-class, Anglo-Saxon Protestant ideas about what ought to be taught and about what children should want to learn. These ideas work reasonably well when the lessons of the school are reinforced by the lessons of the home. But because these ideas and the assumptions on which they are based are so alien to the lives of the millions of disadvantaged urban children who fill our city schools today, there is a vast psychological distance between the clientele of today's urban schools, the students and their parents, and the suppliers of education—teachers, administrators, and school board members.

This psychological gap manifests itself in a number of ways. One is in the high dropout rate, stemming in large part from the inability of many students to see any connection between their studies and their lives. The most dramatic effect of this psychological distance, however, is the violence we have come to fear and expect in our cities. I suspect that much of this violence really amounts to a ghetto version of a PTA meeting. Poorly educated parents and poorly educated teenagers who do not know how to reach a city hierarchy, which is separated from them by a host of cultural differences, seize the only means of communication readily available. Riots are an expensive way to talk, but white people are finally listening after decades of ignoring the quieter voices from the ghetto. Officials in city hall and in the board of education offices are now seeking to respond to needs that have been pointed out so forcibly that they cannot be ignored. There is a new understanding that the squalor and ineffectiveness of slum schools hurt everyone, not just ghetto-dwellers.

Those who are ready to act, however, face a set of powerful obstacles—a major one being money. To grasp the crisis in our urban schools, we need to understand the elementary economics of education today. The key lesson is that it takes more money to run good schools than poor ones, that education costs more in the city than in the suburbs, and that the cities, by and large, lack the money needed to improve their schools. Pressed to supply a wide variety of services at costs far higher than those in suburban communities, they have less money left for education.

An Office of Education Cooperative Research project in 1967 showed that the cities spent an average of 65 per cent of their local tax dollars on nonschool services, leaving only 35 per cent for education. In the nonmetropolitan areas, these percentages were reversed. The suburban areas had 65 per cent of their funds available for the schools.

For many cities, the contrast is even more dramatic. To give a few examples: In the State of Pennsylvania, communities outside the metropolitan areas spend only 22 per cent of local tax funds on nonschool items. The city of Philadelphia spends 58 per cent. In San Francisco, 71 per cent of local tax funds are required for nonschool items, while the state-wide figure is 49 per cent. The figure for New York State is also 49 per cent—but the city of Buffalo spends 76 per cent on nonschool items.

Concurrently, while the demands on the city's services and revenues have been increasing, its tax base has been decreasing, as one corporation after another has heeded the siren song of handsome new industrial parks developed in the suburbs.

In Baltimore, for example, the number of tax dollars behind each pupil dropped 19.3 per cent during the last five years while the property value per pupil in Maryland's suburbs and rural areas increased by more than 10 per cent. In Cleveland, the same comparison shows a 10 per cent drop in the dollars behind each pupil for the city while the suburbs and rural areas increased by almost 5 per cent.

Thus the proportionate amount of money available to the city schools has been decreasing at the very time that the need for money has been increasing and as educational problems have become more intense.

Analyzing public expenditures in thirty-five metropolitan areas for 1964–65, Dr. Seymour Sacks of Syracuse University found that the central cities, on the average, spent $50 more for every citizen than the corresponding suburban areas. Despite this higher over-all expenditure, however, these same cities spent about $50 *less* per citizen on education.

The gap between what the cities need for education and what they can spend on it stems from what social scientists refer to as "municipal overburden." In essence, this term refers to the high costs of public services in the city as compared to other areas—services such as police and fire protection, sanitation, traffic control, street maintenance, and welfare. It costs the city more than the suburb to provide these services because of the complexity of the city itself, and because the city has large concentrations of poor people who make special demands. In addition, some services are needed for commuters, who do not pay their share. Though some cities assess taxes on commuter income and on retail sales, such arrangements make problems for the city in its attempts to hold business and provide employment opportunities.

Dr. Sacks's analyses indicate that the price of "municipal overburden" has increased from about $53 for each city resident in 1957 to more than $100 in 1965. Summing up the fiscal dilemma imposed on our cities by suburban sprawl and our new patterns of living in one place, working in another, a report published not long ago in *Nation's Cities* concluded:

> No city government collects anywhere near enough money of its own to take on the whole job of coping with all the problems that confront it. One reason . . . is that few states let the cities collect enough taxes, even if they want to. The second reason is that few cities like to collect any more taxes than they have to; they would rather get grants-in-aid from the states or from Washington. The third reason is that most cities are afraid to raise taxes for fear of speeding the exodus of industry. The fourth reason is that the cities' only exclusive revenue source is the property tax, and most states make their cities collect most of their property taxes, not on land (which is undertaxed) but on improvements (which are already so overtaxed that the tax inhibits even some of the most needed improvements). The fifth (and perhaps the biggest) reason is that in this country, local government is stuck with enormous costs that in other countries are paid as a matter of course by the central government, so, paradoxically, the local tax burden in most cities is too high even though the tax take is too low.

In brief, municipal finance—whether for education or for other purposes—is in something of a mess. Complicating the fact that cities do not have enough tax money to distribute, and must in consequence shortchange their schools, is the additional fact that big-city schools are more expensive to build and operate. Land and construction costs are higher. Because so many of their schools are in poor and therefore uninviting neighborhoods, cities must pay higher salaries to attract new teachers and hold experienced ones. Furthermore, because such a high proportion of city children come from culturally and economically deprived backgrounds, educating them properly requires a host of special supplemental services that the city cannot afford.

The plight of the city does not arise just from unplanned development, subsidized ugliness, and other policies that have helped drive the middle-income family away. The cities have also eroded their financial base through poor land use, blanketing some of the most desirable real estate in the United States—land close to the city center—with slum buildings and tracts reserved for automobiles. Fully 50 per cent of the Los Angeles downtown area is monopolized by streets and parking lots; in Atlanta, 54 per cent; in Boston, 40 per cent; and in Denver, 44 per cent.

In short, the cities—especially the older ones, which are prohibited from further expansion by suburban boundaries—have in the past wasted the most valuable financial resource they have: their land. By making better use of it, they not only could make the city a more attractive place in which to live but could generate the extra tax revenues needed to provide first-rate education for all their citizens.

Better use of the land also suggests the feasibility of a new partnership between the cities and private business. Not even the combination of local, state, and federal governments can provide the huge sums needed to renovate all of our cities and improve city education. But the cities themselves could do a major share of the job if they harnessed the profit motive to their own goals and matched it with the significant support available from federal sources.

The financing of urban schools thus turns out to be dependent, at least in part, upon the solution of the larger financial crisis of our cities. Urban schools will not be adequately financed until we manage to lift some of the immense economic pressures under which cities are forced to operate.

Cities will have to convince their state legislatures to allow them to shift the present structure of property taxes from the value of *buildings* to the value of *land*.

To make this distinction clear, I would ask you to imagine two buildings: one a new, thirty-story office or apartment building, and the other a fifty-year-old, three-story tenement. Both can occupy precisely the same amount of land. Moreover, as anyone familiar with the central portions of any of our major cities knows, structures of both kinds are often within easy walking distance of each other. You can find obsolete, substandard housing within a few blocks of the United Nations building in New York, within a few blocks of the Capitol in Washington, and within a few blocks of Marina City in Chicago.

Thus, shabby tenements for the poor and exclusive high-rises for the affluent frequently are built on sites that offer the same advantages—proximity to major shopping, cultural, and financial centers;

proximity to diverse means of transportation fanning out from the central city in all directions; and, often, proximity to some attractive, natural feature such as a lake or river that drew people to settle the area in the first place. The land beneath both tenements and high-rises, in sum, has the same "site-value."

As presently constituted, however, property taxes neglect this site-value almost to the point of ignoring it. Cities tax an expensive high-rise heavily, but tax a rundown tenement lightly—even though both occupy tracts that are equally desirable from the standpoint of convenience and desirability.

In essence, this approach considers the value of the building to its owner, not to the city, and confuses property taxes with income taxes. Its result is to discourage the improvement of valuable land close to the center of the city.

It is more profitable for a slum landlord to let his aging tenement sit and decay, while he pays low taxes on the building and the site, than for him to develop the site or sell it to a private builder who will. The city pays in several ways: through the loss of the tax revenue that good housing or commercial construction on that site would bring; through the loss of middle-income families who might both live and work there; and finally, through the excessive prices cities must pay for underassessed slum land to convert it to better use. To quote from the report of a conference of thirty-three urban experts published in the April, 1967, issue of *Nation's Cities*, "Nearly a third of all the people of Manhattan still live in railroad flats that were banned before 1900, and these slums are so underassessed and undertaxed that it has cost an average of $486,000 an acre to buy them up for demolition!"

I do not mean to suggest that the cities should immediately increase taxes on close-in slum dwellings. Such an action would force the eviction of the poor. Faulty public policy operating over a period of decades has built the city slum, and the mischief cannot be undone overnight. My point, rather, is that the present structure of property taxes has fostered the urban ghettos and at the same time discouraged sound development; it has made slums good business, and it has made city renewal bad business. Thus the cities have added to their problems while undermining their own ability to deal with those problems. Tax revision holds the promise of bringing to the city the capacity to meet its problems of health, education, and welfare more adequately and of providing some funds to be added to those from the federal government in order to subsidize housing for the poor. The power to tax may indeed be the power to destroy, but I would argue that it is also the power to build. The cities' inability to wield that power intelligently is forcing them to destroy themselves.

Shifting the basis of property taxes, however difficult it may prove to be, is only one of the things that must be done. Another requires a complete reorientation on the part of state legislatures with respect to education. For present state formulas for aid to the schools—adopted in another era and adapted to other circumstances—are in effect deliberately designed to shortchange the cities.

In the words of Drs. Alan Campbell of Syracuse University and Phillip Meranto of Southern Illinois, "the state-aid system actually works to intensify rather than to resolve the educational crises facing large city school systems."

This is true because our present state-aid systems were designed to cure the problems of the past, rather than those of the present and future. Thus, from the geographical point of view, our fiscal problems in education today are almost exactly the opposite of the pattern of seventy years ago. Writing at about the turn of the century, social historian Ellwood Cubberley pointed out that city schools at that time were in much better shape than their nonurban counterparts.

> In two-thirds of the States of the Union no adequate provision is made for the maintenance of the smaller schools of the state, and usually these are maintained in a most unsatisfactory manner and at a sacrifice entirely out of proportion to the local benefits received. On the other hand, the cities with their aggregations of people and wealth are able to maintain excellent school systems on a relatively small expenditure. . . . There is little excuse for a system of state taxation for education if the income from such taxation is to be distributed in a larger proportion of the communities best able to care for themselves.

At the turn of the century, the cities were able to "care for themselves," while the suburbs and countryside needed help. Yet today, seven decades later, the formulas for the distribution of state aid still discriminate against the large money-starved cities at a time when it is painfully clear they cannot "care for themselves" any longer. Indeed, there is evidence to show that today, state-aid formulas *increase* the gap between superior suburban schools and their underfinanced urban counterparts. In one of his studies on school financing, using figures that apply to the year 1962, Dr. Sacks states:

> Clearly, suburban school systems benefit increasingly more from the present system of state aid to education than do central cities, both because they have a higher enrollment ratio and a greater average grant per pupil. On a per-student basis, the cities average $124.91 in aid from their state, while the suburbs get $165.48, a difference of $40.57 for every student. Because of the difference in enrollment ratio, the relative difference is considerably larger on a per-capita basis than on a per-pupil basis. The mean per-capita aid for education is $20.72 while the comparable figure for outside central city areas is $37.66, a difference of $16.94 per capita.

Another way of stating Dr. Sacks's observation is to say that, in 1962, each suburban school child in the United States had one-third more money from the state invested in his education than his fellow student in the city. This imbalance of support continues today, although it is important to note that some states have made significant moves to change it. Among these are Massachusetts, Pennsylvania, and Iowa.

I have risked the reader's impatience by citing all these figures because it seems to me that although the press and other media of public debate have called attention to the urban problem, the precise dimensions and anatomy of that problem have only infrequently been examined. If we are ever to have fine city schools drawing strength from the cities themselves, rather than from desperate experiments and crash programs financed by foundations and the federal government, we must restore to cities the financial and political power to solve the problems thrust upon them.

What, then, of the schools themselves? Must we wait until cities have ironed out all their other problems before attacking the problem of the slum school? Obviously not. There is much that can be done, if we bring imagination and will to the problem, if we bring parents, educators, and public officials together behind a campaign to improve all our schools, beginning with those in the ghetto but extending to every school in every city in the nation.

Let us see what each individual and each city can do.

First, we must recognize that the ghetto school needs not just as much financial support as the suburban school, but much more. We must realize that it must provide special services that have sometimes been considered educational "frills"—services such as counseling and guidance, small classes, remedial instruction, the latest teaching methods and equipment, and psychological, medical, and dental aid. This is not a matter of coddling slum children; it is facing the reality that the job cannot be done otherwise.

Second, we vitally need a new approach to involving the parent in his child's life as a student and in the school itself. Too often, school, to the ghetto resident, is a hostile fortress of white authority. Too often, the parent has little faith in either the school or the learning process. And too often, the parent does not understand his necessary role as a counselor, as a reader of stories, or simply as a person interested in his child's school life.

We need to give parents a part in school planning, school decisions, and school operations, involving those parents in their children's progress in the classroom. For school boards, principals, and teachers, such involvement must go far beyond an occasional PTA meeting or the once-a-year school open house. It means permanently established programs in which parents become a part of the formal school structure, as aides and as participants in the decision-making process.

Third, new kinds of school district organization might be developed, in which some or all school district functions are decentralized. Metropolitan school boards that establish subdistricts within their system might very well find that they have gained a better handle on policy, for the larger a district, the more likely it is that policy decisions are made by administrators.

School boards might also look to several kinds of subcontractors when considering the development of such subsystems—educational corporations, foundations, universities, local community groups, and perhaps others. In the beginning of any such arrangement, some contractors would probably do well, some might do badly. In either event, decentralization could bring to school administration the opportunity to try different patterns of school organization and different systems of learning—and to compare the results. At least equally important, it could be an effective mechanism for involving parents in the conduct of the schools.

Fourth, we must create the opportunity for effective performance by the children of the poor, and the expectation of it. Cultural disadvantage need not foreshadow poor academic achievement. Children sense a school's lower expectations and grow to demand less of themselves because the school demands so little of them. Schools are not custodial. Children are there to learn, not just to be kept off the streets.

They will learn best if they are taught by specially trained teachers. Beyond expressing our national need for more teachers of every description, we have done little to focus upon a kind of teacher preparation that is necessary to serve the children of the poor. In general, our colleges and universities train teachers for ideal classrooms, and, although some classrooms in the slums may be excellent in their buildings and equipment, their human environment cries out for special attention of every kind.

A share of the guilt for this irrelevant teacher education must be borne by the profession itself. Somehow the idea of service to those who need it most has been obscured by the drive for better teaching salaries and conditions.

Further, city school systems must adopt assignment policies that will guarantee slum schools their share of experienced, able teachers. We must counteract the tendency of experienced teachers to choose the least demanding schools as soon as their years of service entitle them to transfer. We must also change the policies of schools and teacher organizations that tend to confront the slum child with the inexperienced, uncertified, and impermanent teacher.

But, in addition to more and better teachers, slum schools also need volunteers and paid teacher's aides to supplement the work of the fully trained teacher. Added personal attention from adults really can do as much as any other service can to lift the potentialities of the children of the poor. Pupil-teacher ratios might be established at a level of twenty to one—at only slightly greater cost than the present arrangement—if we had each group of twenty attending class half a day instead of each group of thirty-five attending class all day, and if we provided opportunities for the group not in class to study, use language labs and computer instruction, and go on field trips chaperoned by volunteers and teacher-aides.

Fifth, we need to consider wholly novel organizational and other arrangements to change the basic character of the urban school. For example, consortia, such as are developing on the college level, might be developed for junior and senior high schools—perhaps even for elementary schools. All schools could have open enrollment, and students would attend several schools in a given day or week. The advantages might include a stronger curriculum, the elimination of duplication, and instant desegregation.

Space might be made available in ghetto schools for such commercial establishments as grocery stores and beauty parlors, thereby providing new services to the community, part-time job opportunities for students, and extra revenue for the school system.

Students might be offered a new set of choices, so that no student is confronted with the rigid alternatives of either being in school full time or out of school altogether. It seems to me a strange affair to require every boy and girl to be a full-time matriculating student without regard to individual needs and interests and problems—and to offer part-time programs to youngsters only when they have encountered such social disasters as pregnancy or jail or dropout. Perhaps we need to develop a range of options, both in attendance requirements and in the kinds of programs that lead to the diploma. The combinations of work and study that can be offered to high school students are infinitely variable, and most of them remain unexplored by many high schools.

We might in effect subsidize local businessmen—for example, cabinet makers, TV repairmen, printers, or cobblers—by providing rent-free space in the schools with the proviso that they conduct a class or two in their specialty each day.

In any case, we must move toward changing inner-city schools from 9-to-3-o'clock citadels, where all human life vanishes with the dismissal bell, into highly visible neighborhood resources that teach parents as well as children. The inner-city school can create community where there is no other focal point for a common life and shared interests. That would mean, among other things, staffing our ghetto schools so that they can remain open from morning to late evening, offering adult instruction in everything from reading to making the most of the shopping dollar.

We might dream, in fact, about creating not an "education park" but what might be called a "living park": a building that would integrate retail stores, banks, a medical center, restaurants, offices, and apartments; a building that would not only house and employ people but would at the same time educate their youngsters from preschool through high school.

Think what a dent we could make in big-city segregation—racial, social, and economic—if, instead of having a bus driver bring fifty children to school, their own fathers and working mothers brought them to the office. The children of bankers, dentists, secretaries, butchers, elevator operators, accountants—black and white, rich and poor, blue-collar and white-collar—all going to school in the same place.

And a school, moreover, receiving the benefits of an enlightened tax policy—a policy which would tax central city land in such a way that high-income business properties would replace low-income slums. Such a school would be part of a school system that could afford to surround the building with recreation space, sponsor a community orchestra, organize sports. It would exist in the midst of the business and cultural life of the city; while training people to participate in the one, it would enrich the lives of its students with the other. It would be open day and night to serve both children and adults.

For some reason, the popular conception of an "education park" has come to mean a massive structure similar to the schools we already have, but enrolling 10,000 or more students in order to achieve a combination of integration and efficiency. Such a school makes no sense at all, unless it provides each child with a totally new set of opportunities not found in the school he now has:

Opportunity for facilities that would be impossibly expensive to place in separate, smaller schools.

Opportunity for programs requiring highly specialized teachers not available in sufficient numbers to staff all schools.

Opportunity to take courses that attract too few students to make them practical for most medium-sized schools.

Opportunity for services in health, recreation, counseling, job placement, education of the handicapped, and other areas, most of which are neglected altogether or only partially provided in the usual school.

Opportunity for community involvement in the school and school involvement in the community, so that the student uses the school as a bridge to the city and the city becomes his classroom, with all the variety it has to offer.

Opportunity for parent use of school facilities and for the enlistment of parents in the cause of the education of their children.

Any school that achieves these objectives will reach out to the best in the city, rather than lock its doors against the worst at 3:30 in the afternoon. It will find ways within a much enlarged student body to give each youngster the feeling that he belongs and that somebody knows his name. Without being a neighborhood school in the traditional sense, it will create an atmosphere of neighborhood in the city which does not exist there now. Such a school may be 3 miles long and 300 yards wide, as has been suggested for a portion of New York City. Or it may be 60 stories high and integrated with business and dwelling facilities. It will be different in every city, because every city has a different history, a different population mix, a different relationship to its suburbs and to its state government, and different resources of money and imagination.

But whatever the form of the city school of the future, it will depend on more than the planning of educators alone. It will require educators to forge new alliances with city planners, architects, politicians and precinct captains, industrialists, chain-store operators, and all the people who make a city run.

Working relationships must be established with a range of other groups and organizations, public and private alike. This kind of intermingling of interests has advantages that go beyond economic efficiency, vital as that is. It provides new stimulation and new understanding, an opportunity to share common concerns and perhaps to arrive at some new approaches together.

A campaign to prevent dropouts, jointly designed and administered by the schools and such groups as the Urban League, the local community action agency, the PTA, and the boys' clubs, seems almost certain to reach and hold more youngsters than one conducted by the schools alone. One that used dropouts themselves in its planning and recruitment would be even more successful, even though its planners might have some difficult meetings.

To raise the level of urban education across the board will require money; but money is not enough. We will need teachers; but teachers are not enough. We will need research, and educational research is already giving us new teaching techniques, new methods of evaluating academic progress, and a host of additional aids in educating the slum child. But research is not enough.

What is enough?

Perhaps the answer to that question will emerge only when every American recognizes that educating the slum child as a way of breaking the chain of poverty is in his own immediate, direct interest. For this is one of the lessons that your city and all the cities of the United States teach: that our well-being, our safety, the very quality of our lives and those of our children are bound up with the lives of countless other men whom we will never know and may never see.

The city is indeed a teacher, and it has been teaching us that the ghetto school perpetuates a poverty, an injustice, and a weakness that daily saps all our lives.

It is time we learned our lesson and put it to use.

2. The Mind of the Black Militant

by Bayard Rustin

Bayard Rustin is executive director of the A. Philip Randolph Institute, a leading civil-rights organization. A top organizer of the 1963 march on Washington, he also led the New York school boycott of February, 1964—the largest civil-rights demonstration up to that time. In Memphis, Tennessee, he organized the march of sanitation workers following the assassination of Martin Luther King, having previously been, for seven years, a special assistant to Dr. King. Mr. Rustin has served as race relations secretary of the Fellowship of Reconciliation and as the first field secretary of the Congress of Racial Equality (CORE). A pacifist and conscientious objector, he has been arrested twenty-four times in the struggle for civil rights and is one of the movement's most eloquent strategists of nonviolence.

The problems of the school, we have been told, are intimately related to those of the city. Commissioner Howe said that we cannot have good schools if we have bad cities. I would agree with this statement, but I would carry it a step further: We cannot have good cities unless we have a good nation. And to have a good nation, we must face, once and for all, the problems of poverty and race. Only through the formulation of a national program to eliminate poverty and racial discrimination can we lay the basis for a good, let alone a great, society.

There is no longer any denying that this country is in the throes of a historic national crisis. Its implications for education are so frightening that even now the American people have not yet fully grasped what is happening to them.

The grim data are still coming in. In the summer of 1967, thirty of our cities, big and small, were wracked by racial disorder; scores of citizens, almost all of them black, were killed; thousands were injured and even more arrested. Property damage exceeded a billion dollars; total income loss is incalculable.

The greatest toll, however, is not in property damage or even in lives lost. Nor is the greatest danger that the violence will go on indefinitely, any more than the Civil War did. It is that the aftermath of that war will be repeated, that, as in the Compromise of 1877, the country will turn its back on the Negro, on the root causes of his discontent, on its own democratic future.

Why does the republic find itself at a crossroads? What is actually happening?

Several newspaper columnists and television commentators have already begun to draw comparisons between the ghetto uprisings and the French, Russian, Algerian, Irish, and Black African independence revolutions. Some Black Power advocates have proclaimed the beginnings of guerrilla warfare and see the urban Negro as a counterpart to the Viet-Cong. And, in Paris, it has become fashionable to speak of the *révolution des noires* in the United States.

The preconditions for an authentic independence revolution are completely lacking, however. American Negroes have no geographical focus for nationalist sentiment, nor do they constitute a popular majority struggling against a relatively small, white colonial group. More aptly, the situation can be described as a form of social revolution. The phrase "social revolution"—widely used by civil-rights leaders—designates fundamental changes in social and economic class relations resulting from mass political action. Such action would be democratic. That is, it would aim to create a new majority coalition capable of exercising political power in the interest of new social policies. By definition, the coalition must be interracial.

As a minority, Negroes by themselves cannot bring about such a social revolution. They can participate in it as a powerful and stimulating force or they can provoke a counterrevolution.

If, however, the comparison between Harlem and Algeria is misleading, the term "race riot" is similarly unilluminating and anachronistic.

This is not to deny the importance of antiwhite hostility. One has only to hear the sick racial epithets "honkey" and "whitey" to recognize the deep and bitter hatred that is loose on the streets of the ghettos. But if white blood was what the rioters thirsted for, they didn't go very far to get it. What they assaulted were the symbols of white power—police and property, the latter embracing the entire ghetto.

Any real effort to understand the educational meaning of these events must begin with an examination of the mentality of the black activist and the psychological factors that will inevitably face those who attempt to do anything constructive about ghetto conditions—and specifically ghetto schools. The mentality of the activist influences both those who, by their constructive, concrete behavior, are attempting to influence the schools in a positive direction and those who, by virtue of their militancy, exercise a substantial veto over anyone else who attempts to act in the community.

At the outset, it is essential to understand that Negroes are not only "exaggerated Americans," as Gunnar Myrdal said, they are also inevitably ambivalent. A good illustration of this is the total confusion surrounding my friend Stokely Carmichael, who has been accused of being a racist. I happen to disagree with Mr. Carmichael's strategy and tactics; but he is not a racist. He is *ambivalent*, and so appears to be fostering a new form of black nationalist racism.

The racist says, "No matter who you are, what you have done, what your capabilities are, what you have accomplished, you are like that and I am like this—stay away from me. I do not choose to recognize you as a man."

This is not what Stokely Carmichael says about white people. You have to know him and to know the dynamics of ambivalence to understand what he is saying. Actually, he is saying, "I recognize you for your accomplishments and for what you really are, but, knowing from experience that you are not going to recognize me, I cannot endure another injury from you. Therefore, before you have an opportunity to injure me, get the hell out of my way. I hate you. I do not want to have anything to do with you." This is protective negativism, but it is not racism.

Unless one understands that this basic negativism is an effort to be loved, one cannot understand ghetto psychology. Those who are teachers will understand this, and so will those who are mothers, because ghetto rioting can be compared, fundamentally, to a child's tantrum. The child in tantrum ought not to be slapped by his mother, for the child is simply saying, "Mother, something hurts. You do not understand me. I need to be loved. There is something wrong and I need your help." And so he kicks and screams in order to get the attention he needs.

The "tantrums" of the underprivileged are caused by a series of problems. Ghetto people, for example, feel that they have been boxed in by other people—not because they deserve it—but because other people disrespect them. Consider Harlem. With wealthy Westchester to the north, Central Park to the south, the East River on one side, and the Hudson River on the other, there is no way for the community to expand. Already overcrowded, its population continues to grow. The same is true elsewhere as well. In fact, the population of our urban ghettos is increasing by half a million each year. Within these tightly confined areas, the whites—whether they are wanted, loved, or loathed—must fight the ghetto's sense of compression.

So long as people lack mobility—economically, socially, and politically—intruders from the outside world will be regarded ambivalently. Police, teachers, and small businessmen comprise the fundamental outside groups that the Negro community depends on and, therefore, in a certain sense, likes. Resentment at being boxed in, however, turns this liking into loathing:

Resentment of the policeman—because telling a man in a box to behave is tantamount to telling him to accept his unemployment, his lack of education, and his slum housing.

Resentment of the teacher—because, no matter how great his or her contribution, the ghetto child still lags years behind in reading and mathematics.

Resentment of the white small businessman, Jewish or otherwise—because, no matter how good a man he may be, his installment selling (which makes buying possible for the poor) also means an over-all higher price.

All such resentments stem from and contribute to this "boxed-in" feeling from which the Negro in the ghetto can find no escape. The constriction, the sense of no place to go, the lack of outlet, sharpens resentment and amplifies every petty dislike into instant hate.

People in the ghetto are practical. They do not look to what is promised. They see right through what white people call "progress." Ghetto people measure progress very cunningly. They know that there are more Negro youngsters in segregated classrooms now than there were before the 1954 Supreme Court school decision.

They know that the gap between the median income of whites and that of Negroes has broadened. They know that the present proportion of unemployment among Negro males is double that among white males and, among Negro teen-agers, it is three times as high as among white teen-agers. Right now, the national Negro unemployment rate is 25 per cent. For sixteen- to nineteen-year-olds in ten areas surveyed, it is over 39 per cent, compared with 10 per cent for white teen-agers.

Nor is there any evidence that Negro teen-agers do not want to work. Whenever job programs have been announced, they have turned out in large numbers, only to find that the jobs weren't there. In Oakland, a "job fair" attracted 15,000 people; only 250 were placed. In Philadelphia, 6,000 were on a waiting list for a training program.

What Negro teen-agers are not inclined to accept are dead-end jobs that pay little and promise no advancement or training. Many would prefer to live by their wits as hustlers or petty racketeers—their version of the self-employed businessman or salesman. That their pursuit of this distorted entrepreneurial ideal only mires them deeper in the slum proletariat is not the point. They want to be part of the white-collar organization man's world that is America's future, not trapped behind brooms and pushcarts.

Ghetto people, both young and old, know the slums are still there, and that they are worse than ever, with more rats and more roaches in them. They know that even minimally decent health care is lacking. (In 1964, East and Central Harlem, comprising 24 per cent of Manhattan's population, accounted for 40 per cent of its TB deaths and 33 per cent of its infant deaths; in Bedford-Stuyvesant, which contains 9 per cent of Brooklyn's population, the respective figures were 24 and 22 per cent.)

One grows weary of citing the same hideous figures time and time again—figures showing that life in the ghetto has been getting worse rather than better in the last ten years. I will try on this occasion to bring it all home through a less familiar set of horrifying statistics.

In 1930, according to analyses made by Drs. Paul M. Vincent and James D. Haughton of the New York City Board of Health, pregnant Negro women were twice as likely to die in childbirth as pregnant white women. In 1964, the mortality rate of Negro women in childbirth was *more than three times* that of white women.

In 1940, fourteen times as many nonwhite mothers had their babies delivered by midwives as did white mothers. In 1960, the figure was *twenty-three times* as many.

In 1950, the infant mortality rate for nonwhites was 66 per cent higher than for whites, but in 1964 it was *90 per cent* higher.

Black activists know, too, that the problems in education are equally staggering, and they see still less progress in coping with them. The fact is that the educational system is no longer as capable as it once was when it comes to preparing ordinary, uneducated citizens for productive roles in society. People from Eastern Europe who came here in 1900 could, when given a minimal public education, find jobs and become part of the productive system. Today, however, people coming out of Mississippi, even though they know the language and the culture of the United States, need more than a minimal education to take their place in the advanced technological society. The present automation revolution is so pervasive and complex as to leave no room for the uneducated or the semi-skilled. A once-over-lightly education is not enough.

Technology, in short, demands a higher level of competence from both schools and people than it did a mere generation ago. Activists know this, and for that reason they recognize that ordinary measures to improve the schooling of ghetto children are not enough. This accounts for the intensity of their concern with education. This is why the schools have become a primary target of the ghetto activist.

The black militants, looking at housing, looking at employment, looking at health care, looking at education, also understand something else that many whites do not. They recognize that in the great period of civil-rights struggle, between 1955 and 1965, all efforts were directed toward the Negroes in the South—that the 1963 march on Washington, the 1964 civil-rights bill, and the 1965 civil-rights bill were all directed toward the Southern Negro. In fact, there has not been a single victory for ghetto Negroes in the past fifteen years, not a single thing they might point to that makes the ghetto look different, that means more money is coming in or that their children are being better educated. Is it surprising, then, that activists in the ghetto are thoroughly convinced our society does not intend to do away with racism and economic disadvantage?

From this conviction flow a series of corollaries. First, the Negro sees this society as one that responds only to violence. The chief lesson that young Negroes are learning today in the ghetto is: to achieve, create violence.

To illustrate their contention, they point to Mr. A. Philip Randolph, a most respected Negro, who for five years headed a committee in New York for upgrading the police in the Harlem and Bedford-Stuyvesant areas. For five years, I was secretary to that committee and nothing happened. However, two weeks after the riot in Harlem, a Negro, Lloyd Sealey, was promoted to police captain.

Or they cite the situation in Chicago, where Negroes rioted because they wanted to use the fire hydrants to keep cool. Dr. Martin Luther King had been in Chicago two years. He had won not a single concession, except a housing commitment on paper, which was subsequently not honored. But, less than 24 hours after the Negroes rioted, Mayor Daley was traipsing through the ghetto, distributing eight-dollar sprinklers and promising two new swimming pools.

Again, they mention Watts. There, a bus line had been sought for many years because there was no decent transportation system. After the rioting, the establishment rushed in talking about building a hospital and a decent transportation system. One of the young men said to me at the end of the riot, "Mr. Rustin, I don't know what you have been here for. You should go back to New York because we won, and, if you don't believe me, you go out into that street; there are so many sociologists, educators, and economists here, you will trip over them." I would certainly not have tripped over them prior to the riot.

What is happening is simple. Society, by waiting for riots to occur before responding to needs, deprives the more responsible Negro leaders of any possibility of leadership. Why should anyone join the NAACP or the Southern Christian Leadership Conference? Society has systematically taught ghetto people that the methods used by Mr. Wilkins and the late Dr. King are useless.

Reduced to violence and robbed of leadership, the Negro activist is struck by still another reality—the shift of public attention away from these problems. Instead of turning its energies toward a solution of these problems, white America has turned away. After about 1965, most intelligent Americans would have argued that civil rights represented America's most pressing problem. Today, however, attention has shifted to Vietnam. Here, again, the Negro finds himself the victim of discrimination, for the war has diverted more than attention—it has diverted resources that might have been used to eliminate the ghetto from American life.

Worse yet, the Negro activist looks at Vietnam and finds proportionally more Negro Americans there than whites. He sees society, which is unwilling or incapable of dealing with racism and unwilling or incapable of dealing with poverty, pouring its youth and its money into war. The activist concludes that this society is dirty and rotten and that it ought to be wiped from the face of the earth—a drastic conclusion, which results finally in what might be called "frustration politics."

Those who are frustrated, who feel they cannot free themselves and cannot escape from the box in which they find themselves, turn on those who visibly represent the outside world. Since teachers are, in fact, among the most visible representatives of the outside world, they often bear the brunt of the attack. Pressure tactics will not solve unemployment or eradicate slums, but they can give the local board of education and the teachers a hard time—a substitute satisfaction. It may be impossible to get at those in the Pentagon who are sending the boys to Vietnam, but it is relatively easy to strike back at those who run the schools. Thus frustration politics results in such demands as:

Get rid of all white teachers in the ghetto.
Employ only Negro principals in the ghetto.
Win the right to establish the curriculums in ghetto schools.
Take over the ghetto schools completely, and destroy all central control over urban school systems.

I do not agree with all of these demands, particularly the last, for, if control of ghetto schools can be captured by a local group of Negroes, the same sort of thing could be done by any other minority group. What would some other groups that I can think of do if they gained control of the schools? Put in a John Birch curriculum? Insist on only white principals who are Catholic or Protestant, but not Jewish? I cannot agree with this in principle.

Even if one did, however, there is an even more fundamental problem with the politics of frustration—a sense of the hopelessness of it all. Ghetto radicals see the problems of housing, schools, jobs, health, and police as so interrelated and so complex that it appears to them that *no* program is, in fact, workable.

In New York, for example, this negativism is based on the history of the local school situation over the past ten years. Every year there has been a new gimmick. First it was buses; the next year it was the Allen Plan. Now these are forgotten. The following year it was talk about education parks. Last year it was the More Effective Schools program. This year it's decentralization. Next year it will be still another gimmick. The fundamental reason educators have become involved in this gimmickry is that they do not seem to understand that unless there is a *master plan* to cover housing, jobs, and health, every plan for the schools will fall on its face. No piecemeal strategy can work.

There must be a diversion of federal funds simultaneously to schools, housing, jobs, and health. We must eradicate our worst poverty—not the poverty in Harlem or Watts, but the poverty in men's imaginations. The middle classes who think string, Scotch tape, and spit will get us out of our present dilemma must be convinced otherwise. Even compensatory education, isolated from adequate housing, decent living conditions, and good neighborhoods, is useless.

What is needed is something more far-reaching, more imaginative. We must begin by accepting the idea of a *national plan to eradicate the ghetto*. We must have national priorities and we must adjust the scale of our thinking to the scale of the problem.

The only proposal that so far comes close to achieving this is the "Freedom Budget for All Americans" proposed by A. Philip Randolph. This proposal is truly inspiring in its scope. It is more advanced than any other antipoverty and full-employment proposal. But it is also, precisely because of its scope and vision, the most practical. It not only sets priorities and timetables, it indicates how the necessary money can be made available. This budget is a carefully designed, economically feasible program for the obliteration of poverty in ten years. Signed by more than 200 leading Americans, and based on the work of prominent economists, the document recognizes that "the federal budget is the most powerful single instrument of national economic and social policy." It urges an expansion of federal spending from $104 billion in 1967 to $135 billion in 1970 and $155 billion in 1975. It shows how, without cutting back—indeed even with expanded—spending on space, technology, and international programs, it is possible to concentrate billions on housing and community development, on education, health services, and all the other desperate needs in our urban centers. Nor does the Freedom Budget merely bandy about billions without showing in detail how the productive force of the economy can be harnessed to produce these new billions. As it states, these proposals "will seem excessive only to those who do not appreciate the growing productive powers of the U.S. economy, under conditions of sustained full employment and full production."

The Freedom Budget is not dependent upon more than a continuation of present productivity trends in the society. It does not call for "socialization" of the economy—indeed, it implies virtually no change in the present division of responsibilities between private enterprise and government. Essentially, the Freedom Budget calls for the addition of $18.5 billion per year to federal domestic programs for a ten-year period. This sum—enough to wipe out the ghettos forever and to complete the eradication of poverty in the United States—is only one-thirteenth of the *increase* in economic output that we can anticipate by 1975. In short, the Freedom Budget indicates that, if we really mean it, we can end the urban crisis by allocating about 7.5 per cent of our annual economic growth for the purpose, and we can still have the other 92.5 per cent for other purposes. This is why I speak of the need for national priorities.

There is, unfortunately, no room here to describe in detail either the statistical basis or the reasoning behind the Freedom Budget.

Nor is there room to spell out its concrete proposals in the field of employment, housing, education, and urban development. Suffice it to say that this document is absolutely essential reading for anyone seriously concerned about the crisis in our cities and their schools.

Economic and social deprivation, if accepted by its victims as their lot in life, breeds passivity, even docility. The miserable yield to their fate as divinely ordained or as their own fault. And, indeed, many Negroes in earlier generations felt that way.

Today, young Negroes aren't having any of this. They don't share the feeling that something must be wrong with them, that they are responsible for their own exclusion from this affluent society. The civil-rights movement—in fact, the whole liberal trend beginning with John Kennedy's election—has told them otherwise.

These young Negroes are right: The promises made to them were good and necessary and long, long overdue. The youth were right to believe in them. The only trouble is that they were not fulfilled.

What they and the American people absolutely must understand now is that these promises cannot be revoked. They were not made to a handful of leaders in a White House drawing room; they were made to an entire generation, one not likely to forget or to forgive.

Unless the nation is prepared to rearrange its priorities, to set a timetable for achieving them and to allocate its resources accordingly, it will not be taking its own commitments seriously. Surely it cannot then turn in amazement to responsible Negro leaders, whose pleas for large-scale programs it has failed to heed, for an explanation of the consequences.

3. Pressures on the Urban School

by George B. Brain

George B. Brain is dean of the College of Education at Washington State University. A former superintendent of schools in Baltimore and, before that, in Bellevue, Washington, he is a past president of the American Association of School Administrators and a former chairman of the Educational Policies Commission. He is the author of numerous articles and monographs in the field of school administration.

Human problems abound wherever large concentrations of people live. If these problems are to be solved, they deserve the most serious thought and study by all the citizens living in metropolitan areas, and not just those residing in the urban cores. Educational progress requires that educational leadership know something about the demography of our cities. Unless we take the time to grasp the essential demographic trends, our attempts to solve our school problems will founder.

In 1790, the U.S. population stood at 4 million. By 1967, it had reached nearly 200 million. By 1980, the Census Bureau estimates it will increase to 275 million. But today's population is unlike yesterday's, and tomorrow's population will not be identical with today's. Population is not just increasing; it is changing. For example, greater percentages of Negroes, school-age children, and very old people are forecast for the future. The implications of such population changes are great for public school personnel.

Let us take a look at what has been happening to our twenty-one largest cities. When population statistics are examined for these cities over the twenty-year period 1940–60, we find, perhaps to our surprise, that few of the cities actually gained in population. Suburbs have mushroomed, but not the cities themselves. In cities that did show a population increase, the gain was the result of annexation procedures rather than true growth. The dramatic changes in these cities were not increases, therefore, but shifts in population composition. This is evident from the following examples of population changes between 1940 and 1960:

> New York City recorded a 1.4 per cent *drop* in its total population—but registered a 139 per cent gain in nonwhite population.
>
> Baltimore recorded a 1.1 per cent drop, with a 97.4 per cent increase in the nonwhite population.
>
> Philadelphia declined 3.3 per cent in over-all population, but saw its nonwhite population increase 111.7 per cent.
>
> San Francisco dropped 4.5 per cent in total population, while its nonwhite population increased 326.9 per cent.

These figures confirm the general picture painted by Commissioner Howe in the opening chapter in this volume. What we have is a picture of general stability or slight decline in the total population of our largest cities during the past generation—along with an exodus of white people and an influx of Negroes and other nonwhites.

The next trend of major importance for educators has to do not with the over-all population but with the school population. Here we find that, across the board, enrollment in the nation's public schools—kindergarten through grade twelve—shot up from 15,503,000 in 1900 to some 44,068,000 in 1965, a gain of 184 per cent. This vast increase in the number of young people to be schooled has affected each city differently. For example, New York actually had fewer pupils to educate in 1962 than in 1940, but the trend since then has been upward. Philadelphia, Boston, Pittsburgh, and Buffalo have all had experiences similar to New York's. On the other hand, *most* cities saw their public school enrollments increase rapidly in the past generation. And in places like Los Angeles, Houston, Dallas, and San Diego, public school enrollments have actually doubled and tripled between 1940 and 1965. With a few exceptions, therefore, the past generation saw a significant increase in the numbers of children in the public school systems of major cities. All in all, the increase averaged 22 per cent in our twenty-one largest cities.

This bland statistic, however, does not begin to suggest the drastic nature of the changes that have taken place. For, just as the racial composition of the cities has changed, the complexion of the classroom has also changed. Indeed, more so.

Consider the situation with respect to the percentage of persons under the age of twenty who reside in the twenty-one largest cities. Each decade, the percentage of white youngsters who happen to live in our major cities has declined: from 17 per cent in 1940, to 15 per cent in 1950, to 12 per cent in 1960. For nonwhite youth, however, the tendency has been the exact reverse. Each decade, the percentage of nonwhite youngsters under age twenty to be found in the big cities has increased: from 13 per cent in 1940, to 18 per cent in 1950, to 26 per cent in 1960. More and more, white kids are suburbanites. More and more, Negro and other nonwhite kids are city dwellers.

Because the cities have generally offered nonwhites better health and welfare services than were available to them in rural areas, more nonwhite infants survive in the city than in the countryside. Coupled with higher birth rates, this has meant that nonwhite youth (i.e., under age twenty) now represent a higher proportion of the total nonwhite population than heretofore. And because a higher percentage of nonwhites than whites attend public, as distinct from private, schools, the cities have had to increase their public school enrollments or at least hold the same level, despite stable or even declining over-all populations. In fact, had nonwhite youth *not* dropped out of school in great numbers, public school enrollments in the cities would have increased even more, overloading many already overcrowded classrooms.

Nor is the end in sight. A breakdown of data on nonwhite children by age makes it evident that the cities will soon have even greater numbers and percentages of nonwhite students in their public schools. For example, in New York, in 1940, only 7 per cent of preschool children (age five or under) were nonwhite. By 1950, this figure had climbed to 12 per cent. And by 1960, it had hit 20 per cent. The same pattern is present in other cities, differences being only in degree rather than in kind.

In short, what has happened to the racial composition of public school enrollment in Washington—where the upper reaches of racial imbalance are already being approached—is now being duplicated in other great cities. The process is identical; only the time line differs.

The big-city school population, then, has changed drastically over the past twenty-five years, but what of the schools themselves in which these youngsters spend their days? As Ben Graves points out later in this volume, we are still attempting to school some of our children in facilities built before World War I, and, significantly, the preponderance of school facilities needing modernization are located in the inner city, in precisely those neighborhoods where the nonwhite population is concentrated—i.e., in the ghettos. Patricia Sexton, in her study *Education and Income*, reports that among children living in families with annual incomes of less than $7,000 almost 31 per cent—one out of every three children—go to a school that is fifty years old or older. By contrast, no students in the upper-income half attend schools of this age.

Old and obsolete school facilities hamper educational progress in two ways. Students disadvantaged by poverty, often living in great squalor, are deprived of environmental conditions that might improve their attitudes toward education; they are deprived of the beauty and natural splendor that often surround pupils in other sections of the city. Worse yet, inadequate physical facilities tend to drive good teachers away. Competent beginning teachers, trained in an urban setting, are reluctant to accept teaching assignments in older, obsolete buildings with their depressing, grimy surroundings.

Not only are the buildings old: They are, by and large, inadequately maintained. Most cities make little provision for effective modernization or maintenance, and most systematically defer maintenance expenditures as long as possible. This seems like prudent economizing, but the delayed expenditures come home to roost at a later date and result in more extensive rehabilitation or remodeling work at higher cost. Inflation has eroded 25 per cent of the school maintenance dollar's purchasing power in the past five years. Deferred maintenance, thus, *costs* rather than saves dollars for the taxpayer.

With respect to new construction, also, big-city school systems operate at a disadvantage. It costs more to build a city school than its suburban counterpart. In its recent booklet *The Challenge of*

Financing the Public Schools in Great Cities, the Research Council of the Great Cities Program for School Improvement suggested that state school construction aid be provided for all school districts and that full consideration be given to all factors that cause variations in costs for school construction.

Yet, no state makes allowances for inflation, for differences in site costs, or for differences in school construction costs. According to *School Management*'s "Cost of School Building Index," school construction costs have increased almost 15 per cent over the last eight years. Higher labor costs and strict adherence to municipal building codes also make for higher school plant construction costs in the cities.

The average cost of a school site over the past five years was $68,156 per acre in the twenty-one largest cities, compared to $3,074 per acre in other districts in the states sampled. Consequently, in its *National Inventory of School Facilities,* the U.S. Office of Education reported that 50.6 per cent of all school sites in the twenty-one great cities were less than two acres, compared to 36.9 per cent for the nation as a whole. In some instances, it costs as much to purchase a site in the central core of a large city as it does in most other districts to construct the entire school building. Furthermore, complex procedures for authorizing bond issues and expenditures for school plant construction in the cities tend to create construction delays, which are reflected in increased school building costs.

Despite such handicaps, most cities have capital improvement programs under way which have resulted in the construction of many new educational facilities. For example, since World War II, New York City has constructed 261 new schools, built 102 additions to existing buildings, and modernized 165 school buildings to bring them up to acceptable educational standards. Even so, over the next five years, New York City will require $2.13 billion to build the schools needed to carry out its program of school improvement. Just to meet pupil population growth, Los Angeles requires construction expenditures at the rate of $60 million a year for the next five years. Other cities are faced with similar school construction needs.

This raises the inescapable question of money. The difference between good schools in the suburbs and poor schools in the slums lies not in innate pupil intelligence or in community effort. The difference, to a considerable degree, lies in simple economics—money. Money translated into good rather than poor teachers, adequate rather than inadequate facilities, small rather than large classes, modern rather than antique teaching materials. Where there isn't enough money to buy books or offer instructional programs geared to each student's individual needs, pupils drop out of school in great numbers. Dropouts become unemployables. Unemployment creates poverty. Poverty breeds crime and corruption. Thus, money that should have gone into education in the first place winds up going into welfare payments and crime control.

Where, then, is the money for better schools to come from? As population density increases, the per capita cost of municipal government rises sharply. Police organization, transportation facilities, traffic control, fire protection, waste removal and disposal, sanitation facilities, snow removal, smoke control, supervision of weights and measures, street maintenance, welfare programs, public hospitals, libraries, and museums are a few of the services that increase municipal expenditures in the cities. No one maintains that these services shouldn't be provided. But the fact is that big-city residents expect such services and pressure municipal authorities for more and more.

At the turn of the century and for a few decades later, "municipal overburden" did not represent too great a fiscal problem in our large cities. Schools were supported at relatively high expenditure levels. This is no longer true. Nevertheless, no state today recognizes that the ability to support public education is reduced in school districts where the costs for nonschool governmental services are relatively high. Dr. LeRoy Peterson and his associates, in their historic study *Economic Impact of State Support Models on Educational Finance*, recommend that "adjustments for municipal costs be made in formulas for state support of education." So does the Research Council of the Great Cities Program for School Improvement in its booklet *Fiscal Policies to Meet the Needs of the Great City School Systems in America*. Municipal overburden, as we shall see elsewhere in this volume, clearly erodes a community's ability to support education.

At the same time that nonschool governmental costs have increased, the cities have experienced decreasing tax bases with which to support the expanded municipal functions. In a recent study, Carl Thornblad reported that our cities support municipal functions primarily from local property taxes. With respect to education, twelve of the fifteen largest cities pay well over 60 per cent of the total costs for operating public schools from local revenues. Yet, in these same cities, the property tax base—taxable assessed valuation—has not even kept growth with pupil population, much less with increased costs due to bureaucratic bigness.

The erosion of the property tax base in great cities is the result of many forces. As Dr. Paul R. Mort said, "Great highways through the cities and great bridges are not taxed, even though 90 cents on the dollar may have come from the federal government in the first place." These cities have been compelled to turn large areas of their taxable land into free public transportation arteries. Also, however beautiful the new state and federal office buildings and courthouses might be, they are not taxable. The same holds true for slum clearance and the construction of public housing projects. Even the construction of parks and green areas, needed though they are, reduces the cities' tax capability to support schools.

As the costs of municipal government mount higher and higher and the tax base shrinks, we are told that the removal of property tax limitations would free the cities to cope with their school problems. It is true that most cities are saddled with property tax limitations set by the state. It is also true that removal of these and other fiscal restrictions might give them greater freedom of action. But it must be remembered that property taxes support both school and nonschool government services. Thus, even if property tax limitations were lifted, most of the money thereby released would be likely to go toward noneducational purposes in any event. Lifting the property tax limitation is, by itself, no solution.

The fact is that the big cities pay the bulk of their own educational costs. They receive a smaller proportion of both state and federal support than do other school districts, many of which are more capable of financing education. This is an impossible situation. And it is this imbalance that must be altered.

Financing public education in the cities of the nation thus requires the solution of some complex problems and controversial issues. Inequities in financial support, failure to recognize municipal overburden, failure to recognize costs due to bureaucracy, decreasing tax bases, and lack of access to wealth, failure to recognize program cost differentials, failure to recognize valid costs for school construction—all represent pressing problems to be resolved. What complicates the matter and delays progress is the fact that officials at the local, state, and federal levels all expect someone else to resolve these problems.

Each level of government places the responsibility elsewhere, and the cities, surrounded by proliferating suburban political jurisdictions, find themselves trapped in a snarl of administrative boundaries. The Advisory Commission on Intergovernmental Relations, in its report *Governmental Structure, Organization, and Planning in Metropolitan Areas*, outlined various actions that might be taken by state and federal governments to ease the problems of urban growth beyond local and state boundaries. The recommendations of the Commission were translated into draft bills and included in the Council of State Governments' *Program of Suggested State Legislation for 1962*. These specific legislative proposals were as follows:

1. Simplified statutory requirements for municipal annexation of unincorporated territory.
2. Authorization for inter-local contracting or joint performance of services.
3. Authorization for establishment of metropolitan service corporations for performance of particular governmental services that call for areawide handling.
4. Authorization for voluntary transfer of governmental functions from cities to counties and vice versa.
5. Authorization for the creation of metropolitan area commissions on local government structure and services.
6. Authorization for creation of metropolitan area planning bodies.
7. Establishment of a unit of state government for continuing attention, review, and assistance regarding the state's metropolitan areas.

8. Inauguration of state programs of financial and technical assistance to metropolitan areas.
9. Stricter state standards for new incorporations within metropolitan areas.
10. Financial and regulatory action by the state to secure and preserve "open land" in and around metropolitan areas.
11. Assumption by the state of an active role in the resolution of disputes among local units of government within metropolitan areas.

These proposals run the gamut of local, state, and federal relationships. Steps must be taken to streamline and coordinate relationships along these lines, and specifically those relationships that impinge on education.

The most pressing problem facing both the states and the federal government today is the achievement of equality of educational opportunities at a level adequate to meet mankind's challenges. Aid-to-education plans, then, at both state and federal levels must meet demanding tests. Federal aid to education does not meet the test; nor does a single state's aid-to-education program. Accordingly, it is incumbent upon the federal government and each state to reassess its fiscal school-support programs.

We must be courageous enough to stop the jurisdictional disputes over who is responsible for what, and which agency or level of government will get credit for what, in order to develop contemporary educational programs for our cities. We have always sought to keep education out of politics. In general, that has been a good procedure. But the financing of the schools, the support of school construction, and the need to do new and untried things in the schools depend upon the understanding and support of public officials at all levels of government.

It is a political system that produces the money for education in this country. It is a political system that enacts the legislation establishing the basic requirements for public education.

The vast population shifts within our great cities, the deterioration of our schoolhouses, the growing gap between educational needs and available funds, the increasing tangle of jurisdictions—all these demand a new attitude on the part of educators. The day is over when the educator could say that the schools should not be involved in the political life of the city. If there is any lesson in this depressing data, it is that political activity is a necessity. Only political decisions, influenced by educators, can begin to clear away the wreckage and undertake the reconstruction of education in our great urban centers.

4. Differing Needs for Social Renewal

by Robert J. Havighurst

Robert J. Havighurst is Professor of Education and Human Development at the University of Chicago. He is a member of the American Sociological Association, the American Psychological Association, and the National Academy of Education. A member also of the Board of Directors of the National Society for the Study of Education, he edited the Society's 1968 Yearbook, entitled *Metropolitanism–Its Challenge to Education*. He is the author of *Education in Metropolitan Areas* and *Human Development and Education*.

No pastime is more popular today than complaining about our public education. There is an unfortunate tendency to lay the whole burden of guilt for poverty on the schools. But to blame them for the plight of disadvantaged youngsters is unfair and unrealistic, and can only lead to more difficulties for the schools—and for the cities.

The fact is that our public schools are probably doing as well in their sphere as are local governments, police traffic departments, welfare departments, church federations, and other civic and municipal groups. If this is still not good enough—and it isn't—then we will do more to remedy the situation by examining the data dispassionately than by launching irresponsible broadsides.

In order to look at the problems of the city with some perspective it is useful to see how the American population is distributed among places of various size and character. The four categories given below cover the situation. While these categories are not recognized in census publications or in the usual demographic studies, they are especially useful for educators who are interested in the functions of education in relation to the structure of the population.

1. *Cities of 100,000 or more, containing 29 per cent of the population.* These cities of 100,000 or more are the central cities or co-centers of about 120 metropolitan areas. They are large enough to have suburbs and to exhibit the massive socio-eco-

nomic and racial segregation that have become the peculiar marks of American big cities.

2. *Independent cities of 25,000 to 100,000, containing 8 per cent of the population.* These "independent" cities are the major population centers of intermediate size. There are about 300 of them; none are suburbs. Each of them is a county seat, and those with populations of 50,000 to 100,000 are central cities of the smaller metropolitan areas. They differ from the larger cities in having lesser degrees of socio-economic and racial segregation. They have their own unique problems of urban renewal. Schools in these cities have different functions in the process of social urban renewal than schools in the larger cities.

3. *Suburbs in standard metropolitan statistical areas.* These suburbs contain 30 per cent of the nation's population. They are not independent of the central cities, and their future development is tied in with that of the central cities. There are about 2,000 such suburbs, varying in size from a few hundred to about 100,000 people.

4. *Small cities (under 25,000) and open country, containing 43 per cent of the population.* These small cities and open rural areas have the majority of the school buildings in the country but lie outside the boundaries of our present subject.

In this discussion, we shall confine ourselves to dealing with the first two categories—large and moderate-size cities. It is here that the problems of schoolhouse location, planning, construction, economics, racial balance, and educational policy are presented in their sharpest form.

Most of the domestic troubles of the nation today seem to be concentrated in the 130 cities of 100,000 or more inhabitants. Why are these cities all in trouble? A trip through the slums of any big city provides an unpleasant experience both for the naïve middle-class citizen and for the experienced social observer. Nobody can become so accustomed to contemporary urban slums that he accepts them as "natural." They are unnatural and unhealthy. The U.S. Department of Health, Education, and Welfare recently produced a booklet of charts entitled *Cities in Crises,* which states that, compared to "good" housing areas, the "blighted" areas have:

2.5 times as many police court charges;
2 times as many ambulance runs;
2 times as many fire alarms;
4 times as many visiting nurse calls; and
14 times as many welfare service cases.

In these blighted "inner city" areas are concentrated the unemployment, the illiteracy, and the alienation of our urban society.

The problems of the inner city in the large metropolitan area are many. The most conspicuous problem is physical obsolescence. Large areas of the city are obsolete or obsolescent. Houses have been allowed to deteriorate beyond the point at which they can be restored as human dwelling places. Factory buildings and warehouses are not fit for contemporary industry. Acres of railway yards lie relatively unused. Physical slum clearance has removed the worst of the old, and in some cases new buildings of beauty and usefulness have replaced the old slums. At the same time, however, major mistakes have been made in many cities in the process of urban renewal, and there is still a great deal of tearing down and rebuilding to be done.

Physical obsolescence is matched by civic poverty. The cost of providing public services for transit, police and fire departments, sanitation, parks, schools, and libraries has risen, while taxable resources have decreased. The property tax is no longer sufficient to bear the cost, and cities are searching for new sources of revenue. Some look to the federal government for help, some get help from state government, and some have developed new tax resources.

Increasingly, the central cities provide costly services to residents of the entire metropolitan area, without receiving much in compensation. Thus the central city has sacrificed valuable tax-producing land to make expressways for the use of nonresidents or of residents going elsewhere.

The central city also houses the poor people of the metropolitan area. The people with the least income, the least education, and the least tax-paying ability are also the people with the greatest need for public welfare, health, and educational services.

At the same time, subsidized public housing has been mismanaged by most cities so as to increase the residential segregation of the poor. The central city houses most of its Negroes in ghettos. Some of these are tolerable in terms of pure physical conditions, but many are not. For example, the Pruitt-Igoe Housing Project in St. Louis concentrates into a 57-acre area about 10,000 Negroes in 2,000 households. Over half of these households are headed by women, and over half receive their principal income from public assistance. What was started in 1954 as a grand project to improve the lives of the poor has become a civic embarrassment. At times, the project has had a vacancy rate of 20 per cent, because only the utterly desperate go there for housing. Things are better in many other public housing projects, but never as good as they should be if the planning and policy-making had been representative of American democracy at its best.

The central city has grown rapidly in the proportion of residents who are Negroes. The decade from 1950 to 1960 saw the greatest absolute increase of Negro population in the central cities, largely due to the demand of industry for new workers. Only a few suburbs in a few metropolitan areas have accepted Negro residents in substantial numbers. While all the big cities except Washington and Newark have a substantial majority of white residents, the unfounded belief has grown that "our city will soon be like Washington, with a majority of Negroes," and many otherwise clear-minded people repeat this statement and tend to make it a self-fulfilling prophecy.

The fact is that the Negro population is not increasing as rapidly in the 1960–70 decade in the Northern cities as had been expected on the basis of 1950–60 data. Nevertheless, many cities are suffering from an exodus of middle-income whites, in part a result of mistaken perceptions of the present reality.

The contrast of poverty and wealth in an affluent society stimulates hostility on the part of the disadvantaged group and makes the urban core a center of unrest. This hostility is always latent, and may erupt at almost any moment into riots. It seldom takes the form of active, consistent, and possibly constructive opposition to the political and economic power structure. Therefore, it serves no constructive purpose, beyond the value inherent in any protest movement where there are grounds for protest.

While most cities have some active groups representing civic, church, and business interests who are studying and working on the problems of the city, these groups are handicapped by apathetic attitudes on the part of many citizens, who retreat into their own small neighborhoods and regard events in the rest of the community with a kind of passive aversion. Yet, the behavior of government agencies is not much better.

The cities have numerous public agencies that are expected to cope with these problems. Besides the local city governments, there frequently are planning commissions, commissions on human relations, youth commissions, housing authorities, park and recreation commissions, police departments, public library systems, and public school systems. Seldom, however, do we see a city in which these agencies support one another in a comprehensive, integrated plan for community improvement that has been devised jointly and adopted as part of each agency's program. Indeed, in some cases, as with many public school systems, there is a deliberate avoidance of close cooperation with other agencies of government because of a distrust of "politics" and a belief that the system can perform its own functions most efficiently by keeping its operations distinct and independent.

This, then, is the picture in our larger cities—urban centers with populations of 100,000 or more. The medium-size cities of 25,000 to 100,000 do not have these problems—but they have their own rather different set of difficulties.

There are about 300 cities of this size that are not suburbs or satellites of large cities. Most of these cities are relatively old and rather stable. Many have not changed appreciably in population in the last twenty or thirty years. Some have prospered, due to the growth of one or more local industries that have large payrolls and provide employment for most of the residents. Others have stagnated, as local industry has failed to grow.

The majority of cities in this category have a problem of urban renewal. The old central business district has become obsolete. The courthouse square is surrounded by old buildings, which are not well designed for modern merchandising or for office use. Efforts at external face-lifting and internal modernization only make these buildings barely tolerable. No major capital investments have been made in the business section for several decades.

Meanwhile, a few business concerns with flexible capital and no commitment to the central district have established themselves in modern shopping centers on the edges of the city, where parking space is plentiful, land is relatively cheap, and taxes are relatively low. These shopping centers have little or no aesthetic quality, but they are new, clean, and efficient.

At about this point in the city's evolution, a movement starts for urban renewal, to restore the central business district, and to remove some of the old houses near the center of town, which have become slum dwellings.

But the drive for urban renewal generally lacks the near unanimity of support that it finds in the larger cities, where conditions are so obviously bad that people with civic or economic interests in the central city are agreed that something must be done. In the medium-size city, some business interests have already committed themselves to the new shopping centers, and some big employers may see no advantage in paying taxes to restore the old city center. On the other hand, the merchants who still do business at the center may see urban renewal as a solution of their own problem, but they may not be able to draw up a broad plan of urban redevelopment that would capture the imagination and support of the people of the city.

Often the question of urban renewal in such a city is put to the citizens for a vote. The familiar charges of "socialism" and "domination by the federal government" are brought against the plan. The proposal may fail because there is no concerted local leadership that can secure city planning experts to draw up an attractive and realistic development plan.

Meanwhile, in this kind of city, decisions are being made about the location of such building projects as a new high school or a new public library building or a hospital or medical center. Each decision of this kind is made under the influence of competing forces—some directed outward from the city center and other forces directed inward toward the city center. One agency may build on the edge of the city, another near the city center, thus making cooperation between the two agencies difficult.

From the aesthetic point of view, the city has lost its earlier simple symmetrical structure and gained nothing of architectural value. As for functional efficiency, the sprawl of schools, libraries, hospitals, shopping centers, and churches may have doubled the number of miles that are traveled per year by children and adults going about their daily and weekly routine, compared with what might have been the case in a city that was well designed spatially.

While the middle-size city does not suffer from the social pathology that afflicts the large city, it seems to be developing a unique combination of ugliness and inefficiency.

There is general agreement, by now, on the need for social urban renewal. More is needed than merely tearing down obsolete buildings and physically replacing them. There is need for a new metropolitan design that makes possible the realization of ideals and attitudes that are growing in strength among city dwellers and seeking application in the organization of schools, in the social composition of local community areas, and in the development of the cities' cultural resources.

The following elements of social urban renewal are relevant to school administration and to schoolhouse location and design.

1. *The social mix:* As far as possible, the city of the future should consist of communities that are cross sections of the entire metropolitan area in terms of socio-economic status and racial composition. The basic local community unit should have a population of between 50,000 and 300,000 people. The size of the unit should depend on existing community areas that have a sense and a tradition of common interest and action. All big cities already have some such local community areas with community spirit and varied populations. Often they have community councils and other agencies of communication and decision-making.

It is these mixed local communities that will serve as models for social urban renewal. Though not perfect, by any means, they can use the services of local government, schools, and other agencies to work toward an environment in which all kinds of people will want to live and raise their children.

2. *The urban-community school philosophy:* The quality of the

public schools is the single most important factor in the decision of middle-income people to live in the central city or to live in the suburbs, and to live in one section or another of the central city or the suburbs. Knowing this, educators tend to divide into two groups with respect to their views on the proper ways to operate a school system in the contemporary metropolitan area.

One group supports what might be called the concept of the "four-walls" school. The basic principle is to do the best possible job of educating every child who comes into the school, whoever he is, whatever his color, nationality, I.Q., or handicap. This means building good school buildings, equipping them well, and staffing them with well-trained teachers. At its best, it means being courteous and friendly to parents and to citizens who are interested in the schools, but making it quite clear that the schools are run by professionals who know their business and do not need advice from other people.

It means keeping the schools "out of local politics." Staff appointments are to be made on the basis of merit alone, and promotion of staff on the basis of performance. It means limited cooperation with other social institutions, public and private. Welfare, public aid, and public health agencies are asked for help when the schools need it, but they cannot initiate school programs.

The four-walls type of school system strives for efficiency and economy, and attempts to free the creative teacher to do the best possible teaching job under good conditions. The outside community is regarded as a potential source of complexity and tension if the boundary between community and school is not clearly defined and respected.

The second group supports the "urban-community" school concept. Educators who advocate this believe that the big city is caught up in a crisis which has been in force for years and will last for at least ten years more. They believe this crisis requires the active participation of schools in making and implementing a policy for social urban renewal. This big-city crisis is reflected in feelings of uncertainty and anxiety on the part of parents and citizens. There is danger of a collective failure of nerve, which saps the vitality and flexibility of the city's efforts at urban renewal. Middle-income parents and citizens are tempted to escape to the suburbs, where life seems simpler and safer, especially for children.

The urban-community school attempts to act constructively in this crisis by involving parents and citizens in decisions about school policy and practice. The educator accepts the frustration of working with people who are confused and uncertain about the schools, since he believes the only way to solve the problems of the city is to work on a give-and-take basis with citizens and community organizations.

The urban-community school includes the intraschool program of the four-walls school, but differs at important points on the relationship of the school to the community.

Those who take the urban-community-school point of view believe there is no viable alternative. They believe that the four-walls school actually causes some of the problems of the community through its rigid districting rules and its efforts to keep the public away from the classroom. They believe that the schools, by their policies and practices, either attract or repel people in the local community. Under present conditions, the typical school system repels people whom the central city cannot afford to lose as residents. Proponents of the urban-community school believe that the present trend toward economic and racial segregation in the metropolitan area will continue and the central city will lose quality, unless the schools take a more active part in social urban renewal.

3. *Cooperative functioning of social systems:* There are several social institutions whose cooperation is essential in social urban renewal. They have common interests in the maintenance of a good community, but, in the past, they have seldom worked together. These include local government, schools, welfare agencies, cultural agencies (libraries, museums, theaters, recreation centers), and the churches.

All of these institutions are finding new functions in the big city. Government goes into public housing; welfare goes into youth employment and family-life education; the public library reaches into the local community; a subsidized theater looks for an audience; the churches turn their attention to matters of education and welfare in the local community; and the schools are affected by all of these activities. The building of a vast high-rise public housing project may force the school system to construct a school building that serves only the children of welfare recipients; the coming of a branch library may affect plans for school libraries; a school work-study program may be affected by plans for a Neighborhood Youth Corps project; the development of a community theater group may offer an opportunity for the development of a dramatics program in the local high school.

Each of the institutions in the community develops its own program and needs a good deal of autonomy in order to make decisions and implement them. Yet the effectiveness of each institution is conditioned by what the other institutions are doing and planning.

Some form of communication needs to be maintained among these social systems. They need to cooperate in their planning; and they need to cooperate in some of their programs.

4. *Size of school or school complex:* There are two opposite principles that bear on the question of the size of the big-city school. One is the need to make the school serve a diversified population. This argues for a large school, with students coming to it from a wide area. The other is the need to "take the school to the people"—to make it a neighborhood resource. This calls for small schools distributed throughout the area.

We find both principles applied in the projects for social urban renewal. On the one hand, there is the "education park" in its strict form: a large campus that contains all the schools serving a large area—from elementary school up to community college. Pupils who live a considerable distance from the park are bussed to school. The school does not lend itself easily to local neighborhood uses. Such a unit may serve 10,000 to 20,000 pupils, with a high school enrollment of 2,000 to 4,000.

On the other hand, if the principle of the school as a neighborhood center is followed, the schools will be relatively small and will tend to serve neighborhood areas that are more homogeneous in socio-economic and racial terms than the larger area served by an education park. For young children, this is the kind of school that is favored by most parents—a school within a few blocks of home, to which children can walk in safety.

In practice, we are likely to see a combination of the two principles. There may be an education park with a high school and community college that serve a large area, together with a junior high school or middle school that serves a smaller area, and a primary school that serves an even smaller area close to the park.

This creates a dilemma for the educator, since we know that integrated school experience is as important, if not more so, for young children as it is for adolescents.

The best solution for the near future may be one that is worked out by the school administration in terms of the particular area of the city under consideration. An administrator at the district level, together with a group of school principals in the area, may work with the leaders of community organizations to design the physical pattern of schoolhouse distribution. This group would express the parental attitudes that are consistent with the urban-community-school philosophy. Its plans must be made in the light of the facts of the area—the existing school buildings that will be usable for a number of years, the land available for school park purposes, and the broad city redevelopment plan with its provision for parks, greenbelts, expressways, and public services.

5. *The physical plan of the city*: This is a period of great physical change for the cities—both the large metropolitan areas and the medium-size independent cities. Physical renewal can make the city a pleasure to the eye, as well as a more convenient place in which to carry on the activities of everyday life. The aesthetic factor should weigh heavily in the future development of the city.

The city planning commission in every city, large or of medium size, should have allied with it a citizens commission on the future form of the city. A school of architecture should be chosen to offer advice and expert planning. Local high schools and colleges should study the city plan, which should become as familiar a topic of discussion as the city's baseball or football team, or at least as the city's convention hall.

This already has been done by some of our cities. Probably the average citizen of New Haven is far more sophisticated and has more interest in the future form of his city than the average citizen of Chicago.

When we think of the vast material resources of our cities and our technical competence with cement, asphalt, and structural steel, we cannot feel proud of our cities, but we can be hopeful of their future as places for people to live and work.

Although it is popular just now to look with gloomy foreboding at our big cities, the process of social urban renewal has gone far enough to provide some successful models for imitation and a solid basis for belief that we can succeed with the task. Some of the facts that justify this optimism are the following:

1. Racial integration is, in fact, gaining a residential base in the big Northern and Western cities. Voluntary residential integration is gaining momentum. Every large city has one or more middle-income areas that are becoming stably integrated. Middle-class whites are increasingly favorable toward residential integration, as long as the income level of the Negroes and whites is roughly equal.

Examples of city areas that have stable integration are the Hyde Park–Kenwood district of Chicago and the area between Central Park and the Hudson River in New York. In this latter area, there is a mixture of Puerto Rican, Anglo-American, and Negro residents, with a rather wide range of incomes.

The movement of middle-income Negroes into predominantly white suburban residential areas is gaining momentum. This is aided by one or another form of "good neighbor" pledge, which is being promoted by church and citizen groups in the suburbs.

Open-housing legislation is proving effective in some cities to increase the movement of Negroes into previously all-white areas.

2. Negroes are gaining in socio-economic status and education. During the 1960's, there has been a substantial increase in the proportion of young Negro men and women filling white-collar jobs. This will show in the 1970 census as a large increase in the percentage of Negroes in the managerial, professional, clerical, and sales occupations. Thus, the proportion of Negroes who are able to pay for middle-class housing and to associate with white middle-class people on a basis of educational and economic equality is increasing.

The situation has been clouded by the influence of the Black Separatist movement, which tends to chain middle-class Negroes to the ghetto as an indication of their solidarity with the Negro cause.

But this movement is likely to fail in any attempt to prevent Negroes from integrating into middle-class American society.

3. The inner ring of suburbs is getting ready to cooperate with the central city in social urban renewal. Wherever the central city of a metropolitan area is closely ringed by suburbs, the suburbs themselves are feeling the need for urban renewal, and are cooperating with the central city in planning for development as a metropolitan area.

4. The federal government encourages planning for development and urban renewal on a metropolitan area basis. The trend will increase toward treating the metropolitan area as the appropriate unit for planning of highways, parks, higher education facilities, and control of water and air pollution.

5. School administrators are becoming more favorable to cooperation between suburbs and central cities. The American Association of School Administrators, in its 1967 resolutions, urged combination of the central city and suburbs of large metropolitan areas into unified tax, administrative, and educational units. "At present," the resolution said, "although the different segments of the large metropolitan area function vigorously and efficiently as an operational economic unit, their school districts are multiple and autonomous. This pattern of school organization must be radically and swiftly altered."

All these factors give cause for cautious optimism. The independent medium-size city of 25,000 to 100,000 may lag behind the larger city in its redevelopment. Since the situation is not bad enough in such cities to demand drastic action for urban renewal, they will probably not launch a general movement for renewal. Only those cities with exceptionally good leadership will now move to anticipate the problems of obsolescence and decay that will otherwise worsen over the next twenty years and demand action in the 1980's.

Since the 300 cities in this category are not now in obvious trouble, and since they contain only 8 per cent of the nation's population, they are likely to be ignored by the federal government's most dynamic programs of urban redevelopment, except for the minority that have unusual leaders and are able to take the initiative in planning their own renewal immediately. Nevertheless, our larger urban centers are beginning to bestir themselves. In this there is hope.

The postwar decades have created problems and provided opportunities for American cities. To take advantage of the opportunities, we must acquire new habits and attitudes. We shall have to learn the habit of planning for the physical and social development of our cities. We shall have to learn to cooperate throughout an entire metropolitan area in programs involving the whole range of public and private services. School systems must cooperate with local government, with welfare agencies, health agencies, and business and industry. Suburban and central city agencies must also learn to cooperate.

We shall have to learn how to use educational facilities, television, libraries, transportation, and land more creatively for educational purposes.

We shall have to learn to meet the complexity of metropolitan life with rational positive action. What we do not need are irresponsible, indiscriminate accusations and lamentations.

5. The Decaying Schoolhouse

by Ben E. Graves

Ben E. Graves is directing a study for the Research Council of the Great Cities Program for School Improvement, seeking creative solutions to the problem of outmoded school plant. He has been a newspaper reporter, editor of *Better Homes and Gardens*, vice president of an advertising agency, lecturer in journalism at Drake University, and a senior associate with the Perkins & Will Partnership, architects. An active member of many educational organizations, including the Association of School Business Officials and the Council of Educational Facility Planners, he is on the editorial advisory committee of *Nation's Schools* magazine and has contributed articles to all major educational and architectural journals.

Back in 1857, a new school building was dedicated in a fast-growing section of one of our large Eastern cities. All of us have driven past a similar school, and those of us involved in education would not be surprised by the floor plan. Three years after this school was occupied, Abraham Lincoln became the President of the United States.

The dedication of this school, and the many more just like it (with minor variations in exterior decoration), may seem a bit of interesting but unimportant information, until we realize that, in sixteen of the great cities of the United States, there are still almost 600 elementary schools and more than 50 junior and senior high schools built before the end of the nineteenth century that are still in use today.

If we move into the present century and take the period 1901–20, we find still in use 722 elementary schools and 165 junior and senior high schools—almost 900 separate school buildings. These buildings also appear pretty much alike, with floor plans following a pattern familiar to all educators.

Now, if we total our schools of the Abe Lincoln and Teddy Roosevelt eras, we find approximately 1,300 elementary schools and more than 200 junior and senior high schools—more than 1,500 separate buildings still in use that were constructed before the advent of commercial air travel, television, and sound motion pictures—many of them before the invention of the electric light bulb or the automobile.

Just think of it. In fifteen major cities of this country, 12.5 per cent of all public school buildings were constructed before 1900, and more than 36 per cent before 1920. The first national inventory of school facilities conducted by the U.S. Office of Education reported that, nationally, 30,000 public school buildings and additions containing some 250,000 classrooms have been in use for more than 50 years. These classrooms represent almost one-sixth of all permanent instructional facilities. In addition, there are 42,500 classrooms in 5,000 nonpublic school buildings that have been in use since before 1920. If we start adding the general-use facilities, as reported by the national inventory, we begin to get staggering figures—28,000 school libraries, cafeterias, auditoriums, and gymnasiums in public schools and more than 8,000 such facilities in nonpublic schools have been in service for fifty years or more!

Nowhere is this problem more acute than in the large cities. The age profile of the Buffalo, N.Y., schools is fairly typical of that found in any large urban area. The schools still in use span a building period of 103 years.

In a 1962 report on schools in one of our large cities, educational facilities of then and now were contrasted and this statement made on attitudes:

> The attitude toward children and their education was characterized in general by an attitude of rigidity—the children were marched into school to be seated in rows of desks that could not be moved and which took up every inch of space in the dark and often stuffy room. They were drilled in their studies, grade after grade, with little attention paid to each child as an individual human being different from all other human beings. If a child did not measure up, he failed and was held back until he somehow, if ever, came up to grade. A bright child might skip a grade or two, but that was all the variation possible for him. And the buildings expressed this attitude.
>
> By and large, the school buildings of the period seem to us now to be crowded, cramped, ill-heated, ill-ventilated. These buildings had wooden stairs and corridors, gang toilets in the basement, and classrooms which were dark and drab except perhaps, near a window. They had no playrooms inside and little playspace outside. The

atmosphere inside the classrooms was, in many cases, stale and odorous, hardly designed to assist children in staying awake, or if a window were opened in winter to allow fresh air to enter, drafty and cold.

To some extent these conditions can be explained in the setting of the 1850's. Many other public buildings were little better. But the schoolhouse of the period still expressed an attitude, and it was essentially the attitude that children were of no special concern, that they certainly did not merit a habitation in any way superior to any others. But if such were the conditions in the nineteenth century, there is little excuse for maintaining these conditions into the present day.

One might illustrate such statements with photographs of schools still in use all over the country.

It should be stressed that these statements are in no way an indictment of the work being accomplished in the large cities' school districts. In the field of school facilities, the large metropolitan school districts are accepting a role of leadership in educational planning to meet the challenges of today. They are doing an amazing job, as a matter of fact, when one considers the way neighborhoods are changing or being destroyed by shifting populations and that cover-all approach we call urban renewal. But the fact has to be faced that millions of our children attend schools that time has passed by.

Now, for a moment, let's move up to the late 1920's and mid-1930's. About forty years ago, most of the schools built *prior* to that time were put on replacement lists. Our attitude toward children was changing somewhat, and it was hoped we could gradually replace some of the older plants. Once they were put on these lists, little except preventive maintenance and safety revisions were accomplished. But the best laid plans, the most elaborate plans for plant renewal, suddenly became irrelevant. We were in the 1940's, and school construction slowed and then halted. Our old friends on the replacement lists bowed to the war effort, and all we could do was dream of the great tomorrow.

The war ended and we tried to get back to normal, but found ourselves faced by the postwar baby boom. As we built, we realized we couldn't tear down our replacement list buildings. There simply wasn't—and, I probably should add, isn't—enough money to give all our children schools planned specifically for today's changes in education.

At one of the first meetings scheduled on the subject as part of the "New Life for Old Schools" study, representatives from member cities discussed the problem of old schools. A few quotes from that meeting help to point up the dilemma of the old city schoolhouse:

> Our story is the same as in many other cities: heavy growth in concentrated periods and only enough money to meet the demands of new population growth, but never enough money to replace or modernize obsolescent school buildings.
>
> Fifty-nine buildings, or 29 per cent of our total school plants, were constructed prior to the turn of the century, and eighty-five buildings, or approximately 41 per cent, were constructed prior to World War I.
>
> Since most of the buildings requiring modernization and/or improvements are within the so-called inner core or inner city, a section which no longer has community ties and traditions because of population change and mobility, we are faced with a very real problem in human psychology.
>
> The school plant has suffered because of inadequate funds. Extraordinary repairs have had to be curtailed, and many major educational projects have been postponed year after year, because of lack of funds.
>
> It is evident that, until greater resources are available for capital expenditures and/or the need for providing for new construction to meet pupil enrollment demands diminishes, we must necessarily conduct a restricted program for systematically modernizing school facilities.
>
> The young teacher-graduates of modern colleges and universities . . . expect and seek fully equipped, well-designed, up-to-date classrooms in which to pursue their life work. . . . Their talents are ill-used when they must handle classes of forty to forty-five in outmoded buildings with inadequate facilities. As a result, many have left such conditions to move into suburban schools.

So today we find ourselves faced with old schools getting older. On top of this, we have our 1930 schools—still structurally sound —being left behind by advances in educational philosophies and methods. Who among us could boast that we could have planned a school in 1930 to meet the challenges of today? Almost all of these older buildings have some shortcomings when viewed next to the newer schools planned around, and for, changing educational programs.

It is when the building has been neglected—ignored may be a better word—that we find ourselves in serious trouble. As was mentioned earlier, in many cases the administration, five, ten, or even forty years ago, surveyed the system and marked certain buildings for replacement or abandonment. In too many cases, this simply has not happened. The children keep coming, and the building scheduled for replacement continues to operate while the hope persists that, in a few years, "the old dog" can be given a quick but decent burial. In some cases, hopefully, this will happen. In too many instances, it will not—because one of the problems of the central city is that, even as total population decreases, school population continues to increase. One school superintendent in a major city states that they now have about one additional student for every net decrease of one person in the city's total population. Indeed, this is typical of many other cities. And, as one Board of Education member in New York City said, "If you don't have seats for children, you simply have to keep the *old* building."

So we keep them. We are expecting these 30,000 school buildings that have been in use for 50 years or more to continue to serve us, because we are told that a typical family living in the year 2000 may go to school for only part of their education and for the rest receive televised instruction directly from a central computer. Our libraries may become fully automated to answer queries directly from the home.

Faced with this technology, too many modernization programs are really no more than simple maintenance or rehabilitation programs—changing the green walls to yellow, adding some asphalt tile to the floor (preferably the kind heralded by the manufacturer as "maintenance free"), changing the incandescent lighting fixtures to fluorescent ones, putting acoustical tile on the ceilings of classrooms and, if the budget permits, in the corridors.

When we're finished, the classrooms are still the same size and they still dictate or limit the educational program possibilities. The "administrative suite" may be a little more spacious, but just as inconvenient when it comes to conferences with parents or "troublemakers."

We have spent our money locking the old school right back into its egg crate, restricting new and imaginative educational approaches. So the nation's schools are still locked in a rigid mold poured in the past, with the worst problems concentrated largely in the cores of our major cities. The problem is massive—so massive that if we translate the statistics mentioned at the beginning of this paper into dollars and cents, we come up with incentive figures for manufacturers to join in the development of new products for modernization. We have 250,000 classrooms in use today that are considered inadequate by present-day standards. If we use an estimate of $15,000–$20,000 per classroom for modernization, it would require about $5 billion to modernize the classrooms alone—without even figuring in the general-use facilities. If we assume half of these classrooms should be replaced, we still have an impressive figure—about what it would cost to develop a new giant commercial airplane or a month's expenditure in Vietnam. And the problems of physical plant are only a small part of the over-all crisis in our urban schools!

6. Cities and Schools of the Future

by Charles William Brubaker

Charles William Brubaker is a partner of The Perkins & Will Partnership, an architectural firm. He has worked on many educational projects, including the Jones Commercial High School in downtown Chicago, the Evanston Township High School in Evanston, Illinois, and the Orchard Ridge Campus of the Oakland Community College near Detroit. He is the author of *Designing Territory for Learning in the Multi-School,* a special report recently published in *Nation's Schools*. He is a fellow of the American Institute of Architects and a member of Urban America, Inc. and the Society for College and University Planning.

The future of the school cannot be thought about seriously unless we devote some prior thought to the future of American cities. Where are they going? How are they developing? What are the options available to city planners? These questions all relate, directly and inextricably, to the problems of educational planning.

Jean Gottmann, in a classic study for the Twentieth Century Fund, described the urbanized Northeastern seaboard of the United States. This area, extending southwest from Boston through Hartford, New York, Philadelphia, Baltimore, and Washington, is inhabited by 38 million people. There are an average of 700 people for each of its 54,000 square miles. Gottmann dubbed this region Megalopolis, and we can now begin to see the emergence of comparable clusters of cities in the Midwest, on the California coast, in Europe, and elsewhere. It would appear that we are moving from simple "mono-cities" to complex "multi-cities."

Consider the following frightening possibility. What if the population of Megalopolis (Boston to Washington) were to increase to the density of the District of Columbia, which now has 14,000 people per square mile. If this nightmare ever occurred, then the region would have a population of 760 million—3.8 times the entire population of the United States today!

Of course, there is nothing inevitable, or even probable, about such a development. But many planners believe we have to do more than speculate about it. We must actively intervene to prevent the kind of urban sprawl that leads cities to coalesce, forming larger and larger, more and more complex, units. We might, for example, learn a lesson from Holland, where planners are consciously trying to maintain green agricultural belts and recreational zones between their cities by prohibiting construction. Professor J. P. Thijsse, writing on *Connurbation Holland*, suggests that instead of allowing larger and larger urban concentrations to develop, we "establish the overflow industries and business administrative headquarters preferably in the outer provinces. . . . [The] effect would be to stop migration to the *Connurbation*."

However, in the United States, there are no such large-scale plans, let alone the statutory machinery to enforce them. Thus, urban sprawl continues unabated.

This need not be the case. There are interesting alternatives to this formless growth, quite apart from the one being tried in Holland. The city of Washington, D.C., for example, has studied the possibilities. The National Capital Regional Plan Commission predicts a doubling of the population of the metropolitan area from 2.5 million to 5 million by the year 2000. They identified seven possibilities:

1. Continue sprawl until it covers the entire area.
2. Limit growth to 3 million people.
3. Build 4 or 5 "New Cities" of 500,000 people each.
4. Build 20 "New Towns" of 50,000 to 150,000 people each (following examples set by Reston and Columbia, two planned communities outside Washington).
5. Encourage a ring development.
6. Encourage development of suburban clusters.
7. Encourage development of corridors in a star pattern with six fingers reaching out from Washington—each finger in the star being about 5 miles wide and 20 to 30 miles long, with green, open space maintained between these corridors.

The Washington planners recommend the last plan. A rapid transit system has been proposed to serve the corridors. Reston and Columbia, the highly publicized New Towns, are properly located in the corridors.

It remains to be seen whether Washington actually will follow this plan. But, meanwhile, we are experimenting with a variety of new approaches to planned urban growth. These experiments are important for educators because their success or failure will heavily influence the future of the cities in which the schools of the future will be operated. Building schools for megalopolitan concentrations is one thing; building them for New Cities or New Towns is quite another.

Thus, many people are closely watching Reston—the Virginia community built near Dulles Airport. Planned for 75,000 people on a 6,000-acre site, Reston is having financial growing pains. On the other side of Washington, in Maryland, Columbia is rising. Planned for 150,000 people in villages of 10,000 each, Columbia will have open space between each of the villages. It will offer urban services that no village could, by itself, afford. But here again, we must wait for the results.

Big business has even bolder plans. One builder, William Levitt, is proposing to create a whole city for 2 million people. General Electric and other companies are planning cities, to be constructed by them and equipped with their products and services. Joseph Timan, a Tucson builder, suggests what he calls "Module Cities"—ten clusters of 150,000 people, each located 10 miles from the next one, but organized around a central core for financial, governmental, and cultural activities. He wants to build such an urban cluster for 1.5 million people on a 1,000-square-mile site at a new location. Elsewhere, plans are under consideration for the creation of a domed city near Minneapolis.

Shortly after the turn of the century, Daniel Burnham offered advice to city planners. "Make no little plans," he said. "They have no magic to stir men's blood and probably themselves will not be realized. Make big plans; aim high in hope and work, remember that a noble, logical diagram once recorded will never die, but long after we are gone will be a living insistency." It would appear that city planners are beginning to take this advice.

We can expect, therefore, startling changes in the nature of cities, and we can expect some of these changes to occur within the reasonably near future. These changes will necessarily alter the role of education and the character of our schools. To plan schools on the blind assumption that the cities of the future will resemble the cities of the past—only more so—is to make a fundamental error.

School planning must begin with certain assumptions about the future of the kinds of cities they are designed to serve. This attempt to anticipate change, to plan far ahead, is inordinately difficult. But unless we attempt it with all the intelligence and resources at our command, we shall succeed in building schools, or remaking schools, that are inappropriate to their environment.

Once we have thought deeply about the future of the city, once we are willing to make assumptions about it, we can begin to tackle the two other major considerations in the design and plan for any school. These are (1) the unique nature of the educational program and (2) the unique nature of the site.

Here again, unless we want to build for the past, we should attempt to anticipate the needs of tomorrow. Educational programs, for example, are changing. These programs will reflect the new urban realities, and they will also reflect the rising sophistication of educational theory and technology.

Though the established, self-contained classroom concept continues to dominate teaching at the elementary level, team teaching is now providing effective competition. Many high schools, led by the influential Evanston Township High School, are based on team-teaching ideas. Along with this, we are moving toward modular scheduling, which opens new opportunities for better utilization of time and varying-size groups, including independent study and the use of small and large groups. The total effort is directed toward achieving individualized instruction for each student.

The nongraded schools which Drs. Goodlad, Anderson, and Brown have effectively written about and promoted, continue to gain support. The open-plan "school without walls" is a related concept and enjoys thoughtful consideration.

Individual study is a most significant development. In 1959, Cocking, Perkins, and Brubaker published their study *Space for Individual Learning,* which explored facilities for a program based on individualized instruction. Recently, dial access systems, computer-assisted instruction, and other new media developments have encouraged individual study.

Many of the above concepts challenge the traditional classroom (especially the ubiquitous classroom for thirty students) as the principal place for learning. New learning environments are developing that show the way to tomorrow's school. At the community college level, for example, Orchard Ridge Campus, in Oakland County near Detroit, is a model college without classrooms.

Urban schools, in this era of change, must explore these new concepts, probe, evaluate, and take a stand. The same is true with respect to new instructional media. Large-city systems have an advantage here, since they have sufficient size to support the finest television studios, film libraries, supplemental centers, audio-visual services, information systems, computers, and staff. The small suburban school system can't compete in this arena.

Since the new media tend to involve expensive facilities, their adoption often brings (1) a concentration of services, computers, studios, etc., at a center and (2) dispersal of use by students, since electronic access can be from anywhere.

The media center, tomorrow, will be able to serve many schools at distant locations—elementary, middle, and high schools, parochial schools, colleges—as well as libraries and homes. Once again, however, these developments must be matched for suitability against the nature of the city or community in which the school is located. There is nothing magical about such devices. They can be effective only if they advance educational objectives—and these will make sense only if they grow out of the unique character of the city, Megalopolis, New Town, or other urban center that provides the context for the school.

Whether and how they should be employed also relate to the issue of school size, which, itself, must reflect the kind of community being served. Megalopolitan schools or ordinary city schools are usually large. But what exactly is "large"? A 2,500-student high school was recently considered to be large, but now Evanston Township High School is planned for 6,000 students, and Pittsburgh's Great High Schools are to have 5,000 students each.

How large will urban schools become? 10,000 students? 20,000 students? 40,000 students? Some of the educational-park proposals lead us in this direction, but some planners are concerned that many important values of smaller schools might be lost.

Evanston solves this problem by subdividing the 6,000 student body into four 1,500-student schools—each semi-independent with its own identity, student body, faculty, and physical facilities—including library, science laboratories, dining room, student activities space, and administration and counseling suites. The four schools share specialized facilities such as gyms, a field house, pools, special labs, shops, studios, and a large auditorium.

Perhaps the new media will encourage development of smaller school units, interrelated in large systems. Different kinds of cities or communities, however, will employ different techniques, because they will have—at least in part—different educational objectives.

The school planner must also, of course, respond to the unique character of the site, once he knows where his school or schools are to be located. In the city, land is expensive and, therefore, sites are small and difficult to find. Moreover, the proper *form* for the urban school is not the same as that of the typical suburban school. Urban building forms, for example, are strongly influenced by high land costs. They include compact, loft, high-rise, underground, air-rights, and joint-occupancy structures. The compact building uses land sparingly, is multilevel, and accepts city-size gardens and courts in lieu of spacious lawns. The loft school is also compact and multilevel. It uses large floor areas of air-conditioned space, and provides a high level of flexibility. The high-rise school, in the spirit of the modern office building, is built on a minimum site, and trades horizontal circulation for vertical (elevator or escalator) transportation. Lacking land for horizontal expansion, it grows vertically (as, for example, the Jones Commercial High School does in downtown Chicago). Again, we see the influence of the urban context.

In sharp contrast to the suburban school, which stands alone, unaffected by its neighbors, the urban school does not stand alone and is strongly influenced by neighboring buildings that help create the urban environment. This fact suggests that the city school should be planned *with* other urban facilities, and should be closely related to streets, parks, community social and cultural facilities, and to other educational institutions, as well as commercial and government facilities. Cultural, arts, or community centers are natural neighbors for schools—or the school itself can be considered to be the cultural-education center. Pittsburgh studies have even explored the possibilities of integrating the Great High Schools with commercial areas, along with new rapid-transit stations.

This form of integration will be more prevalent in the planned towns and cities of the future than in the traditional cities of the past and present.

If, then, we begin to tie all these pieces together—changes in the nature of cities themselves, changes in the educational program, and changes in educational media—we can draw a few rough generalizations about the urban schools of tomorrow.

First, I believe that these schools will be interrelated in great systems linked together by electronic and other devices for relaying information, and by appropriate transit facilities for moving pupils. Although the over-all systems will involve large numbers of students (depending, of course, on the size of the community, among other things), individual schools will not need to be large. They can be kept small and can be located conveniently near student residences. Students, nevertheless, will enjoy a high degree of mobility, spending part of their time at a "home base" school, but also moving via rapid transit or other means to specialized program centers.

Second, each individual will have something approximating his own unique program and his own schedule. He will move freely in time and space through a nongraded system. The use of new media will encourage concentration of resources and services at supplemental and regional centers, but will also encourage dispersal of use, since electronic access to information can be widespread.

Third, urban school design will embrace typically urban building forms, such as high-rise, underground, and air-rights construction, but this, too, will depend heavily on the type of urban community involved.

Finally, schools will be integrated with other community facilities. The schools, themselves, will become community centers for education, culture, and recreation, expressing the growing recognition that "living" and "learning" are one. In this way, the schools of the future will mesh with the cities of the future in a new, more fruitful fashion than ever before.

PART II

THE SYSTEM

Between the city and the schoolhouse stands the "system." This invisible, but powerful, reality is a set of organizational relationships. It differs from community to community. In some cities it is so large, complex, and bureaucratized that nobody understands it in its entirety. Elsewhere, it may still be small and more or less manageable. The system, however, is the basic mechanism by which the citizens of any city attempt to translate educational policy into real changes in their children. As such, it is the inevitable focal point of struggle. Conflicting forces—administrators, teachers, parents, the students themselves—fight for control of, or influence over, the system.

In this section, we move from a discussion of that most important (but least powerful) constituency, the children themselves, to a series of hard-headed, forcefully presented suggestions for changing school systems. Professor Preston Wilcox, for example, makes a basic contribution by tracing for us, in practical detail, the kinds of links that can be created between the school and the community. His chapter, "The Community-Centered School," provides a workable model for the post-enclave school of the future, a school that draws parents, community leaders, teachers, administrators, and others together into the educational process. While addressed to problems in the ghettos, it has relevance to urban—and even suburban—schools everywhere. It is impossible, however, to bring parents and the community into a new, more fruitful relationship with the school unless power is redistributed among the contending forces. Thus Fantini and Magat describe a powerful move in this direction—the proposals for decentralization that have triggered angry controversy in New York and other major cities.

This call for local control of urban schools is closely linked to the rising demand for cultural and ethnic diversity, which is part of society's movement away from the standardized education sys-

tems of the industrial past. So, too, is Kenneth Clark's challenge to create alternatives to the urban public school by turning to corporations, trade unions, and even the military for help with the problems of education.

Most of these ideas, in turn, are countered by John Fischer, who offers a ringing defense of public education, along with his own eloquent agenda for change. The section ends with Dean H. Thomas James's thoughtful call for a new look at the functions of the urban school—an end to publicly financed "baby-sitting." In short, within the span of a relatively short section, it is possible to survey most of the major issues that will agitate school boards and administrators in the decade to come.

7. The Disadvantaged Child

by Samuel Shepard, Jr.

Samuel Shepard, Jr., is Assistant Superintendent, Banneker District, St. Louis Public Schools. Dr. Shepard has served as a high school teacher in Kansas City, Missouri, and as an elementary school principal and director of elementary education in St. Louis. A member of the St. Louis Board of Community Services, he has received the Page One Award of the St. Louis Newspaper Guild and was cited for distinguished service to education by the University of Missouri College of Education.

The single central and inescapable fact about the schoolhouse in the city is that during the next decade, at least, it will be principally populated by disadvantaged learners—children with needs that cannot be met adequately by today's public schools.

What is there about these children that renders the schools' present program ineffective? What kind of program will serve their needs? To what extent should educational materials, curricula, and methods be altered to meet their needs? What kinds of teachers and administrators are needed to work effectively with them?

My experiences in the Banneker District in St. Louis have given me a few insights which might have value in our efforts to answer questions like these. I believe I know the disadvantaged child and some of the factors that make him what he is. I have lived and worked among them for many years and know that these people are human beings with all the ordinary hopes, frustrations, joys, sorrows, and desires to escape—feelings not necessarily expressed in conventional middle-class terms but experienced with the same intensity.

Let us piece together a partial picture of the disadvantaged child. Whatever his racial or ethnic background, one can be almost certain that he will be poor and will manifest this poverty in the clothes he wears, his lack of cleanliness, his generally undernourished condition, and his tendency to be suspicious of us, the personification of the more affluent middle class. These, however, are only the external differences. Other, less conspicuous characteristics influence, and perhaps even determine, whether or not our pupil will long remain in school and move up the socio-economic ladder of our nation.

The disadvantaged pupil possesses a decidedly negative self-image. More than likely, his early preschool interpersonal experiences will have been extremely limited and so characterized by either parental neglect, on the one hand, or excessive authoritarian controls, on the other, that he will not see himself as a worthy, loved, and wanted individual. Closely related to this unrealistically low opinion of himself will be his values.

What are some of these values? First, he is not likely to see much good in, or derive much pleasure from, going to school, a place in which he discovers quite early that he is neither liked nor successful. If this child is a boy, and particularly a Negro boy, he will see the school largely as a woman's world, not suited to any self-respecting boy at all. Then there is the matter of pleasing the teachers. Ordinarily, a child in a disadvantaged environment couldn't care less whether he pleases or wins the approval of his teacher. On the contrary, it may even be to his advantage, in so far as status with his peers is concerned, actually to displease the teacher and provoke anger. In a word, his system is not at all similar to that which characterizes middle-class society. Rather, it is a system of standards designed to wring a tolerable existence out of a life filled with limitations, poverty, and reminders of the worthlessness of self. In this life environment, the disadvantaged child daily faces scenes that violate all standards of middle-class morality and that would send the middle-class viewer into prolonged states of shock.

This is a life that places a premium on living at any price and in any way, regardless of whose morality such living violates. Is there any wonder, then, that the disadvantaged child, especially the Negro child, sees life differently and aspires to goals that are alien to those of middle-class Americans? It is important to understand that for such a child a low score on an intelligence test is probably not at all indicative of low intellectual capacity. It is important to hold fast to the expectation that such a child can, and will, in time make a 180-degree turn from his present course of antisocial, antidemocratic, and antihuman development, and begin the long and sure climb that will make him just as valuable, just as responsible, and just as productive as the most middle of the middle class in our great society.

Still another characteristic of the disadvantaged child, which a teacher must be sufficiently skillful to turn into an advantage, is the motivation dynamic in such a child. What forces stir him, push him into action, and inspire him to serious, as well as sustained, effort? Let me assure you that the disadvantaged are just as capable of deep and abiding concerns and extended efforts as are members of any social or cultural group. What is the general motivational principle of lower-class children and youth? You might be surprised to learn that, basically, it is the same thing that stirs anyone and causes him to act. Anybody, anything that any individual, regardless of his socio-economic background, has learned to see as personally enhancing, usually in terms of acceptance by and status within a desired group, will be, for him, motivating.

The key to the hierarchy of values for lower-class youth, especially children of the ghetto, is anything that enables them to earn a living out of their poverty-stricken environment and thereby satisfy the biological demands of the flesh. Status symbols that display satisfaction in terms of quality goods become extremely valuable and, therefore, engender highly motivating forces. In a word, the disadvantaged child or youth is interested in "living high on the hog" or giving the appearance of doing so. What enables him to accomplish this is unquestionably motivating.

Now, what are the implications of this factor in teaching? Does it follow that teachers cannot hope to interest the disadvantaged in the goals and the education necessary to succeed in American life? I would answer with an emphatic no. On the contrary, teachers not only *can* promote such interests but must do so, if our way of life is to endure and prosper.

Let us now consider briefly the task of the administrator of the schoolhouse in the city. For the educational administrator serving in disadvantaged areas, the same problems and difficulties exist as in any area—but to a much greater degree. In addition, he must solve other problems that are peculiar to the socioculturally disadvantaged environment from which the pupils of his school or district come.

One of the most difficult and elusive problems of the administrator serving the disadvantaged areas is his own attitude toward sociocultural disadvantage and toward the children and parents who are its victims. All too frequently, educational administrators, like many teachers, see the socioculturally disadvantaged child as one whose chances for upward mobility are limited not by environmental factors that can be changed, but by unchangeable internal factors such as limited mental capacity. Few administrators or teachers will admit that this is what they believe, but this point of view can be deduced from their actions and from the unguarded expletives they utter as they meet problem situations growing out of cultural disadvantage. How many administrators actually encourage their teachers to get blood out of a turnip and never give up on a child? How many principals are permitted to go along believing that the more pupils they transfer to classes for the mentally retarded (more recently labeled "slow learners") the greater administrative service they are rendering both the children and the teacher, to say nothing of the long-range benefits they are accruing for society? How many administrators accept the perennial complaints of so many teachers that "Johnny just can't learn to read or to do arithmetic or to see beauty and value in the finer things in life and in the pursuit of academic excellence"?

Indeed, how many principals actually regard their assignment to schools in ghetto communities as a sign of being in ill-favor with the higher administrative office? How many times are such assignments in reality a slap on the wrist?

Unquestionably, the educational leader in disadvantaged areas needs, first of all, to solve the problem of his own attitudes. The administrator must learn to see the disadvantaged child as one who possesses as much potential for academic and social success as the well-behaved and nice-to-be-around, nondisadvantaged child. In short, the constructive administrator in such communities must see that the problem of sociocultural disadvantage is basically that of defective motivation on the part of all concerned—the child, his parents, teachers, and principal.

Just as few administrators adequately understand cultural disadvantage and its effects on personality and behavior, so, also, do few teachers. Often, only the more ineffective and inexperienced teachers are assigned to disadvantaged areas; many of the more experienced ones simply won't go or remain on such assignments. Equally often, ghetto teachers have not been given the preservice training needed to enable them to understand or to develop instructional procedures that really work with the culturally disadvantaged. How many teachers, for example, know that the first battle to be won with the disadvantaged (and probably recalcitrant) pupil is that of overcoming the pupil's own negative self-image? How many teachers actually recognize classroom failure or lack of pupil interest in academic activities as a product of environment, not merely a sign of low mentality or downright cussedness? Finally, how many teachers, usually the very personification of middle-class values, virtues, and vices, are inadvertently condescending in their attitudes and interpersonal relations with the children they teach and with the parents of these children?

The educational administrator's second problem, then, once he has mastered his own attitudes, is to help the members of his staff gain a more positive perspective and to get them to change their teaching strategies. This problem, since it is one involving change in values, attitudes, and long-entrenched practices, is not easily resolved.

A third problem facing the educational leader has to do with curriculum. The question of paramount importance here is what kinds of *experience opportunities* does a disadvantaged child need and how can these opportunities be structured into a sequence that is initially compensatory and remedial, but not ultimately limited to a low vocational terminus.

A fourth problem area might well be the very routine of administration and the rut in which it so often places its administrators. Too often, the educational administrator, bogged down with the intricacies and sheer mechanics of running the school or district, doesn't have the opportunity to put on the hat of a supervisor. How many times does the administrator actually visit classrooms in the role of supervisor for the express purpose of seeing what he can do to help the teacher improve teaching and learning? Indeed, how many principals have more than a cursory knowledge of the nature of child development, the content of the various grade levels, and the more modern methods of teaching? How many administrators, themselves, are up-to-date on the newer insights into learning and the kinds of experience situations needed to foster learning by children of sociocultural disadvantage? Finally, how many principals actually know how to teach and what constructive supervision consists of?

Then, of course, there are the thousand-and-one problems that seldom arise in the affluent community: the many, many children who don't eat any breakfast at all, to say nothing of an adequate lunch; the children who come from families in which there is no father and in which the mother, having to work, keeps the oldest boy or girl out of school half or more of the school year to take care of preschool kids; the many children whose families consist of six to ten other children, together with parents and even grandparents or aunts and uncles, all living within two or three rooms that provide no privacy and little opportunity for peace and quiet, to say nothing of a place conducive to study.

Children coming from such homes are bound to bring discipline problems to the school—fights, destruction of school property, disrespect for themselves, teachers, the custodial staff, and even for the principal. The pupils' widespread lack of interest and poor achievement almost inevitably lower the morale and enthusiasm of the teaching staff, with the result that a vicious circle of apathy, discouragement, and perfunctory effort sets in.

Nor should we forget the difficult, almost insurmountable problem of parental fear of, and disgust toward, the school and school people. This fear, often manifesting itself as indifference, apathy, or even outright hostility on the part of disadvantaged parents, makes the school appear to be an unwanted alien island.

Such conditions need not exist. Dr. Havighurst, in his paper, has referred to the infamous federal housing project in St. Louis. There is a school there that has 1,500 youngsters and a faculty of fifty. We haven't had a single teacher transfer out of that school in five years. The percentage of attendance in 1966–67 was 92.4, which is competitive with the city average. Vandalism—that is, breakages into the school and destruction of property—occurred only once in that school year. Of the 1,500 youngsters, only 3 were suspended during the school year. So I say that the cycle of apathy and anger need not exist. As a matter of fact, it is the parents who have made the difference. In the evening meetings that we hold each October with them, we register anywhere from 400 to 550 parents. The cycle can be broken. But it is not easy.

There is, for example, the ever present problem of insufficient funds to support the learning programs or experience opportunities, both within and outside the school, that the disadvantaged child must have if his view of self, his attitude toward school and life, and his ways of behavior are to be turned around and made more positive and compatible with the society as it exists today. How many boards of education have the funds to set up and maintain a Head Start program? How many schools have provisions for giving most of their pupils a good breakfast and hot lunch? How many schools have the funds and personnel to set up and staff extended school programs to meet the needs of both children and parents who are victims of sociocultural disadvantage?

Now, many elementary schools have teacher's aides and other paraprofessionals who can relieve the more professionally trained teachers to offer counseling and individualized instruction. But how many schools have available the services of a psychiatrist, psychologist, physician, counselors, and social workers whenever these services are needed? How many schools have the petty cash to sponsor the much needed social get-togethers for parents, which could improve rapport with them and, indirectly, with their children? And, finally, how many schools have enough teachers to reduce the pupil-teacher ratio to twenty children or fewer per teacher? It may well be that such a low ratio is a must for effective programs with the disadvantaged. These are but a few of the problems facing the educational administrator who serves a community of sociocultural disadvantage.

I would suggest that in coping with these problems we should not prejudge either the kind of learning that we can expect in the disadvantaged or the depth of that learning. Teachers should enter their classrooms unshackled by limited visions and aborted expectations. They should see in each face—whether turned upward toward them with young enthusiasm and respect or downcast and sullen—

the possibilities for real growth and development into responsible and productive citizenship. If they can do this, their vision and expectations will be contagious and will spread to the children. They will heighten the children's own views and hopes for themselves and will result in greater and more sustained effort, positive outlooks, and higher goals. Likewise, teachers should not prejudge the kind or extent of cooperation they can expect from parents. Their response to invitations for them to become partners in the education of their children will correlate with the teacher's degree of sincerity.

It should be at once clear that the urban school must change, not so much in what and how it teaches as in the attitudes, hopes, and interpersonal skills of its teachers and administrators. Whatever materials and teaching methods are employed, a learning atmosphere should be created in which the dominant characteristic is respect and genuine concern. Success with the disadvantaged will depend less upon special materials or special teaching techniques than upon the teacher's own personal warmth and noncondescending air. I would also add that, the more we structure learning situations that are real and meaningful in the lives of pupils, the more we will be able to involve these learners in worthwhile activities that will help them to understand that success in school is their most important business.

The nation must not write off the children of the schoolhouse in the city. We must not envision for them only "life adjustment," low-level academic goals, and vocational semiskills. In fact, the most significant differences between a disadvantaged child and one who is not are those of motivation and orientation toward education. When the disadvantaged child has been helped to see himself as capable of achieving success in school, and has been convinced that such success can, and will, make an important difference in his opportunities to earn the good life, the stultifying effects of parental and other adult defeat and apathy will be removed. This depends, however, on the complete desegregation of all aspects of American life, particularly housing and job opportunities.

In short, I suggest that the key to the whole needed change in the education of the children in the schoolhouse in the city is a corps of understanding, dedicated teachers whose breadth of formal and informal experiences has enabled them to see beyond the present low achievement levels and the antisocial patterns of their pupils. This does not mean that what are needed are soft, sentimental "bleeding hearts." The goal in education for these children, as it is for all children, should not be charity or the provision of excuses for their shortcomings; rather, the goal should be a hardheaded practical one—helping the children of all people enter into the frame of mind necessary for them to help themselves earn a decent living in a society that is growing more technical each day.

8. Resources for Transforming the Ghetto

by Gregory R. Farrell

Gregory R. Farrell is Assistant Commissioner, New Jersey Department of Community Affairs, as well as director of the New Jersey Office of Economic Opportunity. He has been executive director of United Progress, Inc., a community-action agency in Trenton, N.J., and an urban affairs and education reporter for the *Trenton Evening Times*. He has also been a classroom teacher and the assistant director of admissions at Princeton University.

If we look at the crisis in our cities and in our schools, we find that most of what is wrong can be summed up under three broad accusations. We hear these accusations again and again, and no proposals for solutions to our problems can ignore them. They go something like this:

Accusation Number 1: We are moving from Fun City to Ghetto City in a very short span of time. We are building a black ghetto in the old cities, and a comfortable, white, two-car garage ghetto in the suburbs. Faced with this seemingly relentless tendency, we are misappropriating and maldistributing the human and financial resources of an affluent society. We are locating the resources where the problems are not, and the problems where the resources are not.

Accusation Number 2: Even if resources were directed back to those in our cities who need them most, the systems that handle and administer these resources—educational systems, welfare systems, housing systems, governmental systems—are irrelevant to the lives of the people to whom they are supposed to be addressed, perhaps even destructive or punitive in their approach to the consumer. These systems, given greater resources, would merely pervert and misuse them as they have perverted and misused the present limited resources entrusted to them.

Accusation Number 3: The bureaucracy within these systems is so designed and constructed as to attract, reward, promote, and sell mediocrity. This bureaucracy, by virtue of its resistance to change, by virtue of its enormity and cumbersomeness, cannot and will not respond to crises, and is, perhaps, the most obsolete of all the structures of an obsolescent urban center.

I have deliberately attempted to state each of these accusations in an extreme form, in order to try to push the argument as far as possible. Let us now probe each of these three accusations, one at a time, to see not merely whether they are true (for there is some truth in all of them) but, rather, whether the situation is as hopeless as they suggest. Are there constructive solutions to some of our urban ills?

Let us begin, then, with the problem of mismatched resources, the rise of a poverty-stricken all-black ghetto in the city and an affluent white ghetto in the suburbs.

There are really two basic strategies for cracking this problem. One is to disperse the urban ghetto, to increase the geographic mobility of its residents and to help them move to better parts of the city and into suburban areas. The second approach is to gild the ghetto, to seed it with quality, and upgrade it out of existence—attracting white, middle-class families to it, locating new businesses, schools, and cultural facilities in it.

It seems to me that neither of these approaches to Ghetto City or Ghetto Suburb can be carried out in isolation or exclusion. It is necessary to employ both simultaneously as coordinated parts of a total strategy aimed at the improvement of life in *both* city and suburb.

Well, how do you do it? There is no shortage of ideas. Take first the dispersion of the urban ghetto. The problem is to move the present residents out of the slums and attract back the white escapees who have fled to the suburbs. There are a number of ways to accomplish this. In New Jersey, we recently passed legislation that puts the state into the bond business and creates a housing finance agency that will stimulate construction of middle-income housing within the city, while working toward an integrated mix of housing levels within both city and suburb. This is only one way. At the same time, we can work to improve the urban school—that great motivator of middle-class behavior—so that it will attract the middle-class family rather than repel it. We can also provide housing subdivisions open to both white middle-class and urban ghetto residents, so that the Negro slum dweller has an opportunity to live elsewhere, either in the city or in the suburbs and smaller towns that encircle it. There are ways to make this attractive to these communities. For example, it has been suggested by some that we put bounties on the heads of urban ghetto youngsters, so that whichever suburban school system gets them gets the bounty as well. A price of $3,000 a year on the head of a slum child might make him and his family more attractive to the community that now restricts and rejects him.

Going further, it is possible to insure the suburban community against loss in real-estate values that might result from an in-migration of low-income minority groups from the city ghetto. In the meantime, we can work to develop jobs outside the urban ghetto and direct major resources to the transportation problem so that ghetto residents can get to these jobs. Such transportation facilities would help break down the wall that exists between city and suburb —making it possible for people who live within the city to get to jobs in the suburbs more easily, and simultaneously helping those who live in the suburb get to jobs in the city. One might go on listing things that can be done to hasten the dispersal of the black ghetto—promotion of home ownership, for example, through a reorganized FHA program, tax incentives, and the like.

But there is a basic objection to this strategy. Often the objection comes from militant sectors of the Negro community. Simply put, it holds that such efforts merely drain Negro leadership away from the central cities. Some black activists regard movements toward metropolitan government and movements toward dispersal of the ghetto as ways of weakening the solidarity of the black community, ways of keeping Negroes from gaining political power in the central cities. Needless to say, there are also some white groups that regard the dispersal of the urban ghetto with something less than enthusiasm, albeit for quite different reasons. Nevertheless, only by pursuing this twin-pronged strategy can we, in the long run, save our cities.

When we speak of bringing resources to bear on the problems of the urban center, we must concern ourselves with economic resources, with jobs. One of the most interesting ideas to come forth

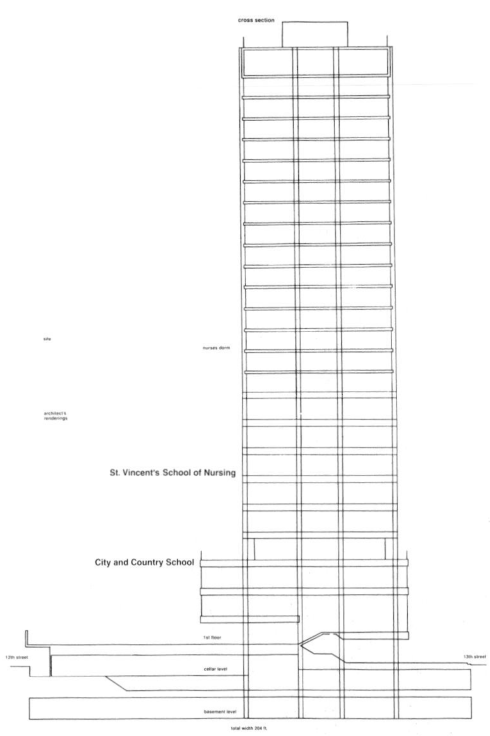

Examples of two new approaches to economy in urban school construction in New York City: *above*—combined occupancy, represented by the proposed combination of the City and Country School and St. Vincent's School of Nursing; *right*—air rights, reflected in the plan to straddle the Hutchinson River Parkway with the new Herbert H. Lehman High School.

Stephen Shilowitz, Architect
(City and Country)
Eggers and Higgins, Architects
(Lehman)

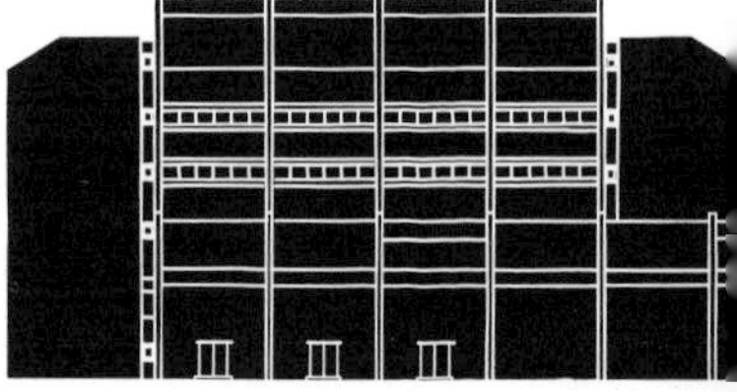

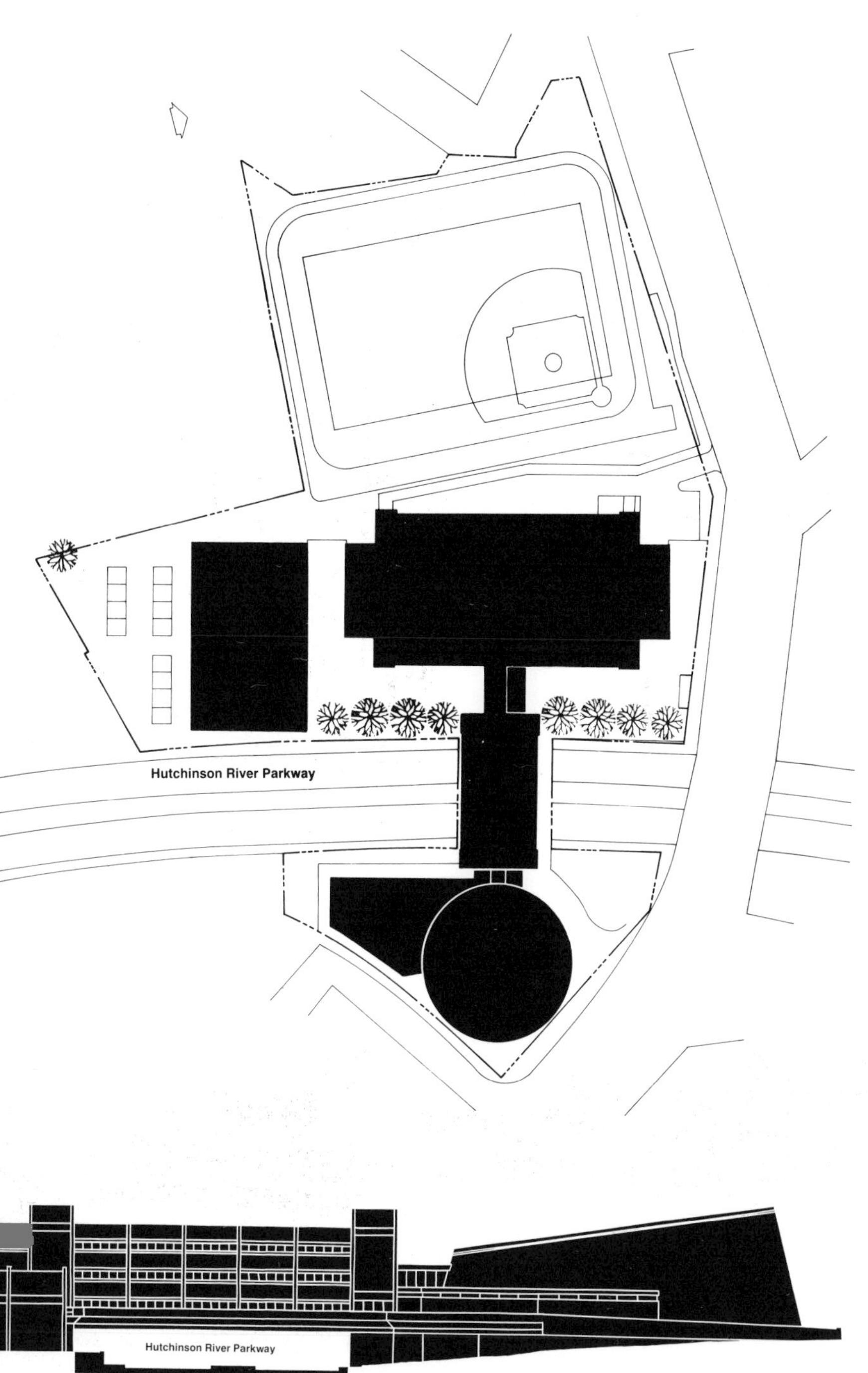
Hutchinson River Parkway
Hutchinson River Parkway

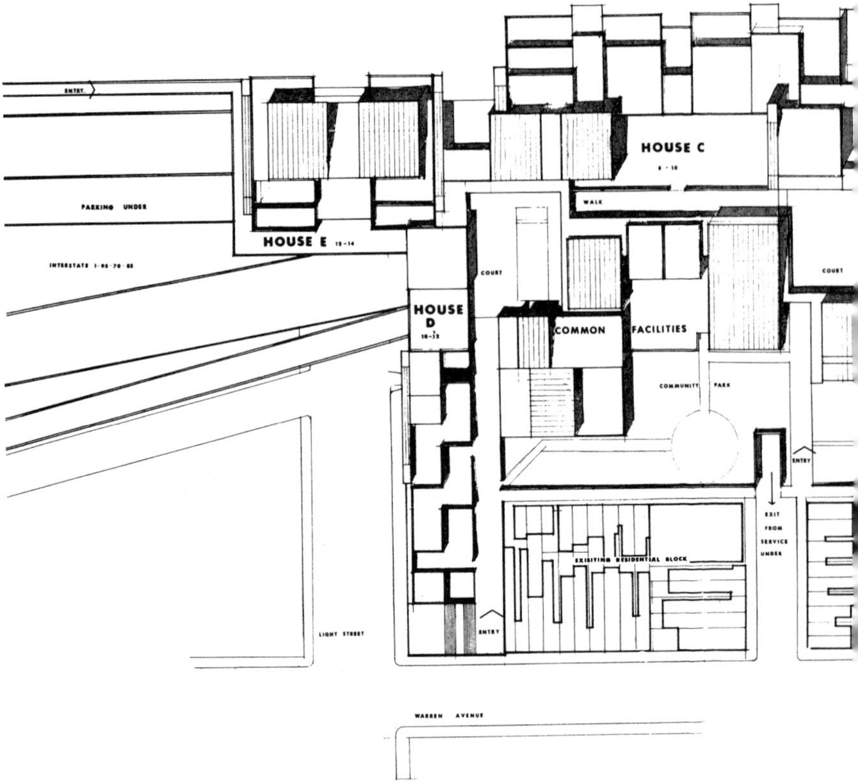

ENTRY

PARKING UNDER

HOUSE E 12-14

INTERSTATE I-95-70-83

HOUSE C
8-10

WALK

COURT

HOUSE D 10-12

COMMON FACILITIES

COURT

COMMUNITY PARK

ENTRY

EXIT FROM SERVICE UNDER

EXISITING RESIDENTIAL BLOCK

ENTRY

LIGHT STREET

WARREN AVENUE

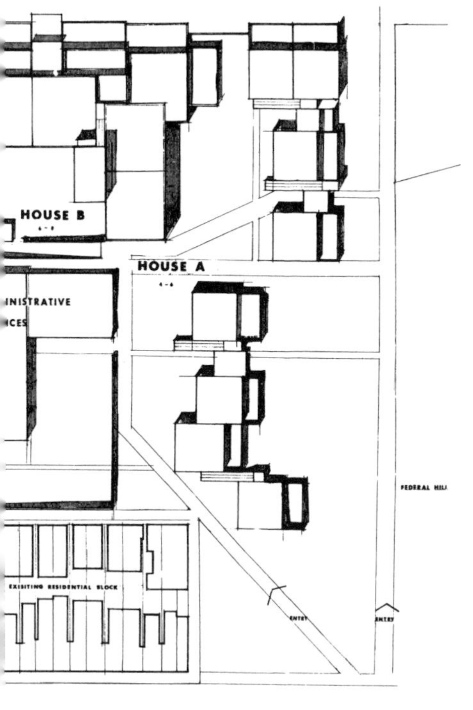

A number of cities are turning to the education park to solve problems of school segregation, plant obsolescence, and economics. This park, proposed for Baltimore, would utilize air rights over an expressway and would enroll children aged four through fourteen.

The CORDE Corporation

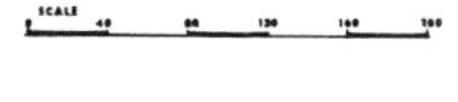

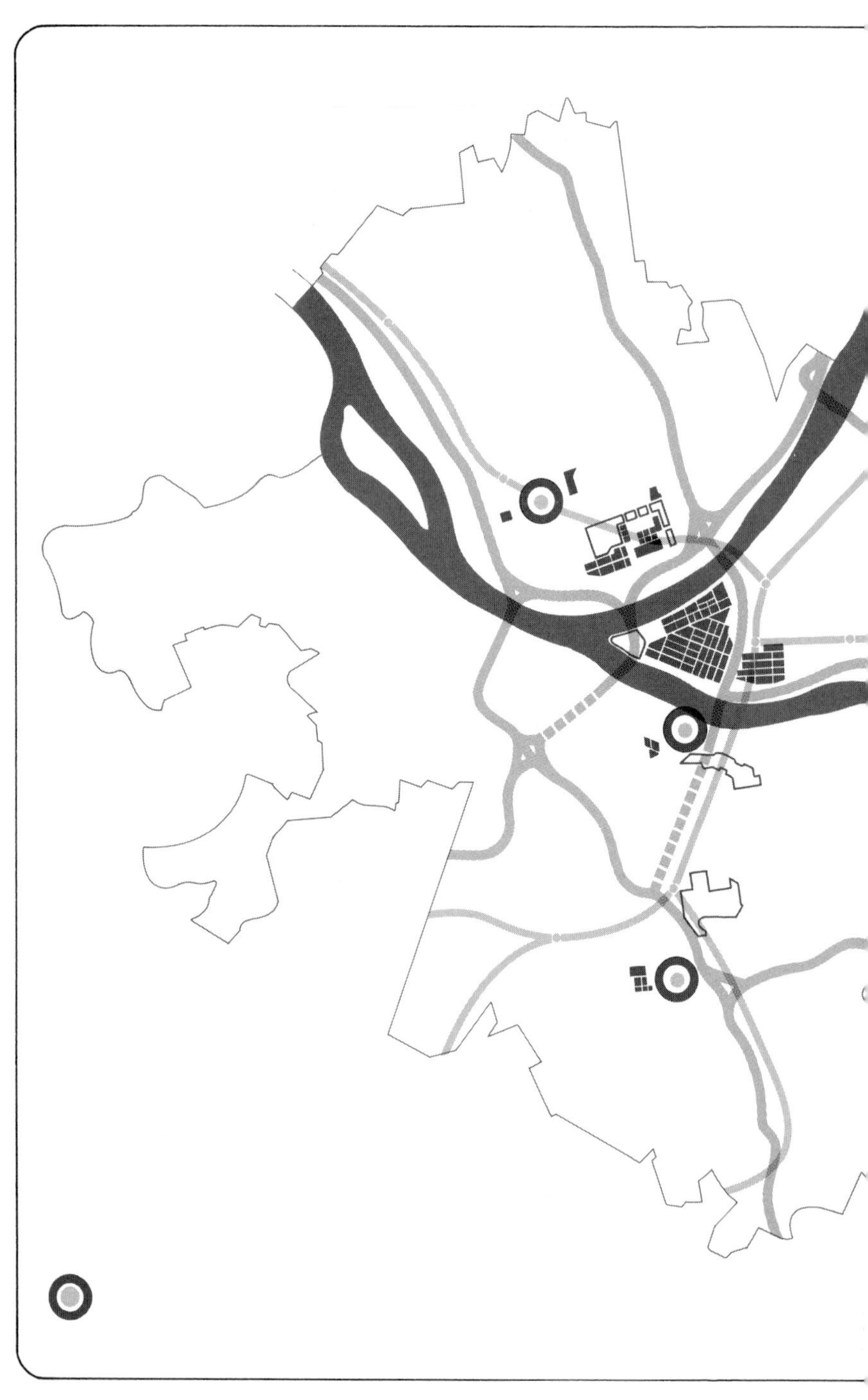

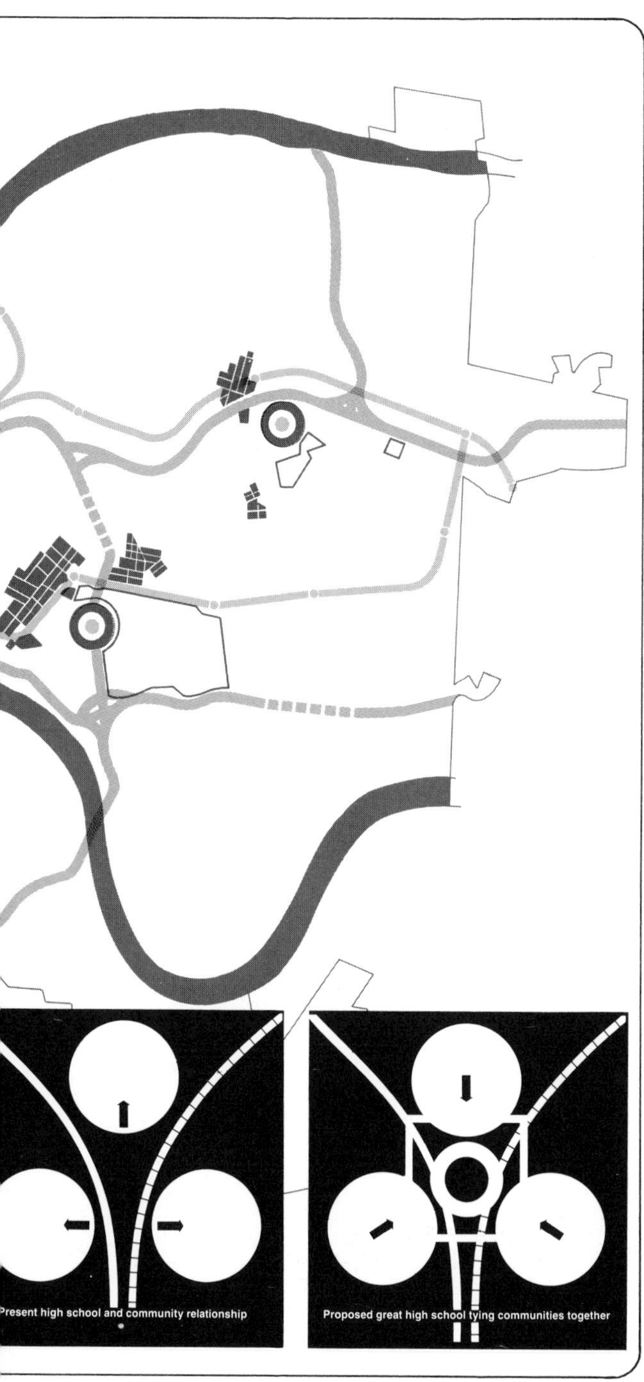

Pittsburgh has taken a different approach to the education park, with its plan to replace 23 existing high schools with 5 Great High Schools of 5,000 to 6,000 students each. The Great High Schools will occupy parklike sites linked to each other by the city's expressways (*dotted lines*) and rapid-transit system (*solid lines*) and to their neighborhoods by pedestrian greenbelts, along which the lower schools will be located (*see following page*).

Urban Design Associates

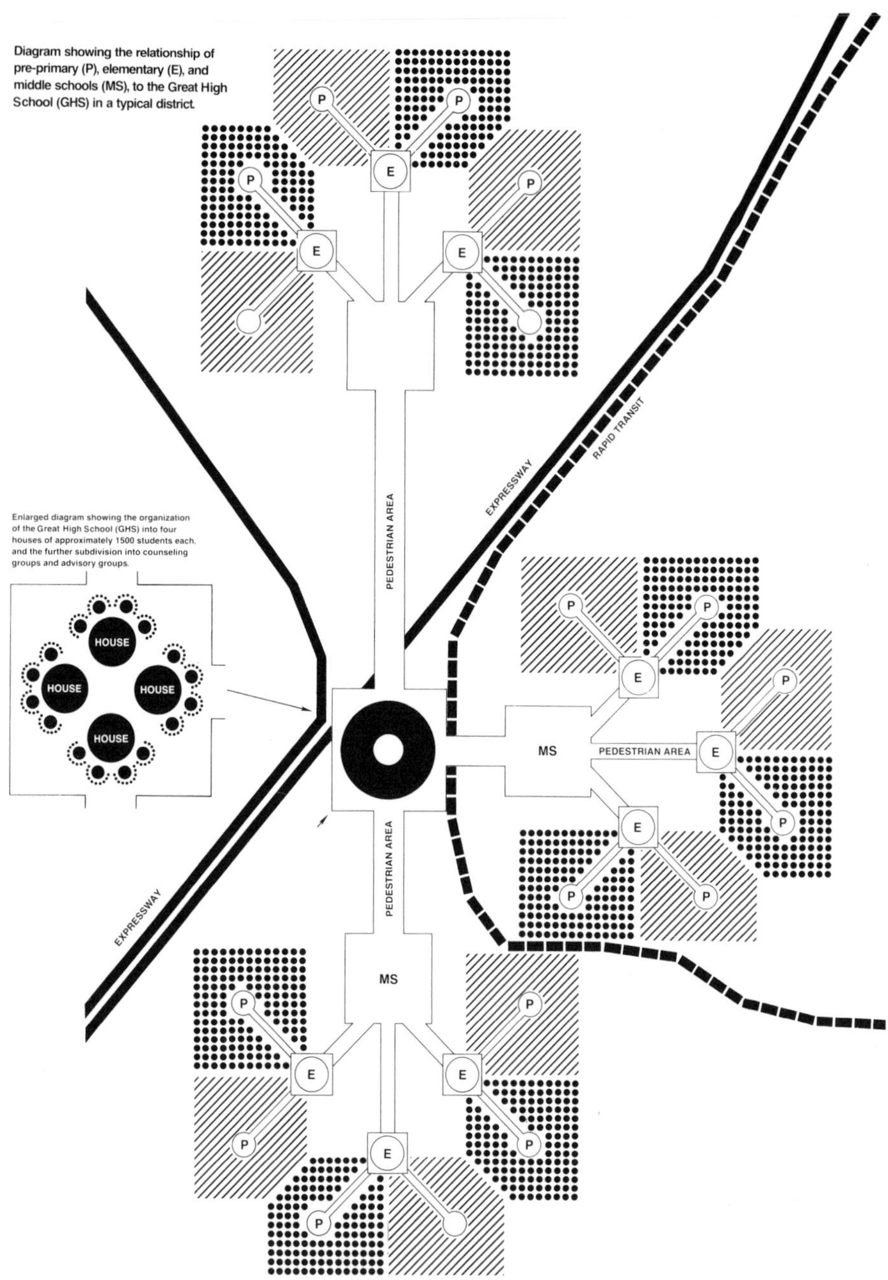

Diagram showing the relationship of pre-primary (P), elementary (E), and middle schools (MS), to the Great High School (GHS) in a typical district.
Enlarged diagram showing the organization of the Great High School (GHS) into four houses of approximately 1500 students each, and the further subdivision into counseling groups and advisory groups.
HOUSE
HOUSE
HOUSE
HOUSE
P
E
MS
PEDESTRIAN AREA
PEDESTRIAN AREA
PEDESTRIAN AREA
EXPRESSWAY
EXPRESSWAY
RAPID TRANSIT

STR
CLOS
8 AM
SCHOOL
PLAY

New York City is planning its proposed Linear City as a total community. A six-mile stretch of the projected Cross-Brooklyn Expressway will be built over an existing little-used railroad cut and, in turn, will be topped by Linear City—a complex of housing, commercial, and industrial facilities, as well as cultural and governmental centers. Educational facilities will be woven through the new community, and pupils will use the rapid-transit system to move from one educational resource center to another.

The CORDE Corporation

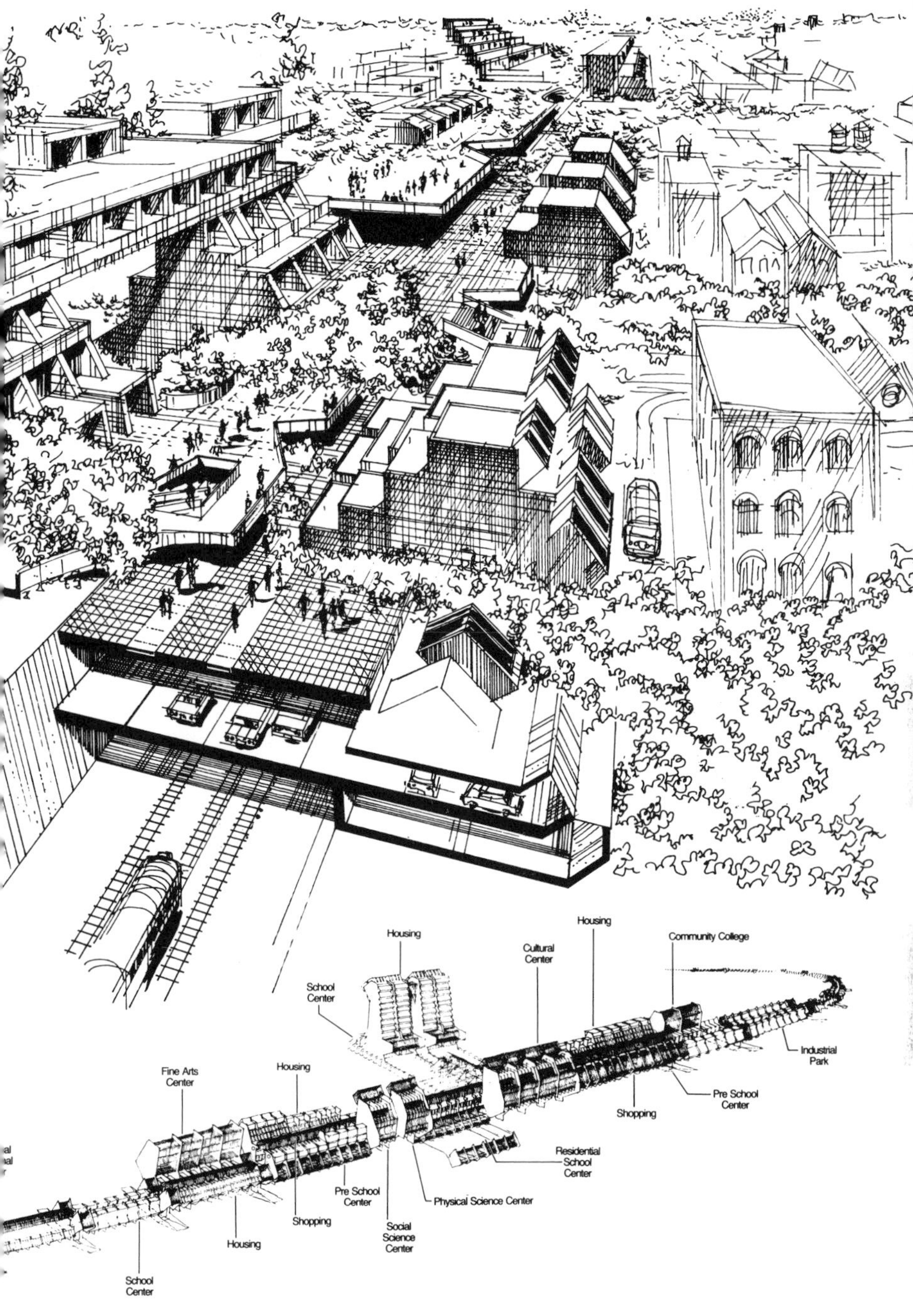
Housing
Housing
Cultural Center
Community College
School Center
Industrial Park
Pre School Center
Shopping
Fine Arts Center
Housing
Residential School Center
Pre School Center
Physical Science Center
Shopping
Social Science Center
Housing
School Center

The New York City Educational Construction Fund is a new agency empowered to build schools and sell or lease the air rights over them, utilizing the income to retire the bonds. Its first project, now under construction, is P.S. 126, a combined school and housing project in the Bronx.

Brown and Guenther, Architects

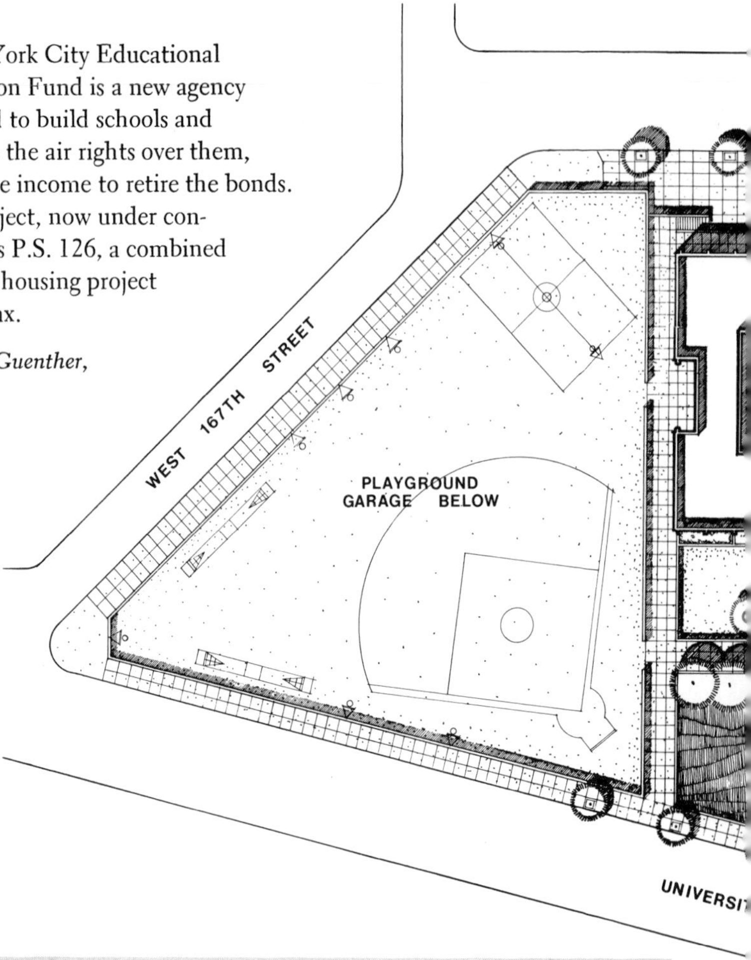

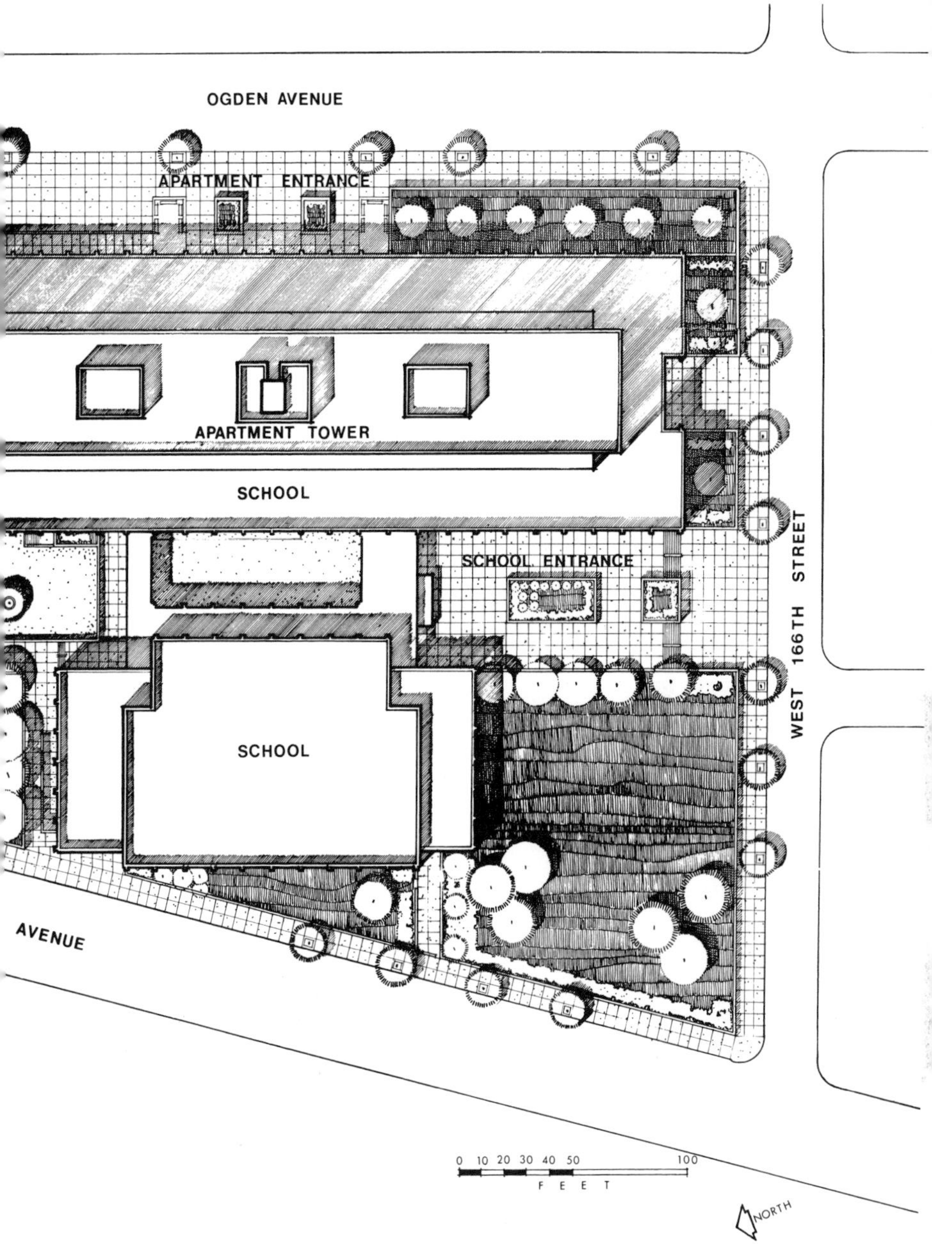

OGDEN AVENUE

APARTMENT ENTRANCE

APARTMENT TOWER

SCHOOL

SCHOOL ENTRANCE

SCHOOL

WEST 166TH STREET

AVENUE

0 10 20 30 40 50 100

FEET

NORTH

A number of cities have turned to the community school concept, in which the school plant serves not only children but residents of all ages. The Conte School in New Haven is a prototype. Its library doubles as a branch public library; its auditorium, as a community little theater. It also houses a senior citizens' center and neighborhood offices of community and city agencies.

Skidmore, Owings, and Merrill, Architects

recently has to do with the role of the city in providing jobs. Here we need to think of the public-service sector of the city's economy as a big economic growth sector. In fact, we might begin to think in terms of the "service city" concept. This means reorganizing our schools or vocational-education institutions to provide workers with skills for a new, expanding service economy—jobs in schools, in hospitals, in welfare agencies, in the full range of service occupations needed by the urban center.

In this sense, government would not be only the employer of last resort but an employer whom one might choose as a first resort, as an avenue to careers of importance. By systematically developing the "service city" concept, we can provide employment where it is now lacking.

Such a philosophy might also create a magnet for talent. This is another of the resources that need to be deployed in the urban battle. We have to recruit the talent. Proclaim the city as the new frontier and bring in the talent. This is what we are not yet doing. At Stanford, I talked with a research assistant who works in the School Planning Laboratory. He said, "You know, we are doing some great things here, but we're doing them all in the wrong places, because the only places we can really get going on our projects are the places that can afford it, and they don't really need us. The places that cannot afford us—they're the ones that need us. But they can't pay for the kind of work we're doing."

This brings us, therefore, to the basic problem of financing. Other chapters in this volume deal with taxation, state- and federal-aid formulas, and other such matters. I need only call attention to the existence of more than 400 federal grant-in-aid programs through which funds may flow to the urban center. The complexities of these programs, the difficulties of using them and putting them together so they make some sense at the local, working level, create an almost impossible problem, as matters now stand. It is a problem that, in itself, requires a major expenditure of resources, time, and talent.

But the art of snagging a federal grant is only part of the story. There is a largely unexplored area that could yield significant resources for the city. Thus, there are many hidden weapons in the governmental structure, within the tax mechanism, within the interest rate, within the financial leverage devices and flow directors in our society, which few of us have taken the time to analyze and understand. I am convinced that the adroit manipulation of those levers and mechanisms could produce major changes in the arrangement of our society and the allocation of great resources to the large urban centers.

Furthermore, we need to remember that government is not the only possible source of succor. There is the vast potential of the private sector, the possibility of the urban development corporation. There is, also, the interest of the computer industry in the problems of education and school management. In assembling resources with which to attack the problem of the urban ghetto, we somehow must make business understand that its future is tied to the future of the city and that, perhaps, morality and good business will very soon be one and the same.

There is, finally, still another technique for attracting major new resources to the city. We need not elaborate much on it. If the other methods suggested here are not employed, this ultimate technique *will* be used—the technique of the riot. Over the past couple of years, it has been by far the most successful way of attracting large amounts of new resources to the cities in a hurry. Let us hope we have sense enough to use the other avenues open to us so that this terrible, final technique need not be employed again.

Thus, the charge that our society is putting its resources into the wrong places at the wrong time is not without justification. But it need not continue to do so. We still have options open to us. Matters are by no means hopeless.

The second charge has to do with the relevance of city systems to their users.

It has been said that the services themselves are producer-oriented rather than consumer-oriented, that they have been designed for the convenience of the distributors of services rather than for those who receive them. They are created in such a welter of jurisdictional requirements that the customer is hard put to find his way through them. Thus, it is said that more resources alone would just heighten the level of their irrelevance. Medicaid is perhaps a good example in the states where it has begun to be implemented. It has become something approaching a national scandal, because the poor still do not receive adequate medical care. Medical costs are rising and the medical profession has benefited enormously, but the people for whom that legislation was originally designed have not. The implementing of Title I of the Elementary and Secondary Education Act is probably another example in which the use of additional, new resources does not accomplish what was intended. In school system after school system, such funds have been used to supplement teacher salaries with after-school payoffs of one sort or another, very carefully designed not to influence the working of the system itself in any substantial way.

There are, however, several approaches to the problems of relevancy. First of all, there is the problem of powerlessness. The systems are irrelevant because the people they are designed to serve have nothing to do with their design. The solution is simply to get those people—the people of East Harlem, the people of the Central Ward in Newark, the people of Watts—involved in the design and control of their own programs. The decentralization of school systems, the installation of black school principals and boards of education—these are efforts to overcome that sense of powerlessness by providing some means of control to the residents who are supposed to benefit from the service systems of the city.

There is an interesting sidelight to this, and that is that the poor have a greater right to this kind of control than even the most benevolent liberals might have thought. This is so because, in property-tax states, or states that depend largely upon property taxes, the poor are actually paying what amounts to a proportional share of the cost of their own support. A recent study at Rutgers entitled *Who Pays Welfare Costs in New Jersey?* suggests that, in fact, the poor do pay their own welfare costs. They support themselves in large measure. I think once they are aware of the fact that they are not mere supplicants but people who, by virtue of the taxes and rents they pay, are supporting a system that supports them, they are likely to become somewhat more vociferous in their demands for control.

There is a danger in this kind of response. Bayard Rustin writes of "frustration politics." Indeed, it might be the most diabolical of all schemes simply to dump the control of urban systems entirely upon the residents of the poverty areas. There is great danger of drowning them in the administration and implementation of many of these programs.

I am not saying that the present focus of power must be retained to insure against the misuse of resources. In fact, it seems to me that any misuse of those resources by ghetto people could not be much worse than the present misuse of resources. I am saying, however, that to dump the full, inordinate load upon them would be no favor and ultimately might be destructive in both a psychological and a moral sense.

What has to be worked out, it seems to me, is a careful releasing of control, to the degree that recipient groups are able to handle and use that control in terms that will not be frustrating to them and to society as a whole.

When we speak of making urban programs relevant to those who are supposed to benefit from them, we need also to bear in mind that this cannot be done merely by tinkering with the cut-and-dried methods of the past. What is needed is considerable imagination.

In Trenton, I once watched a regular first-grade teacher who was working in a Head Start program during the summer. She was a remarkable teacher. She had a sense of adventure; she was teaching children to read, or was at least exposing them to reading, and she was using an experimental method. There were fifteen youngsters, and she had a couple of assistants. All in all, the relationship of that teacher to the class and her sense of adventure and purpose were wonderful to witness.

I went back to see her three months later in her kindergarten class during the regular school year, and she was an entirely different person. A Negro girl walked up to her and put her hand on the teacher's dress. The teacher turned around and slapped the girl across the face, saying, "Don't you ever put your hands on me or anybody else again." It was inconceivable to me that this was the same woman I had seen in the summer Head Start program. She did something else that day. A youngster picked up a book and went to the back of the room with it. It happened to be a youngster who had been in her own Head Start classroom. Yet she went over to that youngster, snatched the book away from him, and said, "Books are for teachers. Go to the back of the room."

That kind of transformation in the quality of that teacher, in her orientation and her personality, would have been unbelievable to me had I not seen it. But consider the difference in her situation. During the summer, she had a classroom of fifteen youngsters; she was involved in a special experimental program; she had a sense of adventure. Back in the school year, she was caught up in the regular system. Several times during that day, she spoke to me with some apprehension about an impending visit from the principal. Several times, she tidied up the room to make sure it would look good when the principal stopped by. Time was taken —at least an hour and a half—in collecting pennies for milk. This was something many of the youngsters couldn't understand, because at Head Start they had gotten it free. Now, those who didn't bring the pennies didn't get the milk, and they couldn't understand. The time taken up in the collection of the money for the milk was time that could have gone for some worthier purpose.

There are many other glaring examples of the deadening influence that the lack of a sense of adventure, opportunity, and experimentation spread throughout the school system. We need, somehow, to open the system, to attempt the new.

In another community in New Jersey, we are running a school for dropouts. It is not called that by name, but is defined as such by its clinical staff. Teen-agers who are in the Neighborhood Youth Corps come in with an average reading level of fourth- and fifth-grade. We use a mixture of nonprofessional and professional teachers, and we use programed instruction. The youngsters come to school for reading, writing, arithmetic, and other subjects for three hours a day, fifteen hours a week, as a regular part of their working experience. To date, the average youngster has advanced 1.4 years in reading level in three months' time, as indicated by standardized tests. That is probably more impressive on paper than it is in actuality, but at least it indicates that the use of nonprofessional teachers in an atmosphere of experimentation and adventure, along with the use of programed instruction, can be made to work. We are probably wasting vast human resources by keeping out of our classrooms teachers who are now barred from teaching in an official way but who could make great contributions.

If we are to make educational services relevant to the lives of young people, we will have to be far more innovative than we have been, even at the cost of our bureaucracies. Perhaps we are not going at this from the right direction at all. Perhaps the school is too unwieldy an instrument ever to change. Maybe, instead of expanding the school to take on more and more of the functions of other institutions, such as the family and the job, we should encourage other institutions to develop their educational capacities. Maybe we should be concerned not solely about the structure, form, and program of the public school, but the educational programs of the other institutions that do the most effective job of educating.

I have yet to hear any really direct line of reaction to the Coleman Report's intimation that the most powerful educative force for youngsters of certain pre-adolescent ages is a peer group. Given that fact, or at least that assumption or tentative finding, how would you then organize an educational process?

These are the kinds of questions that need to be grappled with if we are ever to make our urban services relevant to the lives of their users. They are questions that fall outside the ordinary framework. There is no administrative niche for them. They make professionals uncomfortable. But they just might be the most important questions of all.

This brings us to the next accusation—the charge that our bureaucracies are so mediocre and rigid that they cannot possibly work, and that giving them more resources means only more waste and disappointment. First, let me challenge some of the assumptions in this charge. Bureaucracy is probably the easiest whipping boy to be found, and attacking it may well be the most inappropriate approach to urban change that one could possibly settle on.

If, in fact, it *is* important to nurture and educate youngsters in our schools, it is equally important to nurture and educate the teachers and administrators in those schools. That means we have to engage in new programs of recruitment. We have to take a hard look at the incentive systems that operate within the schools and other service systems. We have to work very seriously to encourage excellence among teachers, administrators, and field-service people. There are several ways to do that.

There are high school and college internship programs designed to lure young people into public service. We are entering an era now in which it is very difficult to tell the difference between the public and private sectors. It is also sometimes very difficult to distinguish among levels of government. People are bouncing back and forth from one to another—from private to public sector, from local to state or federal government, and from one governmental occupation to another. In a sense, it is an era of bounce, and to encourage that, to lend the public service sector some sense of adventure, is perhaps the most important task we have before us. It is also important to make use of the new professional who comes out of business and industry. Perhaps administrators for school systems ought to come out of the business community, rather than strictly through the educational system.

If we are going to attract better and better people into the management of necessary bureaucracies in the cities, we have to give them a more flexible ball game to play in. But not all people are prepared to participate in the new ball game. Probably one of the greatest reasons why administrations do not give adequate discretion to first-rate principals and teachers is because they have not filled their systems with first-rate principals and teachers. There are very few who have the energy, the desire, and the talent to make effective use of that flexibility.

This means that we must reward change within the system. We must encourage experimentation, even when it fails.

In short, I don't think that we can change the bureaucracy by attacking it. I think that, by holding bureaucracy up as whipping boy, we simply create greater resistance on the part of a large number of good-hearted, hard-working people who have expended years of effort and frustration, and who will regard the newcomers and the finger-pointers as babes in the wood. The only way to move the bureaucracy and make it work is to encourage excellence in it, to encourage better people to join it, and to structure the incentive system so that self-criticism and innovation are rewarded.

Three large accusations are hurled at our urban systems. All three have a degree of truth in them. But merely to accuse, to point a finger at the failure of others, to fulminate, is the easy way out. It is much harder to suggest imaginative yet practical solutions to problems. Yet, only through a chain reaction of imaginative, constructive programs can we answer, once and for all, these accusations that do, in fact, cut too close to the truth to be ignored.

9. The Community-Centered School

by Preston R. Wilcox

Preston R. Wilcox is a staff associate of the Education Affiliate of the Bedford-Stuyvesant Development and Services Corporation—an organization that is attempting to put into practice some of the educational innovations described in the accompanying chapter. A former Assistant Professor of Social Work (Community Organization) at the Columbia School of Social Work, Mr. Wilcox identifies himself as an "advocate-theoretician." He is the author of various antipoverty proposals, a participant in the controversy surrounding Intermediate School 201 in Harlem, and a strong proponent of school decentralization.

Who controls the schools our children attend? Who *should* control them? And what is the appropriate relationship between a school and the surrounding community? These questions are increasingly being forced into the headlines today by the devastating failure of our public education systems to educate millions of Black and poor youngsters. Today in the ghettos, angry parents and community leaders are literally demanding the right to shape new educational policies.

This unprecedented demand conflicts dramatically with the vested interests of boards of education, teachers' professional associations, unions, and other groups. The resultant clash has sharpened the issues, trained a whole cadre of educational activists, and raised fundamental questions affecting not merely ghetto schools but all education. It has also drawn long-overdue attention to the concept of the community-centered school. Before examining this revolutionary concept, we need to understand why so many Negroes today are seeking to control the schools in their communities.

Much of the early controversy in New York has centered on control of I.S. 201, a public intermediate school in Harlem. There, educational activists sought to get the New York City Board of Education to implement "other way" integration—that is, the transporting of white students into a Black ghetto to attend school.

When this failed, a community-controlled school was sought. These activists chose to believe that even in a racist society, organized to protect the interests of whites, one could be both Black *and* successful.

At first, the I.S. 201 activists attempted to elicit the agreement of the New York City Board of Education to conduct an experiment in community control of a school. The responses were evasive, perfunctory, or nonexistent. This is not surprising. As in most U.S. cities, the Board of Education is expected to represent *all* the people, and it has an established and unwritten policy that requires consensus. Yet, in most cases, consensus guarantees that the interests of the ghetto will be overlooked. (Until its recent expansion, only one member of the New York City Board of Education was Black and none were Puerto Rican, even though the student population was more than 50 per cent nonwhite.)

Failing to move the Board, the I.S. 201 parents had also carried their integration fight to the Mayor's office. The Mayor, in measured and somewhat professorial tones, gave them a lecture on the tax base of the city, and told them that school integration might stimulate an escalation of the white exodus. This was followed by a visit to Commissioner of Education Harold Howe. Howe, whose provocative paper opens this book, was cordial, concerned, committed to the principle—but apparently helpless to act.

Why do Black people seek control over their local schools? After watching the failures of the present school system, they have concluded that those in control of that system define its objectives in terms of white America. The present authorities use such phrases as "the entire system" or "Negroes aren't the only ones who need better schools." Activists, however, recognize these as euphemisms for maintenance of the degrading *status quo*. The tragic fact is that, regardless of intentions, Black Americans are treated not as full participants in the society but essentially as a group to be considered after the interests of others are attended to. So long as this remains true, school programs will continue to draw heavily on white, middle-class assumptions.

The essence of the struggle, therefore, has been to help the Black and poor residents of the ghettos understand that the present system, in the last analysis, was organized for the protection of "others"—not Black Americans. Indeed, it has been established fairly conclusively on the basis of ethnic composition, performance scores, per capita expenditures, teacher turnover and assignments, and the figures on upgrading of minority-group staff, that many large urban complexes have, in fact, dual school systems—one white and one Black, but both controlled by whites.

The minority-group student thus finds himself in the curious position of being miseducated by a system that represents everybody's interest but his. Such students are ordered to attend school under compulsory education laws seemingly for the express purpose of being convinced of their own uneducability. Those Black students who were able to negotiate the schools had to adopt the views of their oppressors. They had to listen to discussions of history that highlighted the honesty of George Washington but not the fact that he was a slaveowner. In short, the Wasp model was substituted for one with which Black students could more readily identify.

It is this tendency to deliver *generalized* white products into *specialized* Black communities that set the stage for the thrust by Black communities to take control of the schools set up to serve their children. The issue was engaged at I.S. 201. But it quickly spread to at least four other sites in New York, and to Washington, Boston, and Columbus, Ohio. It can be expected to break into the open in the South, as well, before long.

In every instance, a confrontation has occurred between the Black and/or poor and the school system. Note the word "poor," for this thrust is quite unlike the middle-class–oriented drive for quality, integrated education outside the ghetto. It is based on the poor, not the middle class. It seeks to build a constituency among parents and community leaders who, unlike the "Black bourgeoisie," recognize that their own destiny is tied to the plight of the Black poor in a society in which it pays to be neither Black nor poor.

The new thrust for community control of ghetto schools thus represents an important shift in emphasis: from a desire to replicate that which is American to a desire to reshape it. There is in this drive less concern with social integration than with effective education. To bring about effective education, however, it is necessary to do more than simply transfer control or change the ratio of white to Black on the teaching staff. It is necessary to take a revolutionary view of the role of the school in the community.

This brings us to the concept of the community-centered school —the school that functions as an acculturation tool, an educational instrument, and a community center.

As an acculturation tool, the community-centered school serves as a life-orientation vehicle for new students and "newcomers" to the city. It attempts to make viable connections between different homes and different cultures in a climate that respects and cherishes creative differences. It also nurtures similarities. The usual school pattern is to attempt to emphasize similarities and to obliterate differences—the melting-pot approach. Moynihan and Glazer stress, however, in *Beyond the Melting Pot*, that, in fact, the melting has never really taken place.

As an educational instrument, such a school is called upon to help its charges become addicted to the idea of (1) learning for use, (2) developing a sense of functional curiosity, and (3) assuming a large part of the responsibility for developing their own intellectual resources. The skillful teacher brings knowledge to be shared and expanded upon, not just accepted. The normal pattern requires students to memorize teacher offerings and to regurgitate them upon command. The student becomes the depository for the teacher's knowledge, not the enactor, evaluator, and thinker he desires to become.

As a community center, the school takes on the coloration of a freedom school. It becomes: (1) the facility where the community begins to meet its latent needs for recreation and fun; (2) the place where the community begins to formalize its efforts to express itself through art, music, drama, etc.; (3) the locale for shaping community policy as it relates to housing, traffic, health, education, and other social issues; and (4) the arena for developing and implementing mutual-aid programs designed to aid the less fortunate in dealing with their problems.

These four functions, hopefully, are integrated into one program; they shape, and are shaped by, each other. Such a model has implications for the structure, staff roles, selection of policy-makers, and methods of evaluation. More importantly, the educational philosophy must be one that views learning as being lifelong and as taking place inside the classroom and within the community. Such a philosophy accredits and rewards learning-by-doing as the present system rewards learning-by-rote. One of the early innovators of the community-centered school concept, Leonard Covello, stated it this way: "Formulation of school activities, planning of curricula, school administration, classroom techniques, and so forth, result in positive achievements only if and when all educational procedures are developed under constant awareness of the extra-school educational forces active in the background of the students."

The community-centered school is not a new concept. Covello, Principal of East Harlem's Benjamin Franklin High School until 1955, employed it as a means to enable the area's Italians to: (1) acquire the coping and elevating skills—educational, social, and others—to enable them to move into the *corporate* world; and (2) help deepen their understanding of the Italian culture as a tool for contributing effectively within their own *private* world. According to Covello:

> The school must have a thorough understanding, not only of its aims, but of the needs and potentialities of its students. We have discarded the idea of the subject-centered school and developed, as the next step forward, the child-centered school, because we realized the futility of emphasizing subject matter instead of child development. But there is one more step forward. In the concept of the community-centered school, we have, it seems to me, the ultimate objective of all education because it deals with the child in connection with his social background and in relation to all forces, disruptive as well as constructive, that contribute to his education.

Covello's efforts were designed to enable Italian-Americans to become Americanized without experiencing ruthless assimilation. His school was built while Fiorello LaGuardia was Mayor; it was Dr. Covello who introduced Italian into the curriculum of his high school.

The community-centered school, however, has no purpose in being ethnically or racially exclusive. It builds opportunities for students to express and develop their own interests—ethnic interests included. Its thrust is in the direction of imparting citizenship skills along with those of scholarship.

The request, then, for a community-centered school by black communities has its positive dimensions. It is an indication that they feel that they are qualified, that this is their country, too, that they want to get their concerns onto our society's agenda, and that they want to participate directly in their own social and economic elevation. Blacks themselves have made this choice against the grain of the social rhetoric; this is their right in a democracy.

Dan Dodson, Director of The Center for Human Relations at New York University, elucidates this point with greater clarity:

> No nation can maintain the distinction of being democratic if it does not make allowances for cultural diversity. Such differences cannot be "just tolerated." They must be respected and encouraged so long as they have value for any segment of the citizenry. Thus, in a real sense, this opportunity to pursue autonomous goals is a measure of "democratic." No person can make his fullest contribution to the total society with a feeling of compromise about "who he is" because he is a minority group member.

The civil-rightists have campaigned to get Negro history onto the agenda of the school; the Black Power theorists have pushed to get Afro-American history into the schools. The civil rightists want all students—black and white—to understand Negro history; the Black Power theorists emphasize Afro-American history as an identity-building tool for Blacks. Both fail to note that our public education system is bankrupt because it is being controlled by a group of conservative thinkers. White and Black students alike are not being taught citizenship and social responsibility. The emphasis is on "scholarship," despite its lack of social relevance in today's world.

It seems to me, for example, that an honest discussion of the attempted "castration" of Adam Clayton Powell by the U.S. Congress would make an excellent social-studies lesson. A similar critical incident would be the refusal of the press to address Cassius Clay as "Muhammed Ali," and Muhammed Ali's refusal to enter the armed forces. It is the effective teacher's role to help students to relate themselves to the context of our society and to understand their role in shaping it. This doesn't come through memorizing history. It can come, however, through helping students to engage themselves in the issues that touch upon their lives. The community-centered school, as we shall see, helps students—whether white or Black—to do precisely this.

Let us examine the special features of the community-centered school and see exactly what such a school is. We begin with the issue of control.

1. *Redistribution of power.* The community-centered school differs from the traditional public school in that it deliberately shares power with the community it serves. It attempts to define and identify those powers that belong exclusively to the local community, those that belong exclusively to the professionals, and those that should be shared. As a case in point, the community might have the ultimate decision in selecting the principal. The community ought to be able to discern such intangible factors as psychological stance, personal qualities, and commitment to uphold local community interests. The evaluation of teacher and staff performance might be shared with the community. The responsibility for implementation of the educational goals can rest solely with the professional.

The latent function of this model is to build into the local community the skill and competence to develop and establish educational policy and to acquire the skills to measure the effectiveness of the educational program. On the other side of the coin is the opportunity it affords the staff to learn of the community's interests and goals and how to help it acquire the means to achieve them.

2. *Bridging structures.* In order to carve out effective functions, local organizations can be asked to join with parents in "adopting" a piece of the school's program. All participants—organizations and individuals—should be helped to assume a specific function on which everyone else comes to depend.

One organization could spend its entire time obtaining summer camping opportunities for students, while another could assume that of securing summer employment opportunities. Another could focus its attention on securing employment for parents of students. Another could work with local, state, and national legislators to ensure that students on welfare receive decent allowances—an educable income, if you will. Other organizations might "adopt" classes to whom they become responsible for trips, visitations to local organizational headquarters, fund-raising, and the like.

Neighborhood organizations could be urged to use the school as a regular meeting place. There ought to be a "community room," supervised and controlled by the community groups.

3. *Citizen roles.* Local community residents functioning as "foster teachers" can be employed and trained. These persons should operate outside the school, perhaps in a storefront, and should be available to parents and others during nonschool hours. They can train parents to support the education of their children, put them in contact with needed resources, and find ways to relate community activities to the life of the school.

These persons also give local emphasis to the idea that education is an important elevating tool. They become "teachers" outside the school and "foster parents" within the school. An important part of their function is to help individual students in their efforts to bridge the gap between school and home. Naturally, they would expend a majority of their efforts on those students or in those situations where their roles are not already being fulfilled by an interested parent or teacher.

Unlike teacher's aides and assistants who, for all intents and purposes, are extra arms and legs for the teachers, the foster teachers carry out community-parent functions, being advocates on behalf of the community, not the school. There should be a minimum of one such person per classroom, and preferably two.

4. *Parent roles.* Parents who are not employed as teacher assistants (who will not be discussed here) or as foster teachers, or who are not serving on the policy-making school/community committee, should be formed into informal parents clubs based on grade levels. These clubs should meet regularly to plan class trips in conjunction with the class members and to participate in parent training programs.

The latent function of this structure would be to approach the parents as adults in their own right, and to afford them the opportunity to acquire the skills with which one enhances the learning and motivation of one's own children. The parent training should emphasize (1) the transmission of skills, not just the giving of information, (2) the development of parent skills, and (3) an active concern for the personal needs of the parents.

These clubs can also meet the recreational and social needs of the parents, and should be organized by the foster teachers. Students should be expected to know about the parents clubs. Class discussions can be held in relation to them.

5. *Parent-student linkages*. Techniques should be developed so that parents are engaged in what is going on in the classroom through a variety of ways. Most parents want to make their children feel good. How the student feels is largely a factor of the parent function.

Community service projects around local community problems should involve students and parents in data collection—interviewing, surveying, observational tours, etc. The parent and the student may find themselves discussing their communities from different perspectives but out of common experiences.

Students can be encouraged to elicit the opinions of their parents on key social issues and to write reports on their findings. An interviewing instrument might be developed for this purpose. The aim here is to stimulate intellectual exchanges between students and their parents.

Students should be asked to go on tours with their families, visit museums together, etc. Class credit should be accorded for written reports of such ventures. Prior preparation as to "what to look for" on the trip might be included.

Class pictures should be replaced by family pictures, with profits being used to support community activities. Imagine all the families in the third grade showing up at the school to have family pictures taken and then retiring to a class smorgasbord—arroz con pollo, collards, spaghetti and meatballs, Irish stew, gefilte fish, and apple pie! (Most of our schools start with the apple pie.)

6. *Mutual-aid activities*. The caste system favoring professionals in the ghettos has so effectively intervened that the key decisions are often made by them rather than the families they come to serve. The art of decision-making cannot be learned if the opportunity to learn is not afforded.

A mutual-aid committee should be established to deal with community and school problems—behavioral problems, potential suspensions and expulsions, family problems, and the like. Teachers, other staff, and families should present problems to this committee for guidance and assistance. Home visits, referrals, and special programs ought to be set up to deal with these problems.

7. *Economic development.* Credit unions, buying cooperatives, and community fund-raising should be developed as means to create a sense of economic awareness and to stimulate collective economic action. Local fund-raising styles should be employed rather than transporting the Community Chest model into the ghettos.

8. *Legislative action.* The school/community committee can establish a legislative committee that concerns itself with the resolution of those problems that lend themselves to legislative remedies. Locally elected officials can be drawn in for this purpose.

9. *Information and communication services.* A "Parents' Guide" ought to be developed as a means to help parents acquire the knowledge, and hopefully the skills, to help their children exploit the educational offerings of the school. The manual prepared by the Philadelphia Council for Community Advancement is a case in point.

Every family ought to receive or purchase a "parent notebook" emblazoned with the school name. Every insert should be numbered and dated. A history of the school and of the person after whom it is named ought to comprise the first pages. Information as to the structure and composition of the school/community committee and the school organization should be among the annual entries. Over a period of time the book should contain special reports, reading scores at the school, training tools, etc. This notebook can become a "parents' bible"—a tool for developing a continuing understanding of what is going on in the school. During the operation of the West Harlem Liberation School, when P.S. 125 in Harlem was being boycotted, daily news releases were sent to the parents, who anxiously awaited them. In addition, the content of the news releases was interpreted to the students by the teachers. Such material should be written by parents, not professionals.

Parent meetings should be held only after the students have

elicited from their parents a purpose, a time, and a date for the meeting. Another stratagem is to enable parents to call such meetings. The meeting should be held to answer the questions of parents. Informational meetings should be kept small to allow parents time to raise questions and to absorb the answers. Foster teachers ought to have full access to such information so that they might interpret it and enable parents to analyze it.

Teachers, teacher assistants, foster teachers, students, and parents should form the essential horizontal communication linkages. Parents should have easy access to the school/community committee, which, in turn, should deal with the principal. Efforts should be made to encourage the principal to engage in as many nonleadership contacts with parents and community persons as possible.

10. *The school-community process.* The community-centered school depends largely for its success on the degree to which it is geared to problem-solving; citizen, student, and community development; and easy evaluation and communication.

At the beginning of each year, goals should be established as they relate to the academic program, the meeting of community needs, parent development, and program development. "Before-and-after" studies should be included in the plans so as to measure the changes that take place. These changes might be more appropriate indicators than reading levels, attendance at meetings, etc.

The annual meeting of the school-community committee must become an important community event, second only to the graduation ceremony. Tradition-building events should permeate the total community. School holidays should be made locally relevant and draw into participation as many segments of the community as possible.

Career-building ventures should be considered; that is, relationships between learning and future careers should be understood. Class visitations should be made by role models, and "big brother" relationships should be established and nurtured. Leadership opportunities for local participants must be sought with the same zeal with which we decry the absence of leadership in disadvantaged areas.

11. *Student-to-student processes.* Student self-government activities can begin during elementary school years. The student government should have some real tasks to perform and real decisions to make. A focus of their attention might be community-service projects, special interest groupings, recreational activities, career-building clubs, etc.

I have listed elsewhere some techniques for helping teachers to exploit student organizational resources. They are based on the positive strengths embedded within student group relationships. Some of them are as follows:

Permit students to sit anywhere in class they want to. Throw away the alphabetical seating system. Permit students to develop their own sociogram.

Plan for group presentations, with individual responsibility for parts of total assignments to be decided upon by the group members.

Encourage students to assist each other with homework assignments. Provide class time for such assignments.

Encourage discussions among students, with the teacher as an observer and learner.

This has been an attempt to begin to put into one place some of the ideas I have been pulling together in relation to the community-centered school. It would probably take a book to elaborate adequately upon the ideas included herein. I have failed to touch upon the proposed structure for the school, and deliberately so. In a community-centered school, form must follow function. The opposite is true in the traditional school, where function follows form.

The qualifications and kinds of professional staff have been overlooked also. Suffice it to say that prior attention should be given to those staff whose personal interests—art, social issues, community development, and others—coincide with local community needs. The assumption here is that the staff will otherwise meet the professional qualifications for the jobs for which they apply.

The underlying aim of this statement is to restructure the relationship between the school and community by giving prior attention to addressing the parents as adults in their own right. An obvious purpose is to lessen the power of school administrators who are not educating the children, and to develop responsible parent power. The power of the teacher in the depressed neighborhood is a crucial variable. It can be used to elicit parental support of her efforts or to destroy the student because the teacher fails to respect his parents.

If we are serious, therefore, about educating Black children, it is essential to draw their parents, and the community at large, into the process. And if we are serious about the difficulties raised by the "generation gap" in the society as a whole, if we do not wish to see our society torn apart along age lines, as it has already been torn apart along racial lines, we must begin to create community-centered schools.

The fight for local control that has been waged over I.S. 201, therefore, has profound educational implications that reach far beyond a single Harlem schoolhouse. It involves the relevance of education to life.

10. Decentralizing Urban School Systems

by Mario D. Fantini and Richard Magat

Mario D. Fantini is an education program officer for the Ford Foundation. He served as executive director of the Mayor's Advisory Panel on Decentralization of the New York City Schools. A former teacher and school administrator, he has worked extensively on problems of urban education and is the co-author, with Gerald Weinstein, of *The Disadvantaged: Challenge to Education*.

Richard Magat was special assistant to Dr. Fantini in the New York City school study. He is the Ford Foundation's director-editor for publications and public information and has been active in the New York State Citizens Committee for the Public Schools.

On November 8, 1967, a storm broke with full force on the American education community. On that day, a report entitled *Reconnection for Learning* was published. Better known as the Bundy Report, the document dealt with the problems of the New York City school system. Yet, within a few weeks, its proposals for decentralization of that system ignited passions far beyond the borders of New York. The resulting controversy, in fact, has already reached national proportions. It could turn out to be a turning point in the history of public education in the United States.

The Report was drawn up by a committee created in response to a request of the New York State Legislature. This committee, headed by McGeorge Bundy, president of The Ford Foundation and a former dean of faculty at Harvard, took as its basic premise the Legislature's pointed assertion that "increased community awareness and participation in the educational process is essential." This seemingly bland idea, well-grounded in the traditional American concept of local responsibility for free public education, became, in turn, the controversial theme of the Bundy Report.

In surveying New York City's vast school system, the committee found problems so severe and the breakdown of school-community ties so advanced that it called for fundamental structural changes in the administration of our schools. "If this proposal is radical," asserted *The New York Times* in response to the Report, "it is justified by the fact that the situation is desperate. If the cure is drastic, it is necessary because a long succession of moderate reform efforts has failed to halt the deterioration of New York's gigantic school system." (New York City's public schools are responsible for the education of nearly one of every forty public school pupils in the entire United States.)

The heart of the Bundy Report was a plan for massive decentralization that has far-reaching educational and social implications. Before attempting to describe the plan, however, or to interpret its implications, it is necessary to look briefly at the circumstances that gave rise to it.

Administrative decentralization of the New York City school system has been urged for at least a quarter of a century. The first tangible step was taken in 1961, when a new city-wide Board of Education was installed following the disclosure of scandals in the awarding of school construction contracts. Existing but basically moribund local districts—each headed by its own board—were reorganized and reduced in number. The power to appoint district school board members was shifted from the anachronistic borough presidents' offices to the central Board of Education. In turn, the central Board was required to seek the advice of local screening panels chosen by the presidents of the parents associations in the various districts.

All this looked fine on paper, but the plan had basic defects. First, the selection method involving the advice of parents associations was less effective in low-income areas than in middle-class sections. (The "parents association," as now constituted, is essentially a middle-class device and is not consonant with the style of low-income, poorly educated, minority parents.) Second, these local school boards possessed only advisory powers, and their efforts to respond to community demands were often frustrated by the long chain of command leading to the central Board headquarters.

Moreover, the central Board itself was less than enthusiastic about the plan. As Marilyn Gittell wrote in her classic analysis of decision-making in the New York schools (*Participants and Participation*), "The Board of Education has been reluctant to delegate powers to local boards for fear that they would encroach on its own authority." Not until 1967 were these local boards even provided with office space, and they remained largely without professional or supporting services.

The failure of this partial decentralization to make the schools more responsive to parental and community needs did not pass unnoticed. Nor were parents any longer content, as the 1960's wore on, to shrug aside the inadequacies of the city's schools. Well-publicized statistics showed that one out of every five New York City pupils lagged two or more years behind normal reading levels, with even greater reading retardation in the predominantly Negro and Puerto Rican schools. Many other indexes pointed to the need for fundamental change. Dissatisfaction with the schools became bitter.

Furthermore, parents, and especially ghetto parents, began to resist official explanations that placed the burden of failure on the child or his family. Rather, there was an increasing tendency to place responsibility on the schools. Parents accused the schools of being either unwilling or unable to respond to the special needs of ghetto children. They asserted that many teachers and administrators were hostile or negative toward children who did not conform to essentially middle-class styles and values. Expressions of dissatisfaction ranged from talk about a "lack of accountability" on the part of the school system to charges that New York City educators were "colonizers sent down among them by a central office." The collision between tense community forces and the central Board of Education was not long in coming.

The clash took the form of strikes, boycotts, demonstrations, and demands for an independent school district to govern Harlem schools. Similar rumblings came from other embattled low-income areas of the city. There were meetings and petitions, charges and countercharges, even an invasion of the Board of Education headquarters by a "People's Board of Education," headed by a well-known Negro minister and civil-rights activist.

This was the historical context when the New York State Legislature, in 1967, passed an education money bill with a significant string attached. This bill granted the New York City schools a bonus in state aid if the school system could be split into five school districts—one in each borough—instead of a single unit.

This idea originally had been proposed to the Legislature by Mayor John Lindsay. To the surprise of almost everyone, the Legislature, well aware of the controversy that had been raging in the city, adopted the Mayor's proposal and carried it one step further. It attached the condition that the Mayor present a plan for greater community participation in the governance of the city's schools. In effect, the Legislature asked the city to develop a new plan for real—not paper—decentralization.

Amid cries charging political interference with the schools, Mayor Lindsay moved to meet the Legislature's request by appointing a blue-ribbon advisory panel to produce such a plan. The panel members included the president of the New York City Board of Education (then Lloyd K. Garrison, subsequently Alfred Giardino); Mitchell Sviridoff, then head of the city's Human Resources Administration, the coordinating agency for health, welfare, and antipoverty services; Francis Keppel, president of General Learning Corporation and former U.S. Commissioner of Education; Dr. Bennetta Washington, a former high school principal, head of the Women's Job Corps, a Negro, and wife of Walter Washington, the first "mayor" of Washington, D.C.; and Dr. Antonia Pantoja, a social work professor and prominent leader in the Puerto Rican community. To chair the panel, the Mayor called upon McGeorge Bundy, president of The Ford Foundation. A Foundation staff member and one of this chapter's authors, Mario Fantini, was appointed staff director for the study.

In the months that followed, the panel and its staff solicited proposals for decentralization and met with hundreds of individuals and lay and professional groups. It examined the educational problems and studied the demographic, fiscal, legal, and political implications of various organizational configurations. As its proposals began to take shape, it discussed them with various interested parties—particularly civil-rights groups, the United Federation of Teachers, and the organized school administrators (Council of Supervisory Associations).

In the end, when the advisory panel issued its report, Mr. Giardino, who said he was serving not as an individual but as a representative of the Board of Education, expressed basic disagreement with its findings. Arguing that the Board was already committed to parent and community participation and to decentralization, he declared that "serious problems must arise in recasting, in one quick stroke, the largest educational system in the world. . . . We must be reasonably sure," he continued, "that a plan will be successful and [we] do not feel sufficient assurance in the plan submitted. Rather than a rigidly timed and mandated set of procedures, we prefer a more deliberative process of movement and evaluation. Moreover, we believe there are constructive legislative alternatives that can achieve many of the same goals without as many dangers." Mr. Giardino filed the panel's sole dissent.

The basic recommendations of the Bundy panel can be summarized as follows:

1. The New York City public schools should be reorganized into a Community School System, consisting of a federation of largely autonomous school districts and a central education agency.
2. From 30 to no more than 60 Community School Districts should be created, ranging in size from about 12,000 to 40,000 pupils—each large enough to offer a full range of educational services, yet small enough to maintain proximity to community needs and to promote diversity and administrative flexibility.
3. The Community School Districts should have authority for all regular elementary and secondary education within their boundaries and responsibility for adhering to state education standards.
4. A central education agency, together with a Superintendent of Schools and his staff, should have operating responsibility for special educational functions and city-wide educational policies. It should also provide certain centralized services to the Community School Districts and others on the Districts' request.
5. The State Commissioner of Education and the city's central educational agency should retain their responsibilities for the maintenance of educational standards in all public schools in the city.
6. The Community School Districts should be governed by boards of education selected in part by parents and in part by the Mayor from lists of candidates maintained by the central education

agency. Membership on these boards should be open to both parents and nonparent residents of a District.

7. The central educational agency should consist of one or the other of the following bodies: (a) a commission of three full-time members appointed by the Mayor, or (b) a Board of Education that includes a majority of members nominated by the Community School Districts. The Mayor should select these members from a list submitted by an assembly of chairmen of Community School Boards. The others should be chosen by the Mayor from nominations made by a screening panel.

8. Community School Districts should receive an annual allocation of operating funds, determined by an objective and equitable formula, which they should be permitted to use with the widest possible discretion within set educational standards and union contract obligations.

9. Community School Districts should have broad personnel powers, including the right to hire a community superintendent on a contract basis.

10. All existing tenure rights of teachers and supervisory personnel should be preserved as the reorganized system goes into effect. Thereafter, tenure of new personnel employed in a particular District should be awarded by the District.

11. The process of qualification for appointment and promotion in the system should be so revised that Community School Districts will be free to hire teachers and other professional staff from the widest possible sources, so long as hiring is competitive and applicants meet state qualifications.

12. Community School Boards should establish procedures and channels for the closest possible consultation with parents, community residents, teachers, and supervisory personnel at the individual school level.

13. The central education agency should have authority and responsibility for advancing racial integration by all practicable means. The State Commissioner of Education should have authority himself, or through delegation to the central education agency, to overrule measures that support segregation or other practices inimical to an open society.

14. The Community School System should go into effect for

the school year beginning September, 1969, assuming passage of the necessary legislation in the 1968 Legislature.

15. The main responsibility for supervising the transition from the existing system to the Community School System should rest with the State Commissioner of Education. The principal planning and operational functions should be assigned to a Temporary Commission on Transition, which should work closely with the current Board of Education, the Superintendent of Schools, and his staff.

16. The transition period should include extensive programs of discussion and orientation on operations and responsibilities under the Community School System and on educational goals. School board members should be afforded opportunities for training and be provided with technical assistance on budgeting, curriculum, and other school functions.

These recommendations deal with four main problems: the nature of community control of educational policy, the composition and selection of community boards of education, relations between community boards and higher authorities, and the reform of the personnel system. It may be helpful to examine the issues confronting the panel in each of these areas and to understand the reasoning that led to its final recommendations.

Community power: Early in its deliberations, the panel concluded that, if it were to go beyond a mere paper reorganization, it had to propose that substantive power in the areas of finance, personnel, and curriculum be given to local governing units.

Since the Community School Districts were to be quasi-autonomous and would not have taxing powers, they would have to draw their funds from the over-all city education budget. But autonomy without control of the purse would be a charade. Thus, to guarantee that Community School Districts would have flexibility in the way they spent their funds, the panel proposed that they receive lump-sum allocations from the Board of Education. This would eliminate line-item restrictions, so that the community boards could determine their own priorities. Only through lump-sum allocation would Community School Boards have effective power to make their own decisions on such matters as pupil-teacher ratios, the functions of personnel, the number and kinds of books and other instructional materials, the conduct of experimental programs, and a host of other needs and educational strategies.

To insure that districts with special needs receive a fair share, the panel proposed that these lump sums be allocated by a formula that would go beyond per-capita allotment and take into account such factors as poverty, the unemployment rate, and the presence of non-English-speaking children or gifted children. To insure against misuse of funds, the panel outlined a number of auditing and reporting procedures and other safeguards.

Board composition: The choices open to the panel in the difficult decisions regarding composition of community boards included community-wide representation, parent-only representation, and other arrangements that would include professionals. The panel decided on a parent-based system, which it felt would be the most responsive to the needs and interests of children attending the public schools.

The panel proposed a two-stage process for selection of the parent members: Representatives of individual schools would be chosen by an assembly of parents; these representatives, in turn, would select the board members on a basis proportional to the pupil population of each school.

In fixing on a parent-only majority, the panel sought to avoid the danger that these local boards might be dominated by political clubs, by majorities of residents who were not parents, or by sectarian interests that might not hold the interest of public education uppermost.

The panel leavened its weighting in favor of parents, however, with a provision that a minority of community board members—five of eleven—be appointed by the Mayor. This provision reflected a concern for minorities within districts marked by a strong racial or ethnic character—particularly Puerto Ricans in largely Negro neighborhoods. Thus, the Report declared, "It is a real possibility, especially in the early years of the reorganized school system, that a parentally chosen district panel might wholly exclude representatives of minority groups in that district. While we do not hold with proportional representation on Community School Boards, we do believe that total exclusion of minority representation would violate the spirit of community participation in the educational process."

The panel decided on the Mayor as the agent for choosing the centrally selected members, on the basis of his city-wide purview and his prior responsibility for the city's schools, notably in the allocation of the school budget from the total city municipal budget.

Both by admitting parents to a more active role in the educational process and by building a closer link to elected government, the panel sought structural relevance—a school system that would be more responsive to the needs of the citizens. The panel also hoped that, through closer ties with city government, the schools would be able to coordinate their programs with other city agencies, such as its sixty existing planning districts, or its recreation, health, and antipoverty efforts.

Relations to higher authorities: While tipping the balance toward far greater responsiveness to diverse community needs, the panel took pains not to destroy the city-wide integrity of the school system. The reorganized school system, it said, "should insure all pupils and all localities the benefits of the numerous and variegated facilities and services that major urban school systems can offer—ranging from special high schools to costly research, technical services, and logistic support. It should couple the advantages of urban bigness with the intimacy, flexibility and accessibility associated with innovative suburban school systems."

Without diluting the essential independence and decision-making of the community boards, therefore, the panel proposed a number of ties to the central education agency (the Board of Education). These included the latter's authority over pupil transfers (to insure optimum utilization of school buildings throughout the city), over negotiations of the union contract, and, of crucial importance, over integration policy.

Anticipating charges that a federated school system might lead to sectarian pockets—Black Power districts on the one hand, or ultraconservative or segregationist districts on the other—the panel proposed that the central agency be empowered to overrule any actions by a Community School Board "that are judged to be inimical to a free and open society." But the panel said this power ought to follow guidelines established by the State Commissioner of Education. It further cautioned that the central power to curb parochialism or sectarianism should not be interpreted to exclude a reasonable curricular emphasis upon the cultural background of groups that were a large element in a given school—an obvious reference to desires in the ghettos for attention to Negro history and Afro-American studies in the schools.

In view of the city's diversity, the panel provided for the possibility that some districts might wish central headquarters to continue many of its traditional functions. Under the plan, therefore, a district would have the option of handling its own purchasing, curriculum development, and recruiting, or turning to the central Board of Education for these services. Only such clearly city-wide functions as pupil transfers, capital budgeting, integration policy, testing, auditing, and information were reserved exclusively to the Board of Education. The Community School Districts would be given freedom to contract with other agencies—universities, research and development organizations, and other governmental agencies.

In disputes between Community School Boards and the central Board of Education, referee responsibility would lie with the State Commissioner of Education. Implicit in the panel's view was a trust in community responsibility, so the burden of proving irresponsibility or improper activity would lie with the central Board.

Personnel: The personnel power granted to the community would be the right to hire, on contract, a community superintendent of schools. While preserving tenure and centralized collective bargaining, the panel also proposed to place hiring and the granting of tenure at the community level. Its single most important personnel recommendation called for elimination of the central city-wide examination system and its venerable Board of Examiners, established in 1898.

This was intended to insure a wider pool for recruitment of personnel and a more flexible promotion system. In New York State, only two school systems, New York City's and Buffalo's, require examinations for teacher certification beyond the state standards. Not only would centralized examinations be inconsistent with the requirements of effective decentralization, the panel said, but the system had grown obsolete in a market where the demand for qualified teachers outran the supply. The examination system had also produced an inbred leadership system that discouraged flexibility and venturesomeness.

The personnel reforms raised the question of adequate staffing. In a system in which each Community School District had to compete with the others for staff, would teachers flee the ghettos for middle-class districts? The present system, whatever its defects, at least guarantees an adequate number of teachers in the most "difficult" schools by means of an assignment system. For several reasons, the panel was confident that predominantly ghetto districts could, indeed, attract and hold adequate numbers of qualified teachers. It held that:

1. Removal of entrance rigidities would encourage the entry of additional talented teachers from the city, the metropolitan area, and the nation generally.
2. Despite its problems, the New York City school system's salaries are competitively quite favorable, and low-income districts could offer the same salaries as more economically favored districts.
3. The air of reform and innovation under the reorganized system would attract large numbers of men and women who are ready to accept difficult professional challenges.

Although predominantly Negro or Puerto Rican districts might at first seek to staff their schools with more teachers and administrators of their own groups, the panel—again committed to the proposition that most parents want quality education rather than the exercise of power for power's sake—said that professional quality would sooner or later override ethnic considerations in the selection and promotion of teachers.

According to the panel, the best guarantee that the selection of staff would be based on merit rather than race per se would lie in the improved school and community climate that would spring from strengthened cooperation between parents and school personnel. Specifically, teachers would serve in a given district because they chose to be there and were chosen by the community, rather than being assigned there without an expression of preference on either their part or that of the community.

The panel took great pains to insure that the Report's language was conciliatory. Despite its tone, however, the hard bite of its proposals made fierce opposition to the Report inevitable. And, in fact, reaction to the Bundy Report was instantaneous.

The existing Board of Education, represented on the panel by its president, Mr. Giardino, made its opposition felt through his official dissent. But others, too, read in the Report an attack on their positions. Thus, contending elements in the school system quickly made common cause against the plan. The leadership of the United Federation of Teachers, for example, joined with the Board of Education and the Council of Supervisory Associations (a powerful organization representing principals, assistant principals, and other administrative personnel) to oppose the Bundy proposals. (An organization of eighty Negro school supervisors, however, endorsed the plan.) The drive against the proposal was initially spearheaded by the CSA, some of whose constituent bodies assessed their members to raise war chests against the plan. Opponents of the Bundy plan blanketed the city with speakers, brochures, and advertisements. They even established a "hot line" telephone number, which anyone in doubt could call to find out "facts" about the controversy.

In the weeks that followed, the chief lines of attack on the Report were as follows:

1. *The scheme would Balkanize the city.* The creation of two dozen or more quasi-autonomous districts would penalize children moving from one neighborhood to another, because curricula would not be comparable. The system would result in duplication and inefficiency, consuming funds that might better be used in direct improvement of education (e.g., smaller classes and more remedial services). Moreover, the panel had been naïve—if not deceptive—in drawing an analogy between the proposed districts and suburban or small-city school districts.

Against these arguments, proponents of the Bundy plan noted that each district would be required to adhere to state educational standards and that a pupil moving from a district in Manhattan to a district in the Bronx would incur no more of a penalty than one moving from Buffalo to White Plains.

Moreover, the cost of duplication was exaggerated. (The city budget director subsequently estimated it would cost $13 million, or about 2 per cent of the total city education budget.) Furthermore, backers of the plan noted, the present centralized structure had already far exceeded the size at which it might benefit from economy of scale. Instead, it had turned into a wasteful, educationally unsound bureaucracy.

As to the charge that it improperly compared the Community School Districts to suburban or small-town districts, advocates of the plan noted that the Report made no effort to glorify small districts; it simply pointed out that the proposed new districts, which might range from 12,000 to 40,000 in enrollment, would be able to offer the same range of services and curricula as cities like Berkeley, Norwalk, or Evansville.

2. *The plan would deal a blow to integration efforts by creating segregated districts.* During its study, the panel frequently heard this fear expressed, mainly by whites. The panel Report, while supporting the desirability of racial integration in the schools, took the position that, in New York City, integration was a secondary issue. Ten years of efforts to reduce racial imbalance under the prevailing system of New York City school organization had either been beaten down by white resistance or had failed because of population shifts and the general decline of the schools. The panel's recommendation preserved the right of the central Board of Education to mandate integration policies and urged that the state offer individual districts incentives to promote integration. But it said that the long-run value of its proposals for integration must be found in their effect on the quality of public education: "Communities which achieve high levels of pupil performance—in schools that have a favorable climate for learning—will be the strongest possible magnet to draw all kinds of parents back to the city. And nothing less will do the job."

3. *The proposals would produce chaos and turn the schools over to vigilantes and racists.* Columnist Joseph Alsop charged that the decentralization movement was an effort "by the extreme wing of the Black Power movement . . . to take over control of the

predominantly Negro schools in a whole series of big cities." Others voiced similar ideas in more guarded language. In reply, advocates of the plan pointed out that the panel had written a number of strong safeguards into its plan—particularly the requirement that the Community School Districts, no more or less than independent school districts, would be subject to the State Education Law and the considerable administrative powers of the Commissioner of Education. Other checks were provided in the reporting and auditing requirements. The Community School Boards would not, as the plan's opponents implied, be rump bodies but duly elected and selected official bodies. Moreover, the panel proposed a timetable and transition mechanism during which detailed plans for an orderly changeover would be made.

Those who would be "taking over" would not be outsiders or political extremists but the parents of the school children—those with the greatest stake in the educational effectiveness of the system.

4. *Ghetto parents (if not laymen, generally) are incompetent to deal with educational issues.* Lawyer and civil libertarian Morris Ernst, for example, declared that "few of us are capable in time and background of being intellectually involved. . . . We could easily wreck the lives of thousands of our children by giving power to parents who would be called upon to act without . . . highly sophisticated . . . knowledge [about] the great and everlasting problem—the relation of the mind of a teacher to the mind of a pupil."

Proponents of decentralization replied by pointing to the tradition of lay control of public education. They argued that, while members of school boards have the role of reflecting community concerns and needs and of approving educational policy, they are neither required to be versed in the professional aspects of education nor are they supposed to oversee the day-to-day operations of the schools.

Moreover, one of the least discussed and most innovative aspects of the Bundy plan was its recommendation that prospective board members be given preparatory training. Few—if any—school boards anywhere in the country even now provide such training to prepare incoming members for their responsibilities. Beyond this, the panel recommended systematic, intensive programs of education for the community at large on the powers and responsibilities of parents and boards in the new structure.

5. *The personnel changes would deprive ghetto schools of adequate staffs and would destroy the merit system.* As noted earlier, the panel advanced several reasons for its belief that schools would be adequately staffed and, indeed, that staff-community relations would improve. With regard to merit, defenders of the plan noted that teachers still would be required to meet state certification standards, and that the present examination systems had produced an administrative structure in which innovation was not rewarded. Other protections against the spoils system included the requirement that openings be made public and that appointments and promotions be competitive—i.e., that candidates be examined (by interview or test or both) and a record be maintained of the criteria by which they were employed or rejected.

The plan specifically recommended that tenure be preserved and that administrative personnel should retain salary and rank. It also recommended that, at the time the plan went into effect, no tenured person should be transferred out of a district without his consent.

Actually, the Report was only the latest in a stream of studies indicating that the examination system is an outmoded device that rewards characteristics other than educational or administrative merit. As a New York University study, *Teacher Mobility*, noted in 1963, the present system pays off "those with 'stick-to-it-iveness,' [those who] plug along, voraciously swallowing every exam that comes along, and become administrators; those who 'know the system' and 'speak the language' become administrators; the remainder, good and bad, with little success in either passing exams or knowing the system, are denied advancement and fall by the wayside. The school system feeds on its own kind, and many potentially good administrators are lost as a result."

6. *Decentralization would weaken the teachers' union.* Despite the plan's proposal that labor negotiations remain centralized, union leaders argued that the "breakup" of the system would make it more difficult to bargain forcefully. In New York, the UFT increasingly has gone beyond salary issues into demands for a voice

in the determination of working conditions and educational policy. Some union officials believed that this trend would be blunted by the transfer of substantive decision-making powers to dozens of community boards. At the time of the appearance of the Bundy Report, the union's self-confidence was at an all-time high as a result of a successful strike a few months earlier. This strike, however, had exacerbated teacher-community tensions in some areas. Many parents accused teachers of abandoning children for selfish interests. Teachers, in turn, accused parents of serving as "scabs." The union opposition to the Bundy plan, according to Joseph Featherstone's analysis in the *New Republic*, "has the makings of a tragedy, for parents and teachers may not have identical interests, but they do have interests in common against the school administration." Indeed, in a Washington, D.C., experiment with neighborhood control, the head of the local teachers' union has declared, "The parents are demanding, and are going to have, a greater say in the operation of the schools whether the teachers are with them or against them. We want to be with the parents and we have no intention of aligning ourselves with reactionary forces that fear community involvement."

7. *Decentralization is a shrewd effort to foist responsibility for the failure of the schools onto the shoulders of the poor.* Some critics saw in the plan a design by the establishment to let ghetto communities stew in their own juice. According to this thesis, the power structure, unable—or, worse, unwilling—to achieve quality education in the ghetto, would, by surrendering control to the communities, also shift the burden of failure to the victims themselves. Furthermore, the surrender would relieve the establishment of the need to allocate more resources to public education.

There is as little factual data to refute this theory as there is to support it. The panel and its supporters assert that low-income parents, given the substance of participation instead of the illusion provided by the middle-class PTA model, will be motivated to seek high-quality education. Furthermore, what are the alternatives?

What ghetto parents now have, under a centralized system, is inadequate education. The assumption that they are protected only under a system that does something *for* them denies their potency. A so-called hard-headed view holds that giving poor people a role in their own institutions amounts to romanticizing the poor. The Bundy panel contends, on the contrary, that given the freedom and the funds, people—poor or rich—will find whatever technical resources they require. The difference is that they will not be at the mercy of a failing, albeit professional, system. Under community control, it is held, the technicians and professionals would have to perform or be replaced. Of course, a school district might also fail under the proposed reorganization. The point, according to the advocates of decentralization, is that the plan opens a variety of routes through which success may be pursued. As things stand now, children march down the single centralized educational road, and, if they fall by the wayside, there is no alternative.

8. *The plan only deals with administration; it doesn't contain any educational innovations.* Other intellectual critics deprecated the Bundy plan for its alleged lack of "new educational ideas." Members of the Center for Urban Education published a particularly strong "critical analysis" in *The Center Forum,* the Center's newsletter. (The director of the Center, however, disassociated himself from the critique.) The failure of the Center staff to see pedagogical innovation in the plan is, we believe, symptomatic of professional critical myopia. In fact, the Bundy Report did suggest a number of possible innovations. The Report, among other things, touched on bilingual instruction, university-contract skill centers in reading and other subjects, curriculum research centers in individual schools, nongraded school organization, and tutorial arrangements. New career patterns for paraprofessionals and the advancement of teacher's aides to professional status through the ranks of teaching assistant and associate teacher were also discussed. The panel did not include any of these in its recommendations, because to have done so would have been to prescribe detailed styles of education for communities, a common error of educational reformers that is precisely inimical to the principle of community self-determination.

What the Bundy panel did recommend, however—the structural reorganization of school governance—is itself a fundamental educational innovation. Some academic critics fail to see that parental participation—as equal partners and not through the sufferance of professionals—is educationally potent. As the *Saturday Review* noted, "Inevitably the 'education' that results (from having parents participate) will reach far beyond the classroom—into the homes and local institutions of the community."

The same educators who rail against children's environmental handicaps are doing battle against the entry of those great environmental agents—the parents and the community—into the school process. The school is a system. It needs energy, and parents and the community are great energy sources. Not only has formal education failed to tap them but it has so resisted them that this energy is now increasingly working against the professionals. We do not know the full potential of this energy for improving the educational system because we have never tried it, not even in middle-class schools. There is some evidence to be found, however, in Head Start and even in New York City summer school programs in which the regular rulebook is thrown away. In such cases, parents perceive the school as "their" institution, and, whether they continue to stay at home or actually work in the school building, they become true partners with the professional, with all that this implies for student motivation and incentive. At the very least, it is unlikely that students and their families will continue to regard the school as an alien institution, indifferent to their needs. Reconnecting the school with the home is an educational innovation of the first magnitude.

While critics of the Bundy plan mobilized instant opposition, support for the plan grew slowly. (It was not until six months after the plan's publication that a city-wide committee of respected leaders was formed to organize support for it.) Nevertheless, it was clear that there was a great deal of sentiment for some changes along the lines favored by the Bundy panel. The generally liberal United Parents Association, representing some 400,000 members, approved the proposals, with the reservation that the central Board be responsible for curriculum and safeguards against favoritism, bias, or influence-peddling by the local boards.

Support also came from such prestigious groups as the Public Education Association and the Citizens Budget Commission, from several members of existing local school boards, and from most civil-rights organizations.

Although school superintendents in many major cities have given the Bundy Report a cool reception, both Harold Howe, the U.S. Commissioner of Education, and one of his predecessors, Dr. Samuel Brownell, now a Yale University professor and formerly Detroit Superintendent of Schools, have endorsed the Bundy proposals. The approach, said Brownell, "holds promise of meeting some of the fundamental challenges and problems that have remained immune to piecemeal, special approaches heretofore attempted."

Support sometimes came from surprising sources. Predictions that the plan would be embraced by the Parents and Taxpayers (PAT), a New York group that opposes the use of bussing or redistricting to achieve integration, proved unfounded. Mrs. Rosemary Gunning, leader of PAT forces, termed it an "untried hybrid system" and proposed instead a five-borough plan with boards elected by all residents. But 3,000 miles away, California's conservative educational fundamentalist, Dr. Max Rafferty, aligned himself with progressives like Howe. "Every new idea attracts both nutty friends and screwball enemies," wrote Rafferty, "but the [Bundy] proposal is basically a sound one. For too long we educators have been moving in a profoundly unhealthy direction, talking up the advantages of size and numbers and consolidation while at the same time paying lip service to the ideal of education for the individual."

While many critics of the plan opposed it because, in their opinion, it "went too far," there were those who felt it did not go nearly far enough. Some civil-rights groups, for example, argued for *totally* independent community school districts within the city, rather than for the panel's federated plan. They charged that the plan would create a middle-class leadership in the ghettos "whose basic task is to keep the community from getting real control." It was, they said, "a pacification program." This hardly accorded with Alsop's claim that the plan is a surrender to wild-eyed black extremists. The contradiction was seldom noted, however, in the furious clash of opinion aroused by the Report.

The suggestion that the plan does not go far enough is also implied in reservations expressed by Joseph Featherstone, who, while writing in general support of the Bundy plan, believes that even districts of the size suggested by Bundy do not constitute communities in the true sense of the word. He is skeptical about how participatory the board election process would be and suggests that it may be farfetched to assume that voting in board elections will help parents shed their feeling of powerlessness. Bundy plan backers remain optimistic and say that participation goes well beyond the ballot: "Voting is not the sole measure of a participatory system. A decentralized school structure should encourage and create other means of parent participation."

Despite the hot winds of controversy that swirled around the Bundy Report, the idea of decentralization is now beginning to receive the serious attention it deserves—not simply decentralization for administrative convenience but decentralization aimed at bringing parents and the community back into a meaningful relationship with the school.

Several alternative decentralization proposals have been put forward since the Bundy plan—some of them by groups hostile to the Bundy proposals. The Board of Education and the CSA each produced their own decentralization plans. Neither embodied any basic changes in the jurisdiction and powers of the central Board. *The New York Times* called the Board's plan "too little, too late." It would, declared *The Times*, "lead at best to continued divided authority and at worse to an aggravated state of hostilities between local boards and central authority."

The United Federation of Teachers issued a proposal that embodied such elements of the Bundy plan as elimination of the Board of Examiners. But it proposed very large districts, and, moreover, circumscribed their fiscal and personnel powers. Such defects, along with the pungent flavor of some of the UFT leadership's attacks on the Bundy proposals (UFT speakers usually concentrated on denouncing the Bundy plan rather than on arguing their own), cast doubt on the depth of the UFT commitment to the spirit embodied in the Legislature's call for decentralization and community participation.

The Mayor himself greeted his advisory panel's proposals warmly, and the legislation he finally submitted embodied most of the Report's main features. The Mayor's plan exempted high schools from the decentralization, however, on the grounds that "local district perspective is not a sufficiently broad outlook for secondary education." When the Board of Education a few years ago included high schools in its own limited, administratively decentralized districts, the move was hailed as progressive. In a sense, therefore, the return of these schools to exclusive central jurisdiction under the Lindsay plan was a step backward.

The Mayor's plan did not reflect the trust of local communities so strongly evident in the Bundy plan, which provided that any abuses by Community School Boards would have to be proved by the central Board, with the State Commissioner of Education serving as referee. The Mayor's proposal granted the central Board power to intervene, transferring to the community the burden of proving to the Commissioner, through appeal, that intervention was unwarranted. Fred Hechinger, education editor of *The New York Times*, commented that the Lindsay proposals were "calculated to diffuse the growing opposition to the Bundy plan . . . giving to the central Board the authority to decide whether a community is ready for self-government." Critics of the Mayor's modifications argued that this shift would simply create another kind of dependency and dilute the autonomy of Community School Boards.

In an attempt to dispel the destruction-of-merit argument, the Lindsay plan also proposed that the central Board pass on the eligibility of teachers. Since the community board still would have selection and assignment powers, and the Board of Examiners would be eliminated, the Lindsay personnel reform went more than halfway between the *status quo* and the Bundy plan. Thus, while some militant community leaders called it a betrayal, it was as roundly scored by the opponents of the Bundy plan as the prototype itself.

Finally, the New York State Board of Regents also emerged with a set of proposals. The Regents plan included a dramatic and symbolic step—removal of the present Board of Education at the end of the current school year and replacement by a new Board specifically mandated to plan and carry through decentralization. The new Board would serve, in effect, as the Temporary Commission on Transition that the Bundy panel had proposed to supervise the change-over from the old to the new system. The Regents proposed a division of the school system into very large districts (15 of them with an average enrollment of 73,000 pupils). But it made allowances for smaller "temporary" units of elementary and intermediate schools.

The Regents plan would dilute the parental role, however, by providing that the district board electorate consist of all kinds of residents, not just parents. Like the Bundy plan, the Regents' design would liberalize present personnel practices, requiring only state certification as the minimum requirement for a teaching position.

While the Legislature pondered decentralization, troubles plagued three demonstration school clusters that had been established by community groups a year earlier under the Board of Education's decentralization policies. The clusters, which embrace eighteen schools in Manhattan and Brooklyn, were designed as partially self-governing units, each having an elected community governing board that selects a chief administrator for the unit. But they have been beset by the dilemma of responsibility without power, and disruptions in and around them have provided ammunition to opponents of the Bundy plan, who say they provide a foretaste of the problems a decentralized system would bring. On the other hand, proponents of decentralization argue that the very difficulties experienced in the demonstration units prove the need for a plan with teeth, giving each district the kind of autonomy the present projects lack.

The administrator of the lower East Side demonstration unit, a white university professor, resigned after a few months, accusing the central Board of Education of resisting any kind of fundamental change that would shift school control to the community. Under the Board's decentralization plan, he said, "locally elected boards . . . will be held responsible for the outcome, but they will have virtually no power."

In the Intermediate School 201 cluster in Harlem, a controversy broke out over allegedly racist statements made at a memorial service held in the school for the late Malcolm X. Both the acting principal of the school and the two assistant principals had gone on leave prior to this incident. The community board had designated a new principal, but the Board of Education had not yet approved him, and the school was technically in charge of the administrative head of the larger district in which the experimental cluster was located. This ambiguity about who was in charge magnified the tensions aroused by the incident, but within a month the governing board's designated principal was approved, and the furor subsided.

In the Brooklyn (Ocean Hill–Brownsville) unit, a dispute broke out on the issue of the governing board's authority to transfer out of the unit's eight schools a group of teachers and administrators whose performance it said was unsatisfactory. The dispute was marked by walkouts of pupils and teachers, by public arguments between the unit administrator and the Superintendent of Schools, and by warnings by the UFT of work stoppages if the unit persisted in what it termed a "lockout." Here, too, the issue hinged on the demonstration unit's limited authority to run its own affairs.

Of such dependent subsystems, one of the present authors (Fantini) has written in a recent article in the *Harvard Educational Review:*

> They may lack the autonomy and freedom . . . to follow findings through to their ultimate conclusion. More likely than not, explorations into new school patterns call for breaking the rules, and the mother system is frequently unwilling to give her precocious, adventurous children much latitude. . . . The experimental systems also are under pressure to produce results quickly. The mother system, which itself may be in disarray due to years or decades of decline, nonetheless is impatient to evaluate the system, and perhaps vested interests are only too ready to label it a failure if it does not turn out a shining record of extraordinary achievement in a year or two.

Both Mayor Lindsay's plan and that of the Regents required action by the state Legislature. The 1968 Legislature, however, was not in a reforming mood; it rolled back a liberal Medicaid program and surprised almost everyone by failing to liberalize the state's rigid abortion law. Under severe lobbying pressure by the UFT in the final days of its session, the Legislature passed a bill that, in effect, delayed substantive action on decentralization for at least a year. But it did enable the Mayor to appoint four additional members to the Board of Education and does permit the Board to grant additional powers to the thirty existing administratively decentralized districts and to experimental clusters of schools.

Dr. Kenneth Clark, the noted psychologist and the only Negro member of the Board of Regents, said the bill "sacrifices the interests of children in deprived areas to the interests of the [UFT] and the Board of Education." The most serious flaw in the Legislature's inconclusive action, said *The New York Times* editorially, "is the greater danger of day-to-day warfare between the school establishment, which now clearly consists of a coalition of the union and the Board of Education, and the community forces in search of an effective and legitimate role in running their schools."

Despite the legislative setback, the decentralization idea is spreading rapidly across the country. The New Jersey State Commission on the 1967 racial riots called for decentralization of the Newark public schools into small locally governed subdistricts. In Washington, D.C., plans are actually under way for a decentralization project. Decentralization efforts are also being planned in Detroit and Philadelphia. Even in smaller districts that do not suffer from bureaucratic sprawl, the ideal of meaningful parental participation has caught hold. For example, Negro leaders in Mount Vernon, New York—a community of 80,000—have presented a plan for integration of the schools, coupled with a design for elected parent-professional councils. The councils would lack final decision-making authority, but they would have advisory and consultative powers stronger than the most aggressive PTA. The Mount Vernon Negroes regard parental participation as an integral part of their integration proposals, and therefore not negotiable.

There is evidence that Negro professionals may march ahead of their white colleagues in recognizing the potential of parental participation. In January, 1968, at a Harvard education conference, a caucus of Negro educators emerged. Two months later, it crystallized into a formal Black Conference—a strategy meeting of representatives from eleven states that is aimed at community control of public schools.

Moreover, in New York City itself, there is clear evidence that the impetus toward greater parental participation—and improved education through participation—is irreversible. The Mayor's new appointees to the central Board of Education—including its first Puerto Rican member and Dr. Milton A. Galamison, a Negro minister who has led many protests against the Board of Education over the years—are pledged to more meaningful decentralization, including a strong parental role.

Hopeful signs are evident in the experimental districts too. *The New York Times* expressed "measured optimism" in reporting on a spring festival involving students, white and Negro teachers, and neighbors of I.S. 201. But there is even stronger evidence that the promise of participation is on the way toward realization. A fourth locally governed district is being organized on Manhattan's West Side. In the choice of administrators and other supervisory personnel, the existing three governing boards are showing a "cosmopolitan" rather than a parochial tendency. Also, many appointees are rich in human-relations experience as well as professional education qualification. As this is written, in the summer of 1968, the experimental districts have also displayed evidence of an ability to seek and tap a variety of resources to strengthen their educational programs. The I.S. 201 experimental district, for example, has obtained grants not only from The Ford Foundation but also from the Carnegie Corporation and the New York Foundation as well. It has, furthermore, made cooperative arrangements with the Bank Street College of Education, Yeshiva and New York universities, and Queens and Hunter colleges. The prestigious Dalton School, a private school, is conducting a cooperative reading-improvement program with the experimental cluster. Other summer programs include teacher-training for Peace Corps returnees, graduates of elite master-of-arts-in-teaching (MAT) programs, and newly licensed teachers; a special program to facilitate the transition of junior high school pupils to high school; and training of teacher's aides and auxiliaries.

Decentralization as proposed by the Bundy Report was a means to a fundamental reform—the full entry of the public into public education. The president of the National School Boards Association, Mrs. Ruth Mancuso, said recently: "The average citizen feels he's getting further away from influencing anything. We (the schools) have not found many effective ways to relate to the community." And *Education News* noted, "the invisible people also inhabit the wealthy suburb and the dusty farm town. And whether —or when and how—they will influence their schools is a national issue."

The Bundy Report and the echoes it is producing around the country were born of failure in public education. The proposed reforms have been described as last resorts, attempts to cope with crisis, but they deserve the most careful attention for what they promise affirmatively. For too long, we have assumed that all education needed were more *resources*, more *knowledge* of the learning process, and more *ingenuity*. What we have failed to seek are the direct energy and involvement of more people, especially the people with the weakest handhold on economic security and social justice—in short, the people who have most to lose if the public schools fail. When they are joined in the struggle to rebuild public education to meet true public need, then perhaps the other three ingredients will be more effectively mobilized and applied.

11. Alternatives to Urban Public Schools

by Kenneth B. Clark

Kenneth B. Clark is president of Metropolitan Applied Research Center and professor of psychology at the City College of the City University of New York. His research into the psychological impact of segregation was cited by the Supreme Court in its 1954 school desegregation decision. The author of *Youth in the Ghetto, Prejudice and Your Child,* and *Dark Ghetto: Dilemmas of Social Power,* he has won the Kurt Lewin Memorial Award and the Spingarn Medal of the NAACP. A consultant to The RAND Corporation, the State Department, and various foundations, he also founded and served as chairman and staff director of Harlem Youth Opportunities Unlimited (Haryou).

The evidence of a massive breakdown in the efficiency of the public schools in American cities has now become a matter of public discussion. It is no secret that our urban public schools are no longer maintaining high standards of educational quality. To put it bluntly, these schools are inferior, and, so far, no one has found the formula for stemming this rising tide of educational inefficiency.

How do we explain these facts? Our urban schools are spawning hundreds of thousands of functional illiterates who are incapable of playing a constructive role in our society and who cannot be integrated into the economy without costly remedial education, even in such basics as reading and arithmetic. Many of these human beings are doomed to lives of random aggressiveness and self-destruction. Yet, as the negative symptoms in our schools grow more and more conspicuous, the ability to act positively is blocked by the rationalizations and self-serving explanations of many educators.

The problems are explained in terms of the changing racial composition of the schools. The basic racist implications of this explanation are obscured by a variety of euphemisms. The cumulative educational retardation of these young people is explained in terms of persistent racial discrimination, the high percentage of broken homes, and the whole pattern of "cultural deprivation," which allegedly interfere with the ability of these children to learn to read and to understand the language and logic of mathematics.

The common factor in all these explanations, however, is the assumption that the breakdown in efficiency in the public schools is not to be understood in terms of any deficiencies in the schools themselves, in their personnel, methods, or administration, but rather in terms of deficiencies on the part of the present crop of students and their parents. To borrow an analogy from industry: The raw materials are defective, so the product must be defective, in spite of efficient plant management.

Sometimes educators argue that if they were to receive more funds for public education, our city public schools could be made more efficient in spite of the societal, community, and human deficiencies. With more funds, they say, we could have small class size, team teaching, language laboratories, teaching machines, more audio-visual aids, and more impressive windowless schools blocking out the degradations of the ghetto. It is claimed that these educational "innovations" will eventually raise the academic achievement of children in our ghetto schools.

The evidence against this is quietly ignored. It is further obscured by the suggestion that increased compensatory educational programs will somehow provide the answer to the present crisis. Without getting into the current argument about whether these compensatory programs actually do or do not work in the long run, it seems to this observer that we are ignoring the chief problem posed by these programs. In spite of the positive fact that they help some of these children to fulfill their academic potentials, the uncritical proliferation of compensatory educational programs confuses the primary issue—that is, the continued inefficiency of the urban public school system.

The success or failure of these programs—the time, effort, money, good will, and good intentions invested in them—tend to let the regular public school systems off the hook. The administrators of our public schools can point with pride to these programs and deflect attention from the fact that the inefficiency of their schools makes these programs necessary.

Before the influx of minority-group youngsters into urban public schools, the American public school system was justifiably credited with being the chief instrument for making the American dream of upward social, economic, and political mobility a reality. Depressed immigrants from Southern and Eastern Europe could use American public schools as the ladder toward the goals of assimilation and success.

These past successes of American public education seem undebatable. Yet, the fact that American public schools were effective mobility vehicles for white American immigrants makes even more stark and intolerable their present ineffectiveness for minority-group children. Today it appears that the present system of urban public schools is a primary obstacle to the mobility of masses of Negro and other lower status minority-group children.

There remains the disturbing question—a question too painful for many educators themselves to ask—whether the selective process involved in training and promoting educators and administrators for our public schools emphasizes qualities of passivity, conformity, caution, smoothness, and superficial affability, rather than the boldness, creativity, and ability to demand and obtain those things that are essential for solid and effective public education for all children. If this is true—if our system of training and promotion rewards the wrong characteristics—then our hopes for reform are minimal, if not totally futile. In short, we are in bad shape if reform is dependent upon the present educational establishment.

To save our urban schools, we must first demonstrate to the public that the present level of public school inefficiency has reached a stage of public calamity. It must be demonstrated that minority-group children are not the only victims of the monopolistic inefficiency of the present system, but that white children—privileged white children, whose parents understandably seek to protect them by moving to suburbs and enrolling them in private and parochial schools—also suffer, both potentially and immediately.

It must further be demonstrated that business and industry suffer intolerable financial and tax burdens in seeking to maintain a stable economy in the face of the inefficiency of the public schools.

It must be demonstrated that the costs of correctional, welfare, and health services are intolerably high in seeking to cope with the consequences of educational inefficiency—that it would be more economical, even for an affluent society, to pay the price and meet the demands of efficient public education.

It must be demonstrated that a nation that presents itself to the world as the guardian of democracy cannot itself make a mockery of these significant ethical principles by dooming one-tenth of its own population to a lifetime of inhumane misery because of remediable educational deficiencies in its public schools. These things must be understood by the average American if our public schools and our cities are to be effective.

It seems most unlikely, however, that the changes necessary for increased efficiency of our urban public schools will come about simply because they should. Our urban public school systems represent the most rigid forms of bureaucracy. Paradoxically, they are most resilient and innovative in finding ways to resist rational or irrational demands for change.

Why are the public schools so effective in resisting change and so ineffective at educating children? The answer to this question lies in the fact that public school systems are protected public monopolies with only minimal competition from private and parochial schools. Few critics—even severe ones such as myself—dare to question the givens of the present organization of public education in terms of local control of public schools; in terms of existing municipal or political boundaries; or in terms of the rights and prerogatives of boards of education to establish policy and select professional staff, at least nominally or ritualistically if not actually. Few dare to question the relevance of the criteria for the selection of superintendents, principals, and teachers, or the relevance of the entire system to the objectives of public education.

A monopoly need not genuinely concern itself with these matters. So long as local school systems can be assured of stable aid and increasing federal aid, without the accountability that inevitably comes with aggressive competition, it is sentimental to expect any significant increase in the efficiency of our public schools. If there are no alternatives to the current system—short of present private and parochial schools which are, themselves, approaching the limit of expansion—then the possibilities for improvement in public education are limited.

Alternatives—realistic, aggressive, and viable competitors—to the present public school systems must be found. The development of competitive school systems will be attacked by the defenders of the present system as attempts to weaken, if not destroy, public education. This predictable, self-serving argument can be briefly and accurately disposed of by demonstrating that truly effective competition strengthens, rather than weakens, that which deserves to survive.

I would argue further that public education need not be identified with the present system of organization of public schools. Public education can be more broadly and pragmatically defined in terms of that form of educational system that functions in the public interest. Given this definition, it becomes clear that:

An inefficient system of public schools is not in the public interest.

A system of public schools that destroys rather than develops positive human potentialities is not in the public interest.

A system that consumes funds without demonstrating effective returns is not in the public interest.

A system that insists that its standards of performance should not, or cannot, be judged by those who must pay the cost is not in the public interest.

A system that blames its human resources and its society, while quietly acquiescing to the very injustices that supposedly limit its efficiency, is not in the public interest.

Given these assumptions, therefore, it follows that alternative forms of public education must be developed if the children of our cities are to be educated and made constructive members of our society.

In considering alternatives, all attempts must, at the same time, be made to strengthen our present urban public schools. Such attempts involve re-examination, revision, and strengthening of curricula, methods, and personnel selection and evaluation; the development of more rigorous procedures of supervision; reward for superior performance, along with the institution of a realistic and tough system of accountability; and the provision of meaningful ways of involving the parents and the community in the activities of the school.

In spite of the above, I nonetheless suggest the following as possible realistic and practical competitors to the present form of urban public school systems:

1. *Regional state schools:* These schools would be financed by the states and would cut across present urban-suburban boundaries.

2. *Federal regional schools:* These schools would be financed by the federal government out of present state-aid funds or with additional federal funds. These schools would be able to cut through state boundaries and could make provisions for residential students.

3. *College- and university-related open schools:* These schools would be financed by colleges and universities as part of their laboratories in education. They would be open to the public and not restricted to children of faculty and students. Obviously, public students would be selected in terms of constitutional criteria, and their percentage determined by realistic considerations.

4. *Industrial demonstration schools:* These schools would be financed by industrial, business, and commercial firms for their employees and selected members of the public. These would not be vocational schools but elementary and comprehensive high schools of high quality. They would be sponsored by combinations of business and industrial firms in much the same way as various churches and denominations now sponsor and support parochial or sectarian schools.

5. *Labor union–sponsored schools:* These schools would be financed and sponsored by labor unions largely, but not exclusively, for the children of their members.

6. *Army schools:* The Defense Department has been quietly effective in educating some of the casualties of our present public schools. It is hereby suggested that the Department now go into the business of repairing hundreds of thousands of these human casualties with affirmation rather than apology. Schools for ado-

lescent dropouts or educational rejects could be set up by the Defense Department adjacent to camps—though not necessarily as an integral part of the military. If it is necessary that such operations become an integral part of the military, so be it. The goal is to rescue as many of these young people as possible. They are not expendable on the altar of antimilitarist rhetoric.

In my enthusiasm to suggest specific alternatives or competitors to the present public school system, I was even going to suggest that schools be set up by social agencies and foundations. But I thought better of it. I now suggest that the foundations play their most meaningful and traditional role of supporting some of the alternatives suggested above—giving them the initial push.

With a strong, efficient, and demonstrably excellent parallel system of public schools, organized and operating on a quasi-private level, it would be possible to bring back into public education a vitality and dynamism that is now clearly missing. Even the public discussion of these possibilities might clear away some of the dank stagnation that pervades urban education today. American industrial and material wealth was made possible through industrial competition. American educational health may be made possible through educational competition.

If we succeed, we will have returned to the dynamic, affirmative goal of education—namely, to free man of irrational fears, superstitions, and hatreds. Specifically, in America, the goal of democratic education must be to free Americans of the blinding and atrophying shackles of racism. A fearful, passive, apologetic, and inefficient educational system cannot help in the attainment of these goals.

If we succeed in finding and developing these, and better, alternatives to the present educational inefficiency, we will not only save countless Negro children from lives of despair and hopelessness; thousands and thousands of white children will also be rescued from cynicism, moral emptiness, and social ineptitude. We will also demonstrate the validity of our democratic system. We will have saved our civilization through saving our cities.

12. Schools for Equal Opportunity

by John H. Fischer

John H. Fischer, president of Teachers College, Columbia University, served as chairman of the U.S. delegations to the International Conference on Public Education in Geneva in 1963 and the UNESCO Conference on Youth in Grenoble in 1964. Chairman of the board of trustees of the Center for Urban Education, he also serves on the board of Johns Hopkins University and the Institute for Educational Development. He is a member of the National Advisory Council on Education of Disadvantaged Children and of the Visiting Committee of the Harvard Graduate School of Education.

The American public school system is the world's most comprehensive and most fruitful experiment in universal education. Yet, the current performance of our urban schools is so poor and the resistance to change so great, according to some critics, that they propose to replace the public schools with publicly subsidized and competitive independent schools.

Their proposal is by no means irresponsible or irrational, but it *is* based on questionable assumptions. I know of no evidence that for any given group of students independent schools can provide a better education than well-staffed and well-managed public schools. Nor, as far as I can tell, do the advocates of the proposal have any such data. The principal argument for this radical step is that, as city schools are now organized and administered, many of them, and most of those in deprived areas, are simply not providing education of the character or quality their students need and are entitled to receive. To support that contention, there is evidence: the failure and dropout rates of pupils, the transfer applications of teachers, the complaints of parents, and the quiet decisions of the families with broader options, who remove their children by the thousands to private schools or to the suburbs.

To be sure, the schools are often held accountable for failures that they have neither the means nor the opportunity to correct. Not even the best school or the most dedicated teacher can guarantee that all the pupils will finish the year above the grade median.

Nor can every child be assured a place in college, however strongly his parents may demand equal treatment. But the excessive casualty rates of the schools can be neither explained nor excused by statistics. Nor are they all the inevitable result of unfortunate heredity, broken homes, or bad community influences.

The complexity of the situation can be seen in the gaps that separate less fortunate Americans from the majority of their countrymen. Not only are these gaps disgracefully wide; in certain cases they are actually widening. Most of these inequities are related to poverty, many are aggravated by racial discrimination, and all contribute to the handicapping circumstances within which and against which the school must carry on its work. Let me cite a few comparisons.

Nonwhite infant mortality in 1940 was 70 per cent worse than the white rate. In 1960, it was 90 per cent worse. Maternal mortality among nonwhite mothers in 1940 was 2.4 times the white rate. In 1960, it was 3.8 times the white rate.

A Negro boy born in 1962 had as much chance of surviving to twenty as a white boy had of reaching thirty-seven. A Negro girl could look forward to reaching twenty as confidently as a white girl could to reaching forty-two.

In employment, the best years for Negroes only come up to the recession levels for whites. In 1964, a prosperous year when white unemployment dropped to less than 3.5 per cent, the Negro rate was still almost 10 per cent. That was half again as high as the worst white rate since the Depression. These figures are for adults, twenty and older. For sixteen- and seventeen-year-old Negroes, unemployment has not dropped below 20 per cent in ten years.

There is, of course, a close relation between these data and educational conditions. The median years of school completed by persons over twenty-five in 1940 was 8.7 for whites but 5.8 for nonwhites. By 1960, the nonwhites had reached 8.2, still half a year below where the whites had been twenty years earlier. Meanwhile, the white median had risen to 10.9 years.

But, some argue, things are better now than they used to be. They are better, but far from good. In 1960, the percentage of college graduates in the group aged twenty-five to twenty-nine was 15.6 per cent for whites and 5.3 per cent for Negroes. That meant that, in 1960, the Negroes were where the whites had been in 1920. In high school graduation, the gap is closing. The Negro rate in 1960 equaled the white in 1940.

The Selective Service Mental Test is a constant reminder that the educational gap is still tragically wide for our present eighteen-year-olds. The variation among the states is well known, but the differential figures on white and Negro registrants are not as widely circulated. For the country as a whole, the failure rate is about 25 per cent. Between June, 1964, and December, 1965, the rate for white applicants was 19 per cent, for Negroes 67 per cent. Failures among whites ranged from 5 per cent in the state of Washington to 43 per cent in Tennessee. For Negroes, the range was from 25 per cent in Washington to 85 per cent in South Carolina. Those who think that the determining factor is race rather than education might note that Negroes in the state of Washington did better than whites in eight other states. Negroes in Rhode Island surpassed the whites of six other states. The poor showing of city schools is not attributable simply to the influx of Negro children. It is due rather to the failure of the schools to respond to the special problems of American youngsters who are the victims of deprivation, neglect, and prejudice.

In order for the schools to respond as promptly and as effectively as they should to these conditions, it seems to me that three things are necessary: (1) we must reconsider the principle of equal opportunity; (2) we must devise more effective ways to adapt schools to the children they serve; and (3) we must reconstruct existing arrangements for policy-making and school administration.

In the whole American credo, no tenet is more firmly fixed than our devotion to equal opportunity. The race, we say, is to the swift, but it is open to all, and everyone who appears at the starting line is allowed to run. Nevertheless, there are always those who, for no fault of their own, cannot make it to the line before the gun is fired. What we overlook is that "the equal treatment of unequals produces neither equality nor justice."

To offer all children equal education remains a necessary beginning, for, even in our most affluent cities, many thousands still have nothing remotely approaching equality of schooling. But equality among schools is only the first step. We must set our sights not on making schools equal but on devising whatever means are required to enable every child to develop his own potential. Whatever his possibilities, wherever he begins, he should have the help he needs to reach maturity prepared to compete on fair terms in an open society. To live with this conception of equal opportunity, the community must be willing, and the school must be able, to furnish unequal education.

Unequal education to promote equal opportunity may seem a radical proposal, but it is, in fact, a well-established practice. This is precisely what has long been done for physically and mentally handicapped children under the name of "special education." As it has been offered to these minorities, what we now call compensatory education is universally approved. But the largest minority of our children are not the crippled and mentally retarded. They are the millions who suffer the handicaps of sustained deprivation and neglect. The time has come to provide unequal, exceptional education as a matter of deliberate public policy to every child who needs it.

Lip service to the principle of compensatory education in itself will solve nothing. It only points up another puzzling issue, for much of what has been done under this label in the past half-dozen years has proved disappointing. The U.S. Civil Rights Commission, in its report *Racial Isolation in the Public Schools,* describes a number of such efforts and concludes that "the programs did not show evidence of much success." Coleman's massive study *Equality of Education Opportunity* similarly found that existing teaching practices and curricula do little to counteract the effects of isolation or deprivation.

Nevertheless, it would be indefensible at this point to dismiss the concept of compensation as useless. Even though both Coleman and the Commission find that integration may be more beneficial than compensation, the fact remains that, in many cities, complete integration will not be possible in the foreseeable future. Even if it were, many children are so seriously retarded academically that if they could instantly be placed in integrated schools they would still need a great deal of special help. Whether such attention is called preventive, remedial, corrective, or whatever, it must be designed to meet the unusual individual requirements of children for whom present programs are inadequate.

The finding of the Coleman study that may ultimately turn out to be the most significant of all is that students with a sense of control over their own destiny do better in school than those who are convinced that what they do will have little effect on their ultimate opportunities. Ways must be found to create more schools in which children will find that they are respected, that they can be successful, and that what they do does make a difference.

This process must begin early. It becomes increasingly clear that children have a better chance to succeed in school if they are introduced to planned learning experiences well before the age of six. An immediately available "solution," if we want to call it that, for every city is to make kindergartens universally available for five-year-olds and to establish preschool programs for four-year-olds. This step is especially urgent for those most in need of the benefits that such programs at their best can provide.

There is impressive evidence that the level of intellectual capability young people will achieve by seventeen is already predictable for half of them by age four. For an additional 30 per cent, fairly accurate forecasts are possible by age seven. This is no ground for believing that a child's academic fate is sealed by his seventh birthday, but it means that a community that seriously wants to improve its children's opportunities will start them to school early. In terms of sheer economy, it can be seen that, dollar for dollar, the earlier the investment in systematic intellectual development is begun, the greater will be the rate of return.

Some of the early follow-up studies of children in Head Start programs have been interpreted as meaning that such early programs have no effect on subsequent success in the primary grades. It is much more likely that what has actually been discovered is the failure of primary grade teachers to build upon the gains made at the preschool level. Even the best preschool programs will produce only temporary benefits unless the follow-through at the primary level is well planned. Similarly, in the middle grades and the secondary school, curricula and teaching procedures must be designed to build on the progress of earlier stages and to introduce the new emphases appropriate at each level. But our present shortcomings are due less to the state of the pedagogic art than to the state of mind of the artists. Not only teachers but administrators, board members, and parents alike almost invariably approach these new problems assuming that they can be solved without any fundamental change in the nature of the school itself. We should by now be able to see that much of what must be done cannot be fitted into the customary institutional forms.

There are, to be sure, schools that have abandoned egg-crate architecture and with it the image of teachers as interchangeable parts to be distributed, one to thirty children, equally throughout the building. But most schools, even where the need for innovation is most pressing, have yet to make the first break toward anything remotely resembling a teaching team. The utility of the flexible primary unit, in which several teachers work jointly with one group of children for two to four years, has been well demonstrated; but the idea spreads ever so slowly, because it calls for a fundamentally different pattern of professional practice and school organization.

At the secondary level, despite the evidence that adolescents are both able and eager to work on their own, only a handful of teachers will really trust them to learn out of the teacher's sight. Every community, most notably the large city, presents a priceless collection of living laboratories for learning about the modern world and how it works. Yet, in the typical school, respectable education is still defined as what goes on within the schoolhouse walls. Long before De Tocqueville commented on the force of voluntarism in this country, Americans were tapping the committed energy of volunteers to get things done. We have still to learn to apply this magnificent source of manpower and creative effort in a comprehensive way in the public schools.

Now, it might be objected that I have overstated my argument because each of the practices I mention is, in fact, being used in schools. It is true that they are. But I would remind the reader that, almost everywhere, such innovations are considered exceptional. As variations from educational normality, they are still suspect.

The systematic invention and introduction of more promising

school practices is a field, moreover, in which the university should be expected to provide substantial assistance to the schools. More is required, however, than using schools to accommodate the passing enthusiasms of professors or to insure better-prepared, or more judiciously recommended, freshmen.

For too long, university groups have been willing merely to use the schools to serve their own research interests or as convenient populations from which to draw samples. School systems, on their side and often with justification, have resented outside research as an intrusion upon the normal, and in their view more important, activities of the classroom. If school-university association in research and development is to be as productive as present needs require, we shall have to move beyond the practice of viewing each project as a separate *ad hoc* exercise. We must establish mutually agreed-upon long-range policies that respect the needs, interests, and resources of all the participants. We must lay the groundwork for continuing and flexible cooperation at levels ranging from small studies with a few children to large-scale experiments involving entire schools and school systems. The regional educational laboratories offer bright prospects, but additional joint arrangements are necessary. They can be created if the school systems and the universities, particularly in the larger cities, will respond to the imperatives they both face and allocate the necessary energy to the task.

With such cooperation, we can also be on our way toward relieving the most pressing of all the problems of urban education —the better preparation of teachers in city schools. Too many current programs in this field consist of little more than appeals to social consciousness and attempts to "make do" with practices devised long ago for other circumstances. Inspired devotion and humanitarian attitudes are essential in teaching, but they are no substitute for knowledge and skill. Until we mount strong, bold programs of systematic inquiry, experimentation, and evaluation, we shall be retarded both in dealing with the complex pedagogical problems of urban schools and in finding better ways to prepare the next generation of teachers to staff them.

We must also reconstruct the arrangements for school governance. Having spent most of my working years in the schools, twenty-five of them in public school administration, I find limited appeal in this exciting new game called "Get the Superintendent." But, whether one starts from the position of the superintendent, the board, the teachers, the children, or the public, it becomes increasingly difficult to justify the outmoded ways in which we continue to conduct the affairs of city schools.

To call this the decentralization question is to oversimplify. The issue is not whether a particular city should have one public school system, or five, or fifty. The issue is, rather, how to plan, manage, and use all the educational possibilities of the city to meet the pressures of the times, the students' needs, and the public interest. In any city, the public schools are the largest single element in the total educational enterprise, but they are by no means the whole of it. The tradition of separatism that has so long dominated public school policy and administration is clearly out of date. The mechanisms initially designed to protect the schools from partisan or corrupt political influence, however necessary they once were, now tend to isolate the schools from other agencies and to insulate them from normal political processes.

In the city, as in the nation, every important undertaking today has its educational aspect. Many projects have no future at all unless they can count on effective schools. An intricate network of relationships ties the families of every community to its economic, cultural, political, and social institutions. The school is connected in mutual dependence with virtually all of these agencies and many of the families. Yet, among school boards, administrators, and university people, there are many who still think that these connections call for no more than routine courtesies, prudent "public relations," and a vigilant watch against any sign of encroachment on the school's traditional prerogatives.

Urban planning that does not now include educational planning is not only unrealistic; it is irresponsible. Such planning must, moreover, go far beyond perfunctory review of the size and location of new school sites. It must confront questions of curriculum, attendance patterns, teacher supply, financial support—in brief, the whole complex interrelationship between the development of schools and the total development of the city. The need for such planning is crucial, and so is the manner in which it is done. Not only the central planning body but the school authorities, other public and private agencies, and the municipal and state governments must share responsibility for projecting goals and setting timetables, since they must also share responsibility for seeing that the commitments are met.

At the other end of the system, in the individual school, where the whole business succeeds or fails, there are other needs for reform. The demonstrations and boycotts, to say nothing of the thousands of less publicized complaints, that have plagued particular schools are symptoms of deeply serious problems. To be sure, not everyone who criticizes a principal is wholly objective. No doubt there are occasional picketers whose zeal for school reform is diluted by other ambitions. But when all the extraneous interests have been allowed for, there remain the just and proper grievances of parents who often are denied even a respectful reception, much less a voice, in the schools their children are required to attend.

Solutions in these cases would be easier if only the imperfections were more one-sided. At one extreme are the self-appointed groups who would arrogate to themselves a wholly fictitious authority to hire and fire school staff members and to prescribe the curriculum. At the other end of the continuum are that minority of school people who are willing for children to be seen and occasionally to be heard, but who prefer parents to be both invisible and inaudible.

Despite the accumulation of resentment, pride, and defensiveness that encumbers those situations, ways can be devised to involve parents more deeply in school affairs. A first step must surely be to lift the controversies beyond the adversary level. So long as school people and parents view each other as opponents to be defeated, the likelihood of positive results is negligible. What is needed is a sustained, patient effort to build and maintain channels through which each group may express its views and be assured of respectful attention and consideration from the other. A second step is to systematize these exchanges, turning them to constructive deliberation and providing the substantive data necessary to enable the participants to make responsible choices and projections. A third step is a thoroughgoing analysis of the nature of school policy issues to determine at what level the different types can best be handled. Some should be settled within the school, some at intermediate points, and others on a city-wide basis. The heart of the matter is to find the plan and the means by which a city school board can maintain a common floor of opportunity for every pupil in the city and at the same time encourage parents, citizens, and school staff members to apply their own initiative to raising their school as far as possible above the basic level.

The role of the professional staff is, of course, crucial. Teachers must have a major role in determining the programs and policies of the schools in which they serve. In part, this is being accomplished through negotiations between boards and professional organizations. But even where collective action is well established, parallel channels should assure the individual teacher freedom to make his personal contributions to policy and practice, in both his school and the school system.

There are no easy solutions and, very probably, no final solutions of any kind to the educational problems of our cities. But there are vast possibilities still untried, and broad ranges of opportunity open to imagination and bold attack. Yet, it would be a grave error and a stupid miscalculation to think that the public schools should assume these tasks alone, or that they could possibly perform them in isolation.

It is an ironic paradox that the gravest educational deficiencies are often found in the very cities that possess the best resources for correcting them. Yet, all too often, the institutions that harbor these resources—the universities, museums, libraries, scientific agencies, and mass media, all with enormous possibilities for enriching human life—carry on their work with little awareness of the life of the community in which they stand. In the same cities, hundreds of agencies, public and private, with the competence and experience to make critically important contributions to the physical, social, and economic well-being of people, could undergird and supplement educational and cultural efforts.

To be sure, we cannot marshal all these resources without altering existing political and administrative mechanisms. We shall need new laws, new agencies, and new money; but most of all, we need a new vision, newly shared, of what city life at its best might be, and do, and give. Lewis Mumford put it well:

> We must now conceive the city not primarily as a place of business or government, but as an essential organ for expressing and actualizing the new human personality. . . . Not industry but education will be the center of [activity] and every process and function will be approved . . . to the extent that it furthers human development. . . . For the city should be an organ of love; and the *best economy of cities is the care and culture of men.*

13. The Concept of the Educational Clinic

by H. Thomas James

H. Thomas James is dean of the Stanford University School of Education. He is the author of *Wealth, Expenditures, and Decision-Making for Education* and *Determinants of Educational Expenditures in Large Cities in the United States*. As Assistant State Superintendent for Finance and Research, Dr. James developed a standardized system of accounting for the schools of Wisconsin. He has been a consultant to the Interstate Compact for Education and the Committee for Economic Development, as well as to several foreign countries, including Chile, Colombia, and Venezuela.

Public policy in education is determined in very large part by local fiscal resources. This sounds bland and, perhaps, even obvious. Yet, this is an arrangement that can lead only to social disaster. We must find some new ways in which we can make sound public policy decisions about education, and then find the revenue needed to execute that policy. As long as we allow policy decisions about education to be limited by the funds available locally, we face a rising sea of troubles. To understand why, we must look closely at our cities. In doing so, it is helpful to think of them as organisms that grow and change over time. I am convinced that studies of cities along the lines of this organismal model will reveal regularities that should allow us to predict their conditions.

Most of the great cities of this country, and, indeed, of the world, were built in the nineteenth century, and the populations of most of the largest American cities stopped growing early in the twentieth century. The federal census-takers, by 1940, pointed out that this appearance of arrested growth was artificial, the result of arbitrary limits on boundaries. They began to speak of standard metropolitan statistical areas, for it was apparent that, while populations of the great cities were stabilizing and even declining, something larger than the city was identifiable as a population unit, and many of these units, even though not unified governmentally, were continuing to grow around the cores of the great cities.

We have had many proposals that these metropolitan statistical units be unified governmentally, and indeed several have gone a long way in that direction—notably New York, early in this century when the five boroughs were combined, and more recently Toronto, Dade County in Florida, Louisville, and others. Some cities have expanded their boundaries in an attempt to encompass the growth—notably Los Angeles, San Jose, Houston, and Milwaukee. Alaska has taken perhaps the most heroic step toward an early solution of this problem by creating boroughs and subordinating both city and school districts to borough government. This idea seems to have great promise, and the growth of the Anchorage area should provide an early test of the validity of the borough idea. Some professors of education have taken up the cry and have proposed unification of the school districts within greater metropolitan areas as a solution to problems as diverse as tax inequities and racial segregation.

In view of the historical record of our profession for being prone to advocate terribly simple solutions to terribly complex problems, I want to answer some hard questions before jumping on the metro-school-district bandwagon. Perhaps we already have too many special purpose districts, and what we may need is to devise a truly general-purpose, local-type government for our standard metropolitan statistical units, which will control not necessarily the decisions on instruction but at least the fiscal decisions of school districts.

The districts we now have and the ones we may create must, I think, be responsive to two old and well-known popular demands. These are that (1) the services provided by the district shall be efficiently distributed to the children of the district, and (2) the cost burdens bear equitably upon the district's taxpayers. I will consider first some efficiency considerations that have fiscal implications and some equity considerations that concern taxation and distribution of revenues.

The primary function served by city schools in the earlier days of their existence, and perhaps still today, is custodial—providing a safe place for the child to be in an urban world that has no other place for him at certain times. I have suggested elsewhere that we could create a new institution, modeled perhaps on the modern medical clinic, that would diagnose educational problems in individual children and prescribe treatment. The treatment might be as simple as having the child pursue his studies in the traditional school setting; or it might be as drastic as prescribing that he drop out of school to be exposed to new institutional services yet to be invented. (Many of these might be produced in the private sector and for profit.) Another form of treatment might simply allow him to pursue in some instances his own enlightened self-interests. If we could indeed arrive at the latter prescription, we would at long last begin to realize the Platonic notion of education, in which the city and all its rich resources become the classroom and provide the curriculum, while the ends of education pursued by the individual are also the goals of a society governed by such individuals.

The function of the educational clinic would include periodic review of the student's record, with attention also to the process by which he acquires an education, facilitating those conditions that contribute to the process and removing impediments.

Both of these broad purposes—the custodial and the treatment—are attended to now in the public school system and require the personal services of relatively expensive, highly trained professionals. The irrationality and inefficiency of this arrangement is perhaps best illustrated by the fact that the group responding most favorably to treatment—let us say the top 5 per cent in academic achievement—invariably has a record of maximum attendance as well, thus indicating maximum exposure to both the custodial and treatment services; whereas the lowest 5 per cent in academic performance are also lowest in days of attendance. The achievement record of these two groups would almost certainly remain the same if their attendance record were reversed.

So we might profitably experiment along some lines suggested by the assumption that the process of acquiring an education is a normal process that goes on quite independently of whether or not a child is in legal custody of the city school system. Given this assumption, our concern shifts from the normal child responding normally to the stimulation of his environment; for him our concern need be only with seeing that the environment is properly stimulating, with devising ways to minimize the need for personal services in that environment, and with monitoring his responses to see that they continue to be normal.

We then might begin to organize our expensive personal services to maximize their availability to the abnormal child, the one not responding normally to the stimulation of the school environment. We might thus come to some organizational adaptations, like those I suggested earlier, that would be organized for maximum efficiency in diagnosis and treatment of abnormalities, and not at all concerned with custody, care, and feeding.

The advantages of such arrangements become more obvious as we observe how capital investments can be used to reduce the need for personal services as we specify and specialize the functions to be performed. Attractive and efficient laboratories, specialized libraries, video tapes for recording pupil behavior, computer-linked programming, data reduction, storage and retrieval systems for teaching—all point to the probability that substantial capital investments can reduce the time needed to assemble and make readily available rather comprehensive records on each pupil, without the need for continuous surveillance by a teacher.

Furthermore, it seems probable that many a student might progress faster if left to work quite independently through programs planned to meet his interests and aspirations, with only periodic checkups and occasional corrective measures prescribed by a master teacher or by the educational clinic specialists. The teacher in such a system uses her time to facilitate the learning process. This contrasts with present arrangements, for, as classrooms are now organized, much of the teacher's activities—particularly those involving lecturing and disciplining inattentive pupils—may actually distract the child who is trying to concentrate on learning, and interfere with his efforts.

Once we begin to reorganize our schools, the arrangements for the custodial function could be undertaken more rationally, and perhaps we might want to extend it to age groups not now included. It seems perfectly clear from the historical record, that, to the early designers of city schools, the custodial function was perhaps more important than was instruction. Yet we are now learning that children who are better prepared through preschool instruction are better prepared to receive educational services, so that money spent on their subsequent education produces better results than money spent on unprepared pupils. We should, perhaps, face the hard fact that family life is breaking down in many parts of our core cities and that school services extending downward to younger age groups, perhaps as young as two years old, may be the only solution to the problem created by increasing instability in metropolitan family life.

As we probably can organize our large schools more efficiently by further specializing their personnel, so we might also help matters if we further specialize our educational institutions. To date, we have tried generally to meet all expectations for increased educational services to children through general-purpose elementary schools and comprehensive high schools. This tendency almost certainly is inefficient, in so far as it requires high-salaried personnel, trained for rendering one service, to spend time doing something that a less expensive employee could do. It is equally inefficient if it ties up specialized and expensive buildings and equipment when less expensive facilities would suffice. For instance, it probably is more efficient to expand city recreational facilities and personnel, as a response to demands for improved play areas for children, than to ask school districts to make a comparable increase in staff and services. School children visiting a museum are taken through as a unit by the guide while accompanied by their teachers; it would certainly be more efficient to have the guide responsible from the time the children assembled at the school, and leave the teacher at the school to tasks more relevant to her training. It probably will be more efficient, in the long run, to encourage industry to continue its experiments with innovations to capture the school lunch markets than it will be to encourage schools to continue to build their traditional school lunch services, staffs, and facilities. It probably will be more efficient to devise some adaptation of driver training, perhaps utilizing specialized police personnel, than it will be to continue to provide this service through schools at its present, appallingly expensive level.

Up to this point, I have considered how we might improve the efficiency, organization, and management of the metropolitan school by preparing children earlier to make use of its services, by specializing functions so that expensive personnel services and facilities can be more efficiently utilized, and by using capital investments to reduce outlays for personal services. I turn now to a different kind of problem, which is related to equity considerations and governmental arrangements for allocating funds to education.

Across the country, more than half the costs of public elementary and secondary education on the average come from taxes collected by local units of government. This is to say that more than half the costs of education rest on archaic tax structures, mostly involved with property taxation, which are frequently badly —and occasionally scandalously—administered.

The most common result of this arrangement is that the cities most in need of education generally are least able to afford it; or, to state the problem another way, the quality and quantity of education are determined not by social policy but by the money available, so that the poorer a city is, the less likely it is to be able to afford the educational services that might contribute in the long run to its enrichment.

This situation is common in the United States because the legislatures, in granting local agencies of government the power to tax for school purposes, usually defined that power in terms of tax rates based on unequally distributed property values. Through much of this century, state finance has been principally concerned with finding formulas for distributing unequal proportions of sales and income tax receipts to local districts in order to equalize the great inequities resulting from the unequal grants of power to levy local taxes.

The reorganization of school districts also has been pursued vigorously in many states, since these inequities tend to disappear as the size of the districts increases. Much of the bitterness generated by reorganization efforts can be ascribed to resentment over loss of privileged tax positions; districts most privileged under existing arrangements invariably resist reorganization most vigorously and, because the resources they possess can generate political power and influence, they are, more often than not, successful in resisting reorganization. Part of their success is certainly due to the value we tend to attach to decentralized school systems; but much of the discussion of "local control of schools" is really about local resistance to taxation.

In spite of resistance, state efforts to reorganize districts have met with some success; the number of districts is down from about 130,000 in 1930 to about 20,000 today. Most of the large cities have changed sides on this issue, for, while they were once included among the privileged districts in having greater-than-average taxable wealth, many of them now have dropped below the state average. Attempts to create metropolitan school districts extending to the limits of the standard metropolitan statistical units will encounter the same resistance, and for the same reasons.

There is, however, a more rational and effective method for getting at the central problem of more efficient utilization of the property-tax revenue potential. This is the reassertion by the state of its authority to tax property. Such a reassertion would leave undisturbed the highly valued local control of school policy. Local agencies could even retain part of their present power to tax for school purposes. State legislatures would simply reclaim a part of the taxing power they have delegated to local districts by establishing a state-wide rate to be levied on all property for the support of schools. The yield would be drawn into the central fisc and, after being combined with revenues from income, sales, and perhaps other tax sources, would be distributed on a program-budget basis to accomplish educational purposes stipulated by the legislature.

As I indicated before, a child's pro-rata share might be transferred to special schools in the private sector, if he needed their services. If additional purposes were to be defined locally, the local agency would still have local taxing power to finance them; the local voters would decide whether or not to make the additional tax effort. The general effect would be to bring the tax load on property in the islands of privilege up to the state mean. It would equalize the property-tax burden for school purposes among districts. It would put into the hands of the legislature the decision as to what level of property tax could safely be borne for school purposes, and, most importantly, what mix of income, sales, and property taxes is optimum for the support of schools.

The cost of supporting educational clinics could be allocated to the federal government. (It could also be borne by the state, though the federal solution seems preferable to me.) It could be borne either as a direct expense of government, or, if organized in the private sector, charges could be determined as Medicare charges are now determined and billed to government.

To summarize, I have emphasized two general problems of urban school districts: one is inefficiency in the distribution of school services, and for this problem I have commended a reduction in our obsession with taking children into custody, and some drastic efforts to specialize both personnel and institutions; the second is the blind control of educational policy dictated by local availability of resources, and for this I have commended the transfer of control of property tax administration, and the distribution of all school revenues, to the state legislatures. Like most students of school finance, I would then look to the Congress to equalize the burdens of costs of educational services among states, and also for legislation guaranteeing certain minimal services important to the general welfare of all the schoolchildren of America.

PART III

THE SCHOOLHOUSE

We conclude with the schoolhouse—but not the walled fortress or inward-turning monument of the past. For if the school is, in fact, more and more intimately tied to its urban context, then the schoolhouse itself must be seen in a fresh light. It is no longer a matter of mere bricks and mortar but an instrument of social policy—an agent of change.

The implications of this are still just dawning on most of us. One implication is perfectly clear, however: conventional wisdom is irrelevant. As Harold Gores makes plain in his witty and comprehensive paper, all the old formulas, the rules of thumb, the assumptions of the past need to be questioned. Nor will any single new concept serve all purposes.

The combined-occupancy school, described by two authors who have been instrumental in fostering the concept, will be useful in some cities and not others. The education park, which is arousing strong interest all over the country, needs to be seen in the broad perspective supplied by Cyril G. Sargent, John B. Ward, Bernard McCormick, and Allen Talbot. Together they report on applications of the education park idea in a variety of urban settings.

Similarly, we are perhaps ready for some of the novel ideas about play presented here by M. Paul Friedberg, and the sweepingly imaginative proposals of Frederick J. McDonald—proposals that carry us toward a broader conception of what constitutes a learning environment; proposals, in fact, that carry us beyond the schoolhouse itself. For a book about urban education, a book that assumes the city itself to be a teaching machine, this is, as we hope the reader will agree, precisely as it should be.

14. The Demise of Magic Formulas

by Harold B. Gores

Harold B. Gores is president of Educational Facilities Laboratories, a non-profit organization established by The Ford Foundation in 1958 to help schools and colleges with their physical problems. Dr. Gores, who came to EFL from the superintendency of the Newton (Massachusetts) Public Schools, has served on several Presidential Task Forces and Commissions, and is currently a member of the Educational Advisory Committee of *The New York Times*, the U.S. Office of Education Commission on Instructional Technology, and the Building Research Advisory Board of the National Academy of Sciences. He is a past president of the Harvard Teachers Association, and is an honorary member of the American Institute of Architects.

The schoolhouse in the city is being buffeted these days by two gigantic forces. The first arises from a collision of cultures—the poor and the affluent, sometimes oversimplified as black and white. The second is the educational revolution.

Both forces are external, beating in on the schoolhouse from the outside. The cultural collision comes from the streets. The educational revolution springs from university laboratories, federal research projects, and technically oriented industry seeking peacetime markets. Caught in the vortex of these forces, the city schoolhouse, that most numerous and most public of public buildings, becomes an arena of battle.

One of the first to remark on the changing circumstances of urban education was the Heald-Hunt-Rubin Commission. Reporting to the New York City School Board in 1959, the Commission declared:

> In the necessary and continual questioning of municipal operations, the nature and worth of a schoolhouse defy simple analysis. Though it looms as the most frequently created of all classes of municipal structures, and therefore in the aggregate is the most expensive item of capital outlay, it is burdened by having to perform more than the commonly recognized function of serving well the instruction of the young. If the schoolhouse is to produce to the maximum, it must also perform the less commonly recognized, but nonetheless vital, func-

tion of leading the city toward a better and higher plane of living.

The schoolhouse that is only a place where children are taught during the day fulfills its primary function only this much. But there are those who expect the schoolhouse to serve its city in additional ways: it must serve to strengthen the whole fabric of city life by serving its whole community; its architecture should lead the neighborhood on to its own renewal; and it must help to anchor those families who are needed to keep a city in balance culturally and economically, and who are encouraged to desert to the suburbs if the city's schools are dreary and cheerless.

Cities are organic; therefore, they must continually renew themselves. Their growth and greatness may have come about by accident or good fortune; but their decline can be forestalled only by design. Of all municipal structures, the schoolhouse, being the most numerous, holds the key to a city's physical and, indeed, sociological future.

A big city is a wondrous place. The advantages derived from sheer massiveness are manifold. But this same bigness addressed to schooling the young is a handicap. Eminent sociologists and city planners have stated that one square mile is about the largest area to which a resident identifies himself and about which he will take personal action to affect its affairs—provided, of course, there is a channel through which he can act. If the area is much greater, if he lacks a place to be heard, he tends not to act in person or in concert with his neighbors, but, instead, "writes a letter to the editor," puts in an angry telephone call to some branch of city government or, worse, just moves away.

This was 1959, when good manners still required the use of gentle and circuitous language. But what the Commission was really saying, in the bluntness now acceptable in the late 1960's, was that unless schools reorganize they will fail to anchor the middle class to the central city, that the city schoolhouse, a brick fortress glowering at its hostile neighborhood, is one of the principal ejectors of the middle class, speeding them on their way to private schools or to suburbia.

If it were the national intention to empty our cities of parents and children, the city schoolhouse—a masonry fortress afloat on a sea of blacktop, bounded by a hurricane wire fence with two basketball hoops—is the ideal instrument. Add to the hostile schoolhouse the mounting danger in the streets and you have the best combination of the best reasons for getting out of town as soon as you can afford it, if you have children.

And it is happening. Not long ago I arrived in one of our great cities just in time to observe a helicopter hovering over a high school and deploying police cruisers in the neighborhood to quell a riot in the school. When, later in the day, the superintendent of schools said to me, "If we can only improve the schools sufficiently, I think we can save this city," I couldn't help but think of the title of a chapter in one of Amy Lowell's books I read as a boy—"I Spit Against the Wind."

Historically, and with few exceptions, cities have attempted to renew everything except the schools. In the relatively enlightened city of Pittsburgh, for example, they cleaned up the air, built the Golden Triangle, improved housing, cleaned up the river, but they haven't built a high school since 1932. A happy exception has been New Haven, Connecticut, which started its renewal with its schools and may yet become the first slumless city in America.

Philosophical and pedagogical debates can rage interminably, but the moment of truth arrives when a building has to be located and built. A building is a sixty-year decision, which cannot later be erased by taking a vote. It just stands there to serve or to haunt whoever determined where and what it would be. The best tip-off as to whether a city understands itself, what its problems are, and what it must become is what that city is doing about its schoolhouses. When you hear about Pittsburgh's five Great High Schools you know that somebody there has a feeling about what Pittsburgh is going to be. When you hear what Syracuse is planning for its schools, you'll know that someone there has a vision of a new Syracuse. If you could only know one thing about a city to measure its grasp of its human problems, look to the schoolhouse. Moreover, if there is one message about urban education that comes through loud and clear, it is that there is no one solution. If schools are to fulfill their role in revitalizing our cities, a great variety of new art forms in education will be required, and today, for the first time, there is a growing climate of consent for such experimentation.

Let me list some of the new formulas, the new art forms, and the new arrangements that I see emerging:

1. *Formulas for size of school:* Until about 1958, the conventional educational wisdom declared that, ideally, elementary

schools should provide two classes per grade and that high schools, to be efficient, should enroll at least 750 students. If enrollment exceeded 1,250, it was believed, the school would be massive and insensitive.

But we now know that if monolithic line and staff administration (imported by Horace Mann from Prussia more than a century ago) is replaced by decentralized control, by schools-within-schools, by houses, and by subschools a school can then be as large as it needs to be—and still be good. The absolutes no longer apply.

2. *Formulas for size of site:* From time to time, various official bodies proclaim how much land is proper for a school. One of the latest pronouncements for an elementary school is 20 acres, plus an acre for every 100 children. That such a formula, if applied in our central cities, would wipe out the homes of the student body seems to have been overlooked.

We know now, though, that very good city schools can be built on very limited sites, if only we depart from the design clichés of the suburbs. The platforming of space, the use of rooftop playgrounds, the substitution of nylon for blacktop play fields—all these serve to make obsolete the ancient rules of thumb about size of site.

3. *Formulas for organization—6-3-3; 8-4; 6-2-4; 6-2-2-2; and other mystical arrangements:* The Boston Latin School was established in 1635, thereby leading, it is claimed, to the founding of Harvard College a year later, so that Latin graduates would have someplace to go. Whatever the truth may be, as a nation we have enshrined the elementary school since 1642, the free and universal high school since the 1860's, and the junior high school since 1910. Only now are the classic arrangements of schools by grades beginning to crumble, and this is happening principally because the notion of "grade" itself is being challenged.

When New Haven sought to rethink and renew its schools, Cyril Sargent decreed that the sensible and sensitive arrangement would be 4-4-4. New York City is groping toward 5-3-4 on its way ultimately to 4-4-4. But it won't be long before some advanced city decides that a school should consist simply of all the children it is sensible to gather there. School size and composition have suddenly become questions of logistics, not of inherited cultural patterns. Here, too, the old "givens" are becoming unstuck.

4. *Formulas for length of life:* Ordinarily, school buildings are built to last forever—actually for sixty years, which in today's world is the reasonable equivalent. Accordingly, the schoolhouse is still the quintessence of the mason's art—great ceramic fortresses whose chambered interiors are laced with calcium walls. Within, the classrooms are filled with furniture indestructible enough to defy any scholar who may unsheath a jackknife to leave evidence that he once passed through the place. In these schools, much admired by the maintenance department at city hall, nothing yields, nothing nourishes the eye or is warm to the touch. The city schoolhouse, new or old, represents the municipal mind at its cruelest. It is a strange phenomenon: Individually we like children, but as groups—as governments—we don't.

Despite this nuts-and-bolts approach to places of learning, we know some things on which we should act:

1. In view of the mobility of populations, any solution that is incapable of being converted someday to another use is imprudent.
2. In view of the changes likely to occur in the way we teach, any arrangement expected to last sixty years without change is Procrustean where it should be protean.
3. In view of the changing nature of the central city, the building of a conventional schoolhouse should be contemplated only as a last resort. It is fallacious to declare, as we always have, that because there are children to be educated we automatically need a schoolhouse. If there are children to be educated, what we need is space in which to do it. Only if the space is lacking, only if there are no available "roofs" under which we can constitute a humane and supportive environment for learning, do we need a schoolhouse. Indeed, from what I have observed in Cleveland's Supplementary Educational Center (a converted warehouse), many of our cities' children would be better off if they could escape forever the old city schoolhouse.

We know now how to create space for learning that says to the teacher and the child what Plato said to all of us: "That which is honored in a country will be cultivated there." The trouble with schoolhouses isn't their roofs, it's their spirit. A carefully designed office building or other commercial structure can provide an environment in which the child knows he is wanted, that we want him to learn, and that his city has invested in him because it believes he is its future. In the past, we have dealt almost exclusively with architecture; we should also be dealing with the profession of design.

Let us put the question of building costs into perspective. If you build a $1 million high school, its operations budget will be about $1 million every three years. Over a life of sixty years, the actual cost of the building, itself, will be only about 6 per cent of the total cost of fulfilling the purposes for which the building was constructed. Or to put it another way, when you add two teachers to your staff, their salaries and fringe benefits for thirty years equal the cost of $1 million worth of building. Think of the number of city school boards that discuss for five minutes the consequence of adding two teachers and then argue into the dawn about the expenditure of $1 million for buildings. In short, contrary to popular misconceptions, buildings are chicken feed in the educational scheme of things. People are more important—and more expensive—than bricks.

Yet bricks are also important, especially if employed in inventive ways. For example, Syracuse, N.Y., has decided to disperse its core city schools to the periphery. Just as devotees of horse racing require sylvan settings for their tracks, the schools are likewise edging toward the outskirts where, as in the suburbs, the grass is greener and the tulips are taller. As downtown Syracuse locates its elementary schools, and next its junior high schools, out near the city's boundaries, the chances improve that someday the cities and the suburbs will be partners.

In fact, they must become partners, for it is increasingly clear that our central cities can't solve their problems alone. Most of them are inevitably on the Washington, D.C., trajectory—93 per cent Negro school enrollment. Unless unusual solutions are found —and quickly—Washington, D.C., will provide the basic pattern for Northern central cities. The flattening of the curve is up to the suburbs. And it is, indeed, up to the suburbs to reach into the central city, for the central city, being what it is, is unlikely to make proper advances toward the suburbs. Among the variety of new arrangements that must occur, the metropolitanizing of school districts has high priority.

But there are other things that can be done. Let me list a few:

1. In Boston, there is some hope that the public schools and Tufts Medical School will together constitute a medical village—a constellation of schools and housing that will be a viable and safe neighborhood.

2. In New York, the so-called Garrison Law will enable the New York City schools to enter into partnership with the private sector to the end that joint-occupancy structures, housing both educational facilities and apartments—or even light manufacturing—may come about. This may be the first instance growing out of law in which schools will enter the business of creating neighborhoods.

3. Increasingly, I see the development of schools that aren't just for children but for people. To be sure, the young need to be served, but the schoolhouse committed only to the young is too specialized for the city's good. Indeed, if all parts of our cities are to become good places for people to live, committing the schools solely to the young is too slow a process. Adults need the schoolhouse as much as children do. And adults determine what happens now, not a generation hence. To put the matter in bluntest terms, the schoolhouse in the slums should be the people's college, their town hall, their cultural center, their country club, their school.

I view with special alarm the kinds of schoolhouses designed to defend themselves from hostile neighborhoods. The invention of unbreakable glass is not a major contribution to our culture or to school design. Nor, in my view, is the windowless school which, like a Spanish mission, turns its back on the desert. Schools designed to defend themselves from hostile neighborhoods imply that the neighborhood won't improve by the year 2030.

4. In Chicago, there is the beginning of a study based on demographic trends, population movements, birth rates extrapolated forward rather than interpolated backwards, and arrangements with the private and church-related systems that exist, side by side, with the public schools. From my observations, any city that

attempts to plot its future course in education without regard to the companion system of church-related schools is planning in a vacuum. Chicago may well teach us all how to construct a system that will educate all the children of all the people.

5. America's big cities have failed to take advantage of their volume of construction to entice industry to develop modular systems of design and construction based on performance specifications. Pittsburgh is a notable exception to this rule, but, generally, our big cities have not been alert to systems development as have been, for example, the Metropolitan School Board of Toronto, the Catholic schools of Montreal, the University of California with respect to its dormitories, the universities of California and Indiana with respect to academic buildings, and a number of smaller school systems outlying Los Angeles and San Francisco.

It is an interesting question why there is a Valley Winds School on the periphery of St. Louis but not in it, a Barrington Middle School outlying Chicago, a Sonora High School outlying Los Angeles, a Sheldon School in Colorado but not in Denver, a systems school in Athens, Ga., but not in Atlanta, a Nova High School in Fort Lauderdale but not in Miami, and a systems school coming up in Gates-Chili but not in Rochester, or indeed anywhere else in New York State, except a little-known town named Greece. Why this should be so is obvious: Our cities are too complex in their decision-making to respond quickly to advances in the state of the art. From the record, it would appear that the bigger the school district, the less likely it can grasp the advantages of technological progress.

6. Schools are subsystems of government. Unless schools are planned within the total planning of the community, three dire consequences are predictable: schools will be located where someday nobody may live; they will fail to acquire buffer zones and tentacles reaching out to the community and, therefore, will be islands; and they won't get the money, much of which will be coming from Washington under conditions that require total community planning.

In sum, there is no one way to solve any city's educational problems. The intelligent response is a variety of responses. Everything needs to be tried: education parks as in Miami Beach and East

Orange; metropolitan districting as in Hartford and its suburbs; linear solutions as in Brooklyn; joint occupancy as in New York and Boston; the rebuilding of neighborhoods around schools as in New Haven; the creation of educational neighborhoods around our city universities. The alternative is to keep on building schools that lack relevance to their neighborhoods and the larger society.

To end on an optimistic note, it appears that educators are about to get a powerful, new partner—the private sector. Given encouragement, systems-oriented industry—especially aerospace—has the capability of creating the new social invention that our city schools require. Edward Logue, Boston's city planner, says it best:

> The imagination and the drive that has made our system the most productive in the world must be turned to the task of renewing our cities.
>
> Maybe it means we should overhaul the Internal Revenue code to make it as attractive to invest in the slums as it is to buy the tax-exempt bonds or search out oil and gas. If we do, we might just connect up 10 million presently forsaken people with the mainstream of American life. There is still time. Let us make a start before it is too late.

To do less than this is to accept the ancient Malayan proverb: "Better our children die than our culture."

15. The Concept of Combined Occupancy

by Albert A. Walsh and Daniel Z. Nelson

Albert A. Walsh is chairman of the New York City Housing Authority, responsible for the largest low-rent housing program in the United States. This program comprises 150,000 dwelling units, with another 40,000 in construction or planning. He has served as Deputy Commissioner of Housing and Community Renewal for the State of New York. An attorney by profession, he has been a partner of the New York firm of Demov and Morris. As a consultant to the Board of Education of the City of New York on its joint-occupancy school program, he made the study that resulted in enactment of the New York City Educational Construction Fund Act.

Daniel Z. Nelson is executive director of the New York City Educational Construction Fund, the nation's first state authority empowered to finance public schools in combined-occupancy buildings. Mr. Nelson, an attorney, was previously Deputy Coordinator of Housing and Development for the City of New York.

Not only are our cities dotted with ancient, outworn, and educationally ineffective school buildings, they face unusual problems in doing anything about it. The urban schoolhouse, like any other, sits on land, and land is a precious, often outrageously high-priced commodity in our larger cities. This means that finding appropriate sites for new schools is difficult—sometimes even impossible.

"In recent years" says Adrian Blumenfeld, administrator of the School Planning and Research Unit, New York City Board of Education, "an increasingly intense competition has evolved between school planners and community housing agencies, to say nothing of private developers, for available unencumbered land." Blumenfeld tells of one situation in which the same site was simultaneously approved for a middle-income housing project and for a school. Faced with this dilemma, the Board of Education said, "Build one on top of the other." In another case, when a relatively large parcel of land became available on the East Side of Manhattan, the battle, as he puts it, "was really on," with housing agencies, the Board of Education, and private business all fighting

for the land. The intensity of this struggle can be gauged from the fact that the land in question was appraised at between \$40 and \$50 per square foot—or approximately \$1.75 million per acre!

How do cities build schools under such circumstances? One way is to do exactly what the New York Board of Education suggested—to build schools and other kinds of facilities one atop the other. Through such "joint occupancy" or "combined occupancy," school facilities are built into private or public housing projects or even into commercial office buildings. In effect, such schemes provide free sites for schools. In some cases, they may even produce rental income for the school. Any surplus can be poured back into the educational program.

According to a report of Educational Facilities Laboratories:

> New York and Chicago both have created elementary school facilities in public housing projects by altering space originally designed as apartments. And New York is planning two projects, one in a middle-income housing development and the other in a private apartment complex. In both cases the lower floors of the apartment structures will be designed as school space and attached low-rise buildings will house auxiliary facilities such as auditoriums and cafeterias.
>
> A third project, now in the proposal stage, creates a community atmosphere both within and without the structure. The school, on ground and subterranean levels, is topped by a level of commercial shops and four levels of apartments. Two levels of parking are beneath the underground recreational area. There is an interior court and playground. Other community services, such as medical and mental health clinics, are encompassed within the building. All facilities, including the auditorium, gymnasium, and swimming pool, will be available for public use after school hours.
>
> Although New York has a public junior college operating in a high-rise office building, public school space has yet to be built into office buildings. But such a move has been under study in New York for some five years. Specifically, the plans call for construction of a commercial high school topped by a high-rise office building on the east side of the midtown commercial district. It still has not been determined whether the school board will hold title to the site and building or whether the building will be erected and owned by a private developer and the school space leased to the City.
>
> Either way, the Board of Education stands to gain. If it owns the building, rental incomes will more than offset the loss of real estate taxes normally involved when a city takes over property. If a developer owns the building, the City will continue to collect taxes

and expects to recover its share of the cost of the building in the first generation of the building's life.

Or, under newly enacted state legislation, the New York City Education Construction Fund has been created and is authorized to build schools, selling or leasing the air rights above them for apartment or office space. The resulting income would contribute to the cost of the schools.

In Chicago, school authorities have taken a different approach to joint occupancy. The six-story classroom wing of the City's new Jones Commercial High School was designed to support a fifteen-story commercial tower. But erection of the tower will await conclusion of a suitable agreement for sale or rental of air rights over the school to a developer.

The joint-occupancy schemes have advantages other than helping to overcome high real estate costs. Space is freed for parks and playgrounds. Provision can be made for future fluctuations in the size and composition of school enrollments. If enrollments fall off, properly designed school space can be converted to apartment or office use, or vice versa.

The combined-occupancy approach, revolutionary in its implications, has possible application in many urban centers. In the pages that follow, the authors, both of whom are actively involved in New York's experiment with combined occupancy, discuss this promising innovation. Mr. Walsh writes about the legal aspects of the experiment; Mr. Nelson discusses its advantages.

Legal Aspects

The increasingly critical shortage and rapidly escalating cost of developable land in the City of New York, coupled with the intense competition of public and private developers for available sites, has led the New York Board of Education to the concept of "combined occupancy"—i.e., the idea of building schools as an integral part of larger dual- or multi-purpose structures. In short, the Board, some years ago, began to think about building schools in structures that might also house commercial offices, apartments, or other noneducational facilities.

This novel idea permits more productive development of constantly diminishing land resources in metropolitan areas. It reduces —and may even eliminate—capital expenditures for acquiring sites and constructing new schools. It produces revenues from land that would normally be tax exempt—revenues that can, in turn, be used to offset construction costs or to produce additional schools. It permits additional economies through dual utilization of certain areas, such as meeting rooms, open spaces, playgrounds, etc. Finally, it offers, in a combined school-housing development, a challenging opportunity to integrate the entire pupil-teacher-parent relationship in new ways.

Such reasons led the New York Board of Education to explore the feasibility and desirability of combined occupancy as long ago as the early 1960's. It quickly found, however, that there were many legal and administrative obstacles that would effectively prevent the creation of such combined-occupancy school structures. Thus, in the fall of 1965, the Board, with the financial aid of the Taconic Foundation, retained my former law firm to study the legal and economic complications and to come up with recommendations for making the combined-occupancy idea lawful and workable.

Early in our study, we determined that, while piecemeal legislative amendments (such as a 1965 act authorizing the sale of school "air rights" to limited-profit housing companies) could be helpful, the possibility of amending the multiplicity of state and local laws affecting the problems was practically nil. The legal complexities were simply too overwhelming.

The concept of combining public and private ownership as well as public and private uses in one and the same building violates long-standing traditions embedded in both city and state laws. For example, school property, including even the rights to the air space over an existing or proposed school, could be sold or leased only by the city itself, and only at a public auction or by sealed bid, with a maximum lease term of ten years plus one ten-year renewal. The Board of Education in New York, while legally autonomous, does not have legal title to its own schools or school sites and has almost no fiscal independence from the city. Thus, the Board could not convey air rights—the city, itself, would have to do so. Moreover, under state law, at least three separate contracts would have to be competitively let for all public construction—one for plumbing and gas fitting, one for heating, ventilation, and air conditioning, another for electrical work, etc. This single complexity meant, in effect, that each contractor would be separately responsible to the contract-letting agency.

Obviously, few private developers could hazard the time and expense of planning a combined-occupancy structure under such circumstances—with the acquisition of air rights subject to the vicissitudes of public auction, and the control, timing, cost, and profits of construction divided among separate contractors over whom the developer has no control.

Not only did such legal provisions serve effectively to block the creation of combined-occupancy schools, but it was clear that it would be extremely difficult to modify the rules. In particular, we noted the many unsuccessful prior efforts to relax the public-bidding, multiple-contract provisions of the state law. We concluded that, unless some totally new approach were found, it would be impossible to create combined structures under two or more unrelated contractors, one of whom had been awarded a school construction contract on a competitive basis, while the other had obtained independent financing and was developing the nonschool portion of the structure for his own account.

Even if the problem of conveying air rights over proposed schools to private developers could be solved, or a successful auction procedure developed, it was difficult, if not impossible, to envision the school and nonschool portions of a single, combined-occupancy structure being separately owned, designed, and constructed, with different architects, engineers, and prime contractors and subcontractors all working simultaneously on related elements of the same structure without any single, centrally responsible entity. Such a venture would be extremely unpredictable—and hence extremely risky—for the private developer of the nonschool portion. Beset by such problems, the inherent advantages of combined-occupancy, multi-purpose structures are lost.

One alternative involves the leasing of school space in existing or proposed private buildings. While this approach has been used to some extent in New York, it is subject to the limited availability of suitable space in the desired locations, or the ability and willingness of private developers to acquire land in such neighborhoods and build structures designed to meet educational requirements. Even this alternative turned out to be fraught with legal obstacles.

We needed, in short, a drastic way to cut through the multiplicity of laws, ordinances, charter provisions, and governmental jurisdictions. Thus, we came to the conclusion that the desired objectives could best be accomplished through creation of a new public corporate entity (commonly called a public authority) that would be: (1) authorized to finance school site and construction costs through the sale of its own tax-exempt bonds and notes; and (2) able to provide, through contractual agreements with private developers, for the construction of new schools in combined-occupancy structures containing other privately owned, revenue-producing facilities.

Actually, the use of public authorities to finance and construct public or quasi-public facilities is nothing new. The rapid increase in the number of such authorities over the past twenty years has been in direct proportion to the need for increased capital construction at costs exceeding limitations on public debt, and the desire to cut across jurisdictional lines and statutory barriers in order to get a job done somewhat more rapidly than the normal glacial pace of government permits. What was new in our proposal, however, was the inherent partnership between government and the private sector in the financing and development of a single structure containing both public and private ownership and public and private uses.

Understandably, our original concept went through a series of modifications, additions, and compromises during its rather perilous journey through the various levels of state and city officialdom, and in the state legislature. It emerged, at 1:25 A.M., on the last day of the 1966 legislative session (having been amended twice on that day alone), as one of the most complex legislative enactments of that or any other session.

The final version of the act creates a nine-member public authority consisting of the president and four other members of the Board of Education, and four members appointed by the Mayor of the City of New York. By requiring a three-fourths vote on all important decisions, the act insures effective control of the authority—or "Fund" as it is called—by the appointees of the Mayor. The act requires also that certain other actions and decisions of the Fund be subject to approval by various municipal officials—including the Corporation Counsel, the Commissioner of Real Estate, the City Comptroller, and the Budget Director.

In addition to these controls, all matters of site selection, design, and construction of the school portion of combined-occupancy structures are subject to approval by the Board of Education, which must also approve the architectural concept of the nonschool portion.

In order to assure fair and open procedures for the selection of project developers and full disclosure of the terms of their agreements with the Fund, the act provides for prequalification of eligible developers by the Board of Education and approval by the Board and the Corporation Counsel of all contracts, leases, and other agreements between the Fund and its developers.

In an obvious, but perhaps shortsighted, effort to prevent the Fund from usurping the entire school-construction program of the city and the Board, the act limits the Fund's activities to the development of schools in combined-occupancy structures and prohibits the use of its debt-free financing to build separate school structures. Oddly enough, this amendment was insisted on by the Civil Service Union representing certain of the architectural and drafting employees of the Board of Education. Such are the realities of political life!

The most controversial—and potentially damaging—amendment to the original bill obligates the private developer of combined-occupancy structures to let separate, competitive subcontracts for the plumbing, heating, and electrical work. However, since these subcontractors will each be responsible to the developer, who is free to negotiate the general construction provisions of his agreement with the Fund, the major advantages of a single, negotiated contract, with a single entity having the responsibility and authority for timely and satisfactory completion of the work, are preserved.

The law is complicated, but it at least makes combined-occupancy structures possible. Here, then, is how it works.

Upon the acquisition of a site by the Fund, the Fund conveys to a qualified developer the rights and interests necessary to permit him to build the desired type of combined-occupancy structure. This will contain, as a separate but integral element, classrooms and other school facilities designed to the specifications of the Board of Education.

Construction of the school portion of the structure is financed by the Fund through the issuance of bonds or notes. The nonschool portion is financed by the developer independently of the Fund.

When the building is completed, the school portion is released, reconveyed, or leased back to the Fund, with the developer retaining either a fee or leasehold interest in the air or space rights above the school. He also keeps title to the nonschool improvements constructed by him in these spaces. The Fund, which at all times continues to hold fee title to the underlying site, then leases or subleases the school portion to the City of New York for use and occupancy by the Board of Education. In effect, the Board of Education rents the school facilities from the Fund. Such rent cannot exceed the average cost or rental of comparable new public school facilities in the city.

The developer, in the meantime, pays to the Fund the "fair market value" of the air or space rights and other spaces occupied by the nonschool portion of the structure. He must also pay—and this is crucial—an amount equal to the real-estate taxes that would ordinarily be payable on such air or space rights and the nonschool improvements in them. This provides revenue that would have been lost if the site had been used for the school alone.

Complicated though all this may sound to the layman, it is immeasurably simpler and more elegant than the impossible maze of restrictions that made combined-occupancy schools impossible until now. By setting up this new public authority, and giving it the power to deal with developers in the private sector on fair terms, the state has given urban educators a vital weapon with which to attack the problem of inadequate school facilities. Only time will tell how well this weapon will work and how useful it will prove to be in other communities as well.

Advantages

The New York City Educational Construction Fund has been designed as an institution with sufficient built-in flexibility to serve a range of municipal purposes—while serving education first. It is my strong conviction that the Fund will continue to be, for the foreseeable future, an exciting tool for urban improvement.

Let us look at some of New York City's problems on which the Fund will make an impact.

First, there is an acute shortage of land. Most visitors to the island of Manhattan see New York as a vertical town. To many of its residents who live in the other four boroughs and spend an hour each morning traveling to work, New York is a vast horizontal town, built out to its borders. The city is running out of sites for all kinds of construction. It must make maximum use of those that are still vacant and those scheduled for rebuilding. The Fund's program will thus aid the city by stimulating combined uses of land and creating air-rights sites for construction.

Second, rising standards and increasing costs of municipal services make it imperative that the city preserve and enhance its tax base. Yet, wherever most publicly owned facilities (such as schools) are built, the land is removed from the real-estate tax rolls—a major source of the city's income. The Fund's program will create income-producing properties above tax-exempt schools.

Third, the city's fiscal limitations inhibit capital construction at a time when its economic and civic health demands an improved physical plant, especially for schools. The Fund's financing is not a charge against the municipal debt, which is limited by the state constitution. Its program, therefore, promises more schools, built faster, because the schools it finances need not be balanced against claims for other capital construction.

Fourth, the city's economy and its social vigor are linked in a common need for an increasing supply of commercial space, an expanding housing inventory, and more and better educational facilities. To put it simply, the best interests of the individual and society are served by jobs, homes, and schools. The potential for the ghetto, especially, stirs the planner's imagination. Applied with social skill, the combined-occupancy concept could become a way of advancing racial integration by attracting whites into currently segregated, nonwhite areas to avail themselves of schools, jobs, and housing, all located in the same building complex.

The Fund's program will provide combined facilities in an uncommon relationship. The school will be operated by the Board of Education, but owned by the Fund. The facilities above the school will be operated and owned by private enterprise. The intimate association of schools with the adult world could produce unexpected benefits. Middle-income apartments combined with elementary schools could cement an identity of interest between parents and teachers. Office buildings combined with high schools could offer an ideal setting for the Board of Education's "co-op" program, which provides experience training together with skills training. High school students will now be able to work and attend school on alternate weeks in the same building, perhaps encouraging employers to participate in the school curriculum. The relationship of schools to business can be expected to raise our sights even higher in motivating and training youth for careers.

The Fund is an instrument of government known under New York State law as a "public benefit corporation," and more commonly identified throughout the country as a "public authority." It has the power to raise funds by selling bonds and bond anticipation notes to the investing public. So far, it differs in no important way from other public authorities. However, the Fund has two unique sources of income, which will enable it to provide schools at little or no cost to the city. The Fund will receive payments for the use of air rights over the school in the form of either annual income or capital, depending on whether air rights have been leased or sold; in addition, it is authorized by statute to receive payments equivalent to the normal real estate tax on the nonschool portion of the building during the forty-year life of the debt on the school. User lease payments—that is, rentals for the schools—will be required only when a decision has been made, for social or other reasons of public interest, to undertake a combined-occupancy structure that is unable to support the debt service on the school.

The idea of payments in lieu of real estate taxes is novel, to say the least. Its inclusion in the statute makes the entire concept workable, with no real loss to the city. First, unless a facility is built above a school, the school site goes off the tax rolls; second, after the school debt has been paid, the facility produces direct income for the city by paying the normal tax; and third, the shortage of sites suggests that many of these commercial and residential facilities would not be built—at least, not within the city—unless the air rights available under the Fund's program provided the site. In effect, the Fund's program is likened to miniature urban renewal projects without requiring either federal or local cash write-down.

It is, moreover, worth mentioning that the tax-exempt bonds and notes of the Fund are expected to prove easily marketable. They are backed by an unusual security feature—a first lien on state aid for education to the City of New York. No one expects that a call on state aid will ever be made, but the bondholders will be able to clip their coupons, secure in the knowledge that interest and principal will always be paid. From our point of view, this security feature assures us that the Fund's bond and note issues will be able to maintain a competitive position in the market place with those of long-established public authorities.

In this pioneering program, the private developer plays a key role. He is going to pioneer with us in developing and operating compatible uses of the air space over schools. He will have to have experience and ability in school construction, and in the construction of commercial or residential buildings as well, for the combined-occupancy structure he undertakes will be designed and built as a single project.

In most instances, the Fund intends publicly to invite developers to offer proposals. School sites considered appropriate for multiple use by the Board of Education and the Fund will be advertised. Proposals for development of those school sites with combined-occupancy structures will be invited, reviewed, and the best proposal selected. The Fund will base its decision on several factors, including the compatibility of the air-space use with the school itself and with the neighborhood, its financial feasibility, and how well the proposed plan serves the city's long-range social and economic needs.

A few exceptions to public invitation as the chief method of selecting a developer may be made—in instances when a developer has a legal interest in an appropriate site, or, even more rarely, when he has invested considerable money in developing an imaginative design or a novel use concept.

Like all innovative programs, there is much that is tried and traditional in the Fund's program, and a part that is new. For New

York City, synthesis of these elements, old and new, has produced a method of multiple site use to accomplish important objectives.

One may question whether the idea is adaptable to other cities. At present, we in New York do not believe it is necessarily appropriate even to every section of our own city. It may, however, prove a workable tool wherever a city needs an expanded school building program but is inhibited by financial limitations from undertaking it, and wherever a shortage of sites is preventing the construction of commercial and residential facilities necessary for economic growth.

The program is urban-oriented for the skyscraper city. It could one day be made adaptable to suburbia, where scarcity of land is beginning to be demonstrated in the gradual replacement of the one-family house by the two-story garden city, and the two-story garden city by the multistory, high-rise city. It may never be appropriate for exurbia, where the village is only now replacing the farm, and the borders of metropolis are beyond the horizon and this century.

But here in New York City, in 1968—and in the years we see ahead—the Fund's program is a practical way to build the schoolhouse in the city.

16. The Concept of the Education Park

by Cyril G. Sargent, John B. Ward, and Allan R. Talbot

Cyril G. Sargent is a Professor of Education at the City College of New York and president of the CORDE Corporation, a nonprofit organization devoted to community research and development. Dr. Sargent was a member of the Harvard faculty for fifteen years, during which time he served as the director of the Center for Field Studies. He later joined the State Department, where he was chief of the Urban and Educational Development Division of the Alliance for Progress. He is the author of *Educational Administration—Cases and Concepts* and the author or director of school studies, many of which have focused on urban school systems.

John B. Ward is president of Design Management and a director of the CORDE Corporation. A former vice president of Caudill, Rowlett & Scott, architects, he has also served as a vice president of the Corning Glass Works Foundation and a former chairman of the board of education in Corning, N.Y. He is a past president of the New York State Citizens Committee for the Public Schools.

Allan R. Talbot, director of the Urban Policy Center of Urban America, Inc., has served as administrative assistant to Mayor Richard C. Lee of New Haven and as a director of Community Progress, the New Haven antipoverty agency. His book, *The Mayor's Game*, is an account of the politics, programs, and personalities involved in the attempt to rebuild New Haven. He served as consultant to the New York City Housing and Neighborhood Improvement Task Force and directed the study of the education park carried out by the CORDE Corporation for the U.S. Office of Education.

NOTE: This chapter and Chapters 18 and 19 were adapted in large part from the publication A *Report on the Education Park*, issued by the CORDE Corporation, a nonprofit consulting organization.

The education park is not a new idea. As early as the turn of the century, Preston Search, then Superintendent of Schools of Los Angeles, proposed a "school park" for that city. Search, an admirer of John Dewey, was also greatly influenced by European educational practices. He felt that a healthy farm environment, away from smoking chimneys and congested urban conditions, could lead to "unconscious instruction," through the inclusion of such units as a zoological garden, a museum, and a miniature ranch.

Search proposed a 200-acre site which would house the entire school population of Los Angeles in separate but related buildings. The sketches he produced in his book *The Ideal School or Looking Forward* showed gardens, ponds, a school transportation system, and a plan for each school to be a "community by itself and under one management."

He also presented his argument for the school park in financial terms. His theory, frequently cited today, was that Los Angeles tax-papers could save money if the antiquated schools in the central downtown area were to be sold, and land purchased and schools constructed on a 200-acre site on the outskirts of town. He did not, however, discount the idea that the school park might result in increased costs. Search argued that the park would probably save money; but if it didn't, the better education would be worth the increased price. As he put it, "After all, what are we living for if not for our children?" He said also, "The people are not tired of taxation for the schools, but they are tired of taxation without returns."

Search emphasized that his school park would be more than a traditional educational institution—it would be a cultural center, library, vacation farm school, and a meeting place for people of all ages.

Preston Search was obviously well ahead of his time. He called for ungraded instruction, individualized comments by teachers instead of grades, and student seminars. He also proposed a teacher-pupil ratio of one to twenty-four—a revolutionary idea at a time when the average class had more than fifty students.

The basic themes Search established for the park—a pastoral school setting, the school as a community center, and the park as a means of educational innovation—recurred in school planning during the early part of the century. In one way or another, these found their way into a number of specific proposals for variations on or prototypes of the park idea.

In 1928, Radburn, New Jersey, a model community of 25,000 in the New York metropolitan area, provided for a small-scale variation of the education park by combining generous amounts of open space and community recreation facilities with new school construction. The town plan called for a neighborhood development scheme in which 600 families were to be "grouped around interior parkways [park areas], which will be about half a mile long and the width of a city block and in which will be located a school, playgrounds, tennis courts, and community rooms."

At just about the same time, Wallace K. Harrison, the architect, and C. E. Dobbin, Superintendent of School Buildings in New York City, claimed that big cities had only two options: either to put school buildings in a park, or to place schools on top of skyscrapers.

Through the years, the park idea persisted, though the realization was minimal. In the 1920's and 1930's, the emphasis was on coordination of school sites with parks and playgrounds. Later, there was the "campus plan," which advocated a community school in a park setting, to include museums, art galleries, concert and lecture halls, gardens, zoos, water areas, and theaters.

A step-by-step reconstruction of the many variations on the park idea is not intended here. Through the years, however, there were instances of both theoretical park planning and concrete site proposals. By and large, expressions of the park *idea* have been more numerous than actual, physical plans. Here are a few examples:

During the Depression, the Detroit schools proposed school complexes housing 6,000 to 10,000 pupils each, ranging from elementary to high school. One of these, the Roosevelt-Central Complex, was built originally on one site to effect savings on heating costs.

In 1939, Glencoe, Ill., completed a "community-park school" on a 10-acre site. This was a school designed for adults as well as children, and it included a 1,000-seat community auditorium among its facilities.

In 1946, Virginia and Edward J. Matson proposed a school and community center of "fixed and movable" buildings in a garden setting of parks and playgrounds. They proposed a single site for all students from nursery school through junior college. This theoretical site plan was never realized.

It was not until the 1950's that the education park was once more thought of as an economy measure—one of Preston Search's basic arguments back in 1894. Charles Colbert, an architect for the New Orleans school system, proposed a plan for "school villages." He named two goals: first, to effect economy in the building of much-needed schools in the overcrowded Negro slums of downtown New Orleans; second, to provide a superior education program for more than 9,000 students. He hoped that this plan might even bring about some degree of integration—quietly and discreetly. His vision was of a "suburban park" that would provide specialized instruction in a beautiful setting.

Ironically, the only part of Colbert's proposal that was eventually adopted was his suggestion for its site—90 acres in the outlying Gentilly area. The project, completed in 1958, cost slightly over $4 million—about one-third of the projected cost of the originally proposed school village. It was designed to serve about 4,000 students, instead of the 9,000 Colbert had envisaged. Called the George Washington Carver School Park, it now serves 8,000 local Negro pupils in what is basically an oversized—and overcrowded—neighborhood school.

A recent and more successful park endeavor is the Nova Education Park in Broward County, Florida. The Nova park is essentially a physical expression of an educational idea; it is not designed as an economy measure, a community center, a means of providing fresh air and open space, or for any of the similar reasons frequently cited as guiding the park concept. The park is a total education center. An effort has been made to establish strong communication between students and faculty of all the components. The key to the Nova park is an educational research center, which works closely with the teaching staff in establishing educational goals and providing in-service education. The research center and an elaborate television network are planned as the main elements in the entire system.

The Nova park is still under construction. The elements already completed include two elementary schools, an administration building, a senior high school, a junior college, and the beginnings of a new technological university. The students are to be given considerable latitude in charting their own educational programs.

The Nova program provides interesting insights into the potential of the education park, but it has limited applicability to the needs and problems of the larger urban school systems. The school is open on a voluntary basis. It is being developed on an abandoned airport in a rural area. It is faced with no significant racial problem—at least in terms comparable to those existing in Northern cities. Even the Florida climate offers a unique impetus to successful park operation, not only as an inducement to teachers but by removing the problems of inclement weather which, in Northern cities, can make it difficult to move children and teachers.

The New Orleans and Nova education parks are the only two recently built, large-scale parks in operation, although a score are being planned or proposed in other communities. A smaller-scale education park was recently opened in Acton, Massachusetts.

In every case, the shape and organization of the current park proposals reflect specific local needs. In Syracuse, New York, for instance, a prekindergarten-through-fifth-grade park is being planned to strengthen the elementary school program. In East Orange, New Jersey, a kindergarten-through-twelfth-grade park is proposed to replace, eventually, all the schools in that city. Quebec City in Canada is building a kindergarten-through-twelfth-grade park to provide needed new school space in that city. Guelph, Ontario, has completed parts of its 3,000-pupil recreation and education complex. In metropolitan Toronto, the Stephen Leacock Educational Complex, to be completed in 1969, will accommodate pupils on a 7-3-3 plan.

Pittsburgh is planning large high school parks, connected by pedestrian malls to middle and elementary schools located in the surrounding neighborhoods. Albuquerque is considering four primary and middle school parks for 13,000–20,000 children each. St. Louis is looking into the feasibility of a metropolitan education park for all levels. Berkeley feels it has the equivalent of a high school park already, and is exploring a kindergarten-through-eighth-grade park.

From the park proposal of Preston Search to the park planning under way today, the concept has been shaped by the needs and conditions of the community it was to serve. Those needs might be for more open space, educational innovation, community centers, economy, or, in the context of today's problems, school desegregation and integration. Certainly a major impetus for contemporary park planning is that numerous educators, planners, sociologists, and community groups regard the park as a viable alternative to the neighborhood school, which, in its present form, is generally regarded as an obstacle to school desegregation. One of the foremost proponents of the role of the education park in integration is Dr. Max Wolff, who also advocates using the park as part of the "fundamental reorganization of the school system" and "the renaissance of the center city."

The park must also be measured against the need for other improvements in public education. School desegregation is part of a larger issue of educational quality. The park, if it is to be an effective school form, must provide, or at least hold the promise of providing, a higher quality of education than is now possible in smaller scattered-site schools.

And behind this new interest in the park lies an interesting irony. The park, originally developed as an anticity device, must now be evaluated in an urban context as a means, together with other planning tools, of improving the physical condition and quality of life *in* the city.

The park concept has been fluid, shaped by local conditions and often defined in terms of goals, not ingredients. It is significant that, for all the enthusiasm it has generated, few education parks have actually been constructed.

The only two fixed characteristics of the education park are its large size and its consolidation—of age groups, teachers, and facilities. Today the concept is seen as the road to integration, higher educational quality, and cost economies. But when one attempts to relate these goals to the characteristics of large size and consolidation, one encounters questions as well as answers.

A large school complex or facility, when compared with smaller neighborhood schools, has a greater potential for the racial integration of its students. The neighborhood school draws from a restricted geographic area which, in the city, is quite often characterized by a preponderance of one ethnic group—Puerto Rican or Negro in most inner-city neighborhoods. The larger the attendance area, the greater the chance for student diversity and for flexibility in feeder patterns.

Education-park advocates feel that the park, through size and consolidation, can overcome the disparities in facilities and staff that can exist among numerous, smaller schools on scattered sites. In this sense, size is viewed as encouraging equal educational opportunities, a key issue in school desegregation efforts.

A large school complex can offer advantages to a school system that takes its desegregation responsibilities seriously, but it provides no discernible attack on the root causes of segregation. The causes of school segregation are obviously more complex than the size or location of a school. The school population, at best, can merely reflect the population of the city as a whole. In most cities, the population trend is toward an exodus of the white middle class and the in-migration and often ghettoization of Negro and Puerto Rican families.

Schools can and do play a role in determining where people live and the resultant population composition. But that role is just one part of broader considerations involving the availability and quality of housing, jobs, transportation, recreation, and commercial facilities.

In recent years, urban school administrators have learned how fragile, temporary, and frustrating school desegregation efforts can be when they are made in a planning vacuum—that is, without the involvement of other agencies. The local public housing or urban renewal agencies—to cite two of many examples—have just as much influence on who goes to what school as the man in charge of attendance boundaries.

The education park can be nothing more than an interesting idea if it serves an area undergoing unplanned and undirected population changes. Similarly, the park or parks can be rendered impotent as far as integration is concerned if planned for a city becoming predominantly nonwhite and having no discernible or effective public policy to maintain diversity.

There are areas of a city with sufficient stability to allow the park to achieve its potential for school desegregation. There are others where, without awkward gerrymandering of boundaries, the park would result in segregation on a mammoth scale. There are, in fact, some situations where a smaller school would be a more effective means of school desegregation—such as neighborhood renewal areas where the planning and economics of new housing would result in the integration of a new neighborhood school built under the plan.

It is how the school relates to total planning that counts; the size of the school must be dictated by the planning situation.

Any large city is composed of widely divergent sections with equally divergent social and economic conditions and planning opportunities. The choice of school size cannot be governed by generalized claims but by what works to achieve desegregation through joint planning and action.

The relationship of size to educational quality varies; it all depends on the conditions of the comparison. The needs of a community, the condition of the schools it now has, and the kind of new schools it plans to build must be kept in mind. This was the consensus of a panel of nationally known educators convened to help us gauge the merits of the education park. Their opinions seemed to reflect their own mental comparisons with their own school systems. "An exciting educational idea," one called the park. "A circus," said another.

Generally, the panel was favorably disposed. A few liked the park concept simply because it was unusual. Others favored it because the concept had generated enthusiasm, and enthusiasm for any idea, they felt, was at least as important as its intrinsic merits. Most of those who favored the park felt it had the potential for "flexibility" in school planning and programming.

The panel found it difficult to see how the park's size would provide for greater instructional advantages than could be achieved in a 4,000–6,000–student senior high school, or a large (1,500–1,800) intermediate or (900–1,000) elementary school. What they did see were advantages in consolidation of facilities, age groupings, and teachers. The presence of different levels of schools on a common site could lead to a greater continuum in guidance, increased vertical mobility for students, more comprehensive teacher education, and more specialized instructional space. No one was prepared to say that the park was an exclusive path toward the kinds of guidance, mobility, teacher education, and specialized space he thought desirable. Rather, they felt the park could remove a chief obstacle to their attainment, namely the geographic distance normally separating smaller schools and their staffs and facilities.

All members of the panel treated the problem of size with respect. The chief concern was that the park might potentially become an unworkable monolith. Experience with educational institutions of 10,000 or more, which is the scale most contemporary park proposals call for, shows that this size can lead to a breakdown in communications. Ironically, the large size and consolidation that could bring about program flexibility in a park could also lead to administrative inflexibility. Perhaps there is no precise limit on size except for that imposed by our human capacity to deal with it—and this is a fundamental problem of our time.

The basic question posed by the panel is a question that goes unanswered in most park proposals: At what point in size does the park present its maximum advantages? Beyond what point do the advantages of the park diminish and the disadvantages of large size take over?

Many, if not most, of the tangible educational benefits of the park flow from the efficient space utilization that a large student body makes possible. As schools are clustered on one site, they begin to share underused facilities, such as the auditorium. This increases utilization, decreases the cost per child, and parlays the savings into specialized space for new or expanded programs. For example, two elementary schools located on the same site can share one auditorium. The saved space can be devoted to a use neither school could have had if separated. This new use could be anything from a prekindergarten center to a larger school library. As one combines four or seven or nine schools, space utilization increases and the planning options increase to include highly specialized facilities and equipment. This could well mean expanded or unique programs.

As we studied the educational specifications for schools in three cities, we learned there are limits to these windfalls. In some schools, there is a real question, for example, whether these institutions actually need more science laboratories, language centers, remedial reading rooms, or similar instructional space. There is already pressure to build large schools or to cluster schools to provide for increased space utilization and for specialized space allocations. In other words, many of the instructional advantages of a larger school are already being tapped. A larger library or more specialized libraries could be one result of a park. Generally, however, the park would lead to the construction of facilities that a traditionalist might well call nonacademic—such as swimming pools, concert halls, a museum, a fully equipped dental and health clinic, a teen lounge, or a television studio.

Two questions arise at this point: How crucial are such facilities to the education process? Assuming they are crucial, how large does a park have to be before it can contain them?

On the first question, debate is often heard on whether a school system should be providing music facilities, dental care, elaborate recreation programs, swimming, and the rest. In the suburbs and some areas of the city, the debate has meaning because there are alternatives available. A child need not depend on the school for strictly nonacademic activities and services. But many of the city public schools have inherited these responsibilities by default, and debate over whether the schools should provide recreation, or health care, or after-school activities is hollow. If the school does not provide such programs, particularly in low-income areas of the city, then it is often likely no such programs will exist.

The school certainly has an interest in and is directly affected by parental attitudes, a child's diet, his health, his physical activity, and his creative outlets. Such nonacademic considerations influence his school performance. And when this influence is a harmful one, the provision by the school of lunch programs or comprehensive medical care must be considered relevant to the education process.

Increasing the role of the school in the life of the child is one of the advantages of the park most underlined by park proponents. But, just as there are limits to how much a park can provide in instructional programs and space, so, too, are there practical limits to how much a park should do in nonacademic, community-related programs and facilities. There have been proposals for the park to serve as a center for concentrated community services and for recreational and cultural programs. While this may be economically feasible and desirable in a park, it is increasingly recognized that, in many cases, community service centers must be convenient to the people in order to be effective. There is a welcome trend toward locating many service functions where people congregate—at transit stops, in shopping centers, or right on neighborhood streets through bookmobiles or other vehicles. The established success of storefront libraries, neighborhood employment centers, and other such programs must be taken into account in park planning.

Another key aspect of the park's role in other than purely academic matters is its relationship to the community it serves. Any school's responsiveness to the needs and problems of the community is influenced enormously by how the school is administered—how free its administrator is to shape the school's organization and programs not according to some abstract master plan but in the light of actual daily conditions.

A common criticism of city schools is that they are often too rigid and bureaucratic. There is more than a geographic distance between those who set policy, hire, and pass on budget matters in a downtown office and the teachers, principals, and parents who work with or are involved in the schools. The size of the city school system and the distance separating schools are basic components of the problem.

One reform, which has often been suggested, is that principals, with the increased involvement of teachers and parents, be given much greater authority for their schools, even to the point of hiring their own staffs, administering separate school budgets, and establishing their own curricula under an over-all system guideline.

An education park can logically provide this kind of administrative autonomy. The park will require considerable freedom and flexibility in establishing relationships among administrative staff, teachers, pupils, and parents, if only because the downtown office would have no exclusive wisdom on these matters. Indeed, we feel, if the park is not regulated under administrative arrangements based on considerable park autonomy, a school system would be passing up one of its great potential benefits. By creating a large school unit on a self-contained site to replace separated, small school units, the park hurdles one of the great obstacles to logical and controllable decentralization. It would also put administrators, teachers, and special service personnel in closer contact with each other.

How big, then, does a park have to be? How big, that is, before it pays off in the potential for administrative decentralization, or specialized instructional space, or in after-school and community-related facilities?

It all depends on the community. The Nova park has been designed at a 5,000-pupil capacity. The New York City school staff has found that the specialized instructional areas and grade combinations they desire can be achieved in a 10,000-pupil park. In Baltimore, our study showed that significant increases in instructional space can be achieved in a 6,000-pupil park. The size of a park will be determined by the kind of instructional program and related school programs a school system wishes to provide, and what it is willing and able to provide in its scattered-site schools. The residential density and ethnic distribution of a city will also play a role. And related to the question of size will be the economics of park-scale construction.

Preston Search was probably the most forthright of the park enthusiasts when it came to economy. In effect, he said the park would probably save money; but if it didn't, it was worth the increased costs. Our engineering and cost analysis agrees with Search's ideas as far as physical facilities are concerned. The economics of the park are based on size. Size creates economies that save money. Size also creates complexities that cost money. In most cases, the economies of size will at least be equaled by the costs of the complexities.

The economies of size flow from greater space utilization, which results in decreased costs per pupil. In a school complex, opportunities exist not just to maximize space utilization within a school but to remove certain duplications. Auditoriums, cafeterias, assembly areas, administrative space, and boiler and maintenance areas, for example, are facilities that could be consolidated and shared.

Large size also makes possible construction economies. Contracts for large units usually result in lower square-foot building costs because the contractor increases his base for overhead expenses and has many repetitive work items, such as forms and scaffolding. In some communities, architects' fees decrease significantly on a square-foot basis when the construction project is large.

If a park is to provide educational opportunities not available in smaller schools, however, these economies of large size would never be realized in lower costs. They would be transformed instead into specialized facilities and services. In New York City, the Northeast Bronx Park Study showed that 31,600 square feet of space could be saved in a park, as compared with five separate schools. The educational program for the park, however, called for 60,575 square feet of added instructional space that would not have been available or financially possible in the separate schools. In Baltimore, our studies showed that 29,000 square feet in assembly and food-preparation space could be transformed into additional instructional space when six schools were clustered in a park.

The complexities of large scale, at least as they apply to an education park, will also *create* costs a school system would prefer to avoid. The biggest of these will involve the movement of students, teachers, and goods to, from, and within the school.

The park will require service roads and loading and unloading areas. It will also require substantial investments in off-street parking. Normally, a school relies on existing streets to handle transportation, loading and unloading, and parking. But a park of 10,000 students, for instance, would create massive congestion and a severe blighting influence on adjacent areas if these functions were not handled off the regular streets. In all areas, this would require additional land acquisition. In dense, inner-city areas, it would also mean structured parking and loading facilities, which can be expensive. The construction of these facilities, shared by families in adjacent residential areas and by others, would probably be in the best over-all interests of the city. But someone would have to bear the costs.

The park will inevitably result in large transportation expenses. How great will depend on how much student transportation is already under way. But the added costs will have to be borne by the schools, the parents, or by public transit facilities through school subsidies.

Still another major cost factor will be the cost of land assembly and preparation. The only realistic way to compute these park costs is to consider how they would compare with sites for a comparable number of smaller schools. For example, the normal frustrations encountered in locating an adequate school site can be considerably aggravated in the search for a park site. Large tracts of undeveloped land are getting scarce. Where they exist, there is competition from other potential developers—housing, industry, commerce, or other public agencies—that may wish to keep them open. Assuming the schools can get such land, they will most likely find out quickly why the land is still open—perhaps because of poor subsoil conditions, inaccessibility, or rough terrain.

Building a park on already developed city land presents other problems, including family and business displacement. Urban renewal is the best means for rearranging existing land use, but there are few renewal projects where twenty to fifty acres or more are available for a school. Neighborhood renewal projects, therefore, would impose costly restraints on park size, site, and design. Such restraints on size and scale could easily offset any savings of a land write-down.

The issue of park-scale economy is a cloudy one, especially when considered on a general or theoretical level. Despite the claims and enthusiasm of park proponents, there are limitations, questions, doubts, and uncertainties, as we have suggested. The concept is an appealing one, but how does it hold up under real conditions? We have found that only under real conditions, involving specific planning situations, can the benefits and limitations of the education park be usefully assessed.

17. Toward the Education Park: Pittsburgh

by Bernard J. McCormick

Bernard J. McCormick is superintendent in the Pittsburgh public schools, and has previously served as both teacher and principal in that city's schools. A member of the Committee on Advanced Placement, College Entrance Examination Board, he has lectured widely on the importance and problems of advanced placement programs. In the summer of 1967, he served on the faculty of the Salzburg Seminar in American Studies.

Pittsburgh, home of various Mellons and Carnegies, a great university, and the sun-glinting towers of the Golden Triangle, has received widespread publicity for its urban renewal efforts. Less well known are its educational renewal plans. Yet these are a crucial part of the over-all campaign to improve the quality of life for all its citizens.

To understand the scope of the effort, it is important to know a few simple facts: the city puts 75,000 children through its public schools each year; another 46,000 are enrolled in parochial schools, mainly Catholic. These two vast school systems operate side by side. The city, meanwhile, is completely surrounded by independent political subdivisions, with school districts unrelated to the city school systems.

In many ways, Pittsburgh's problems are familiar. In 1950, its population was 675,000. Ten years later, it had declined by about 10 per cent. Since then, the decline has continued steadily at the same rate, the heaviest losses piling up in the twenty to twenty-nine age group. The city has lost nearly 40 per cent of its young adults, the "young marrieds" with their preschool and early school age children. It has suffered the classical flight to the suburbs of the white middle class. Today, of the total public school enrollment, fully 37.5 per cent are Negro.

In grades 9–12, Negro enrollment is presently 30 per cent—but this is concentrated in a relatively few neighborhood high schools where the percentages are higher.

These are the basic statistical elements with which leaders in

Pittsburgh are now working to change the entire face of secondary school education in the city. That "face" needs changing.

The average age of Pittsburgh high school buildings is fifty-three years. The newest was opened more than forty years ago. Structurally, none of them accommodates modern teaching philosophy or technology.

Yet five years from now, every pupil in the Pittsburgh public schools, grades nine through twelve, will attend a school that does not exist today. Five new "Great High Schools," each with an enrollment of from 5,000–6,000 pupils, will house the high school pupils. These pupils now attend twenty-three secondary schools. Construction of the Great High Schools is the first phase of a master plan to renew the physical plant of an entire city from elementary, through middle school, and through high school. The second phase of the master plan calls for the construction of several new middle schools and the rehabilitation and conversion of most of the present senior high schools into middle schools. The middle schools will include grades six, seven, and eight. The third phase, not yet on the drawing board, will be concerned with elementary school renewal.

The decision to house high school pupils in five buildings was made by the Board of Education to achieve three objectives: (1) to provide quality education, (2) to provide totally comprehensive schools, and (3) to provide optimum opportunity for racially balanced schools.

In achieving our objectives, we expect to offset the attraction to the suburbs by offering superior education in magnificent school environments to the children of young parents and by providing a trained and retrained supply of labor to the industrial and business community throughout the metropolitan area.

These are the basic goals of the master plan at all grade levels. This paper, however, will deal exclusively with the first phase, the five Great High Schools.

I define a quality comprehensive high school as one that accepts every child—the swift, the average, the slow, the richly endowed, and the handicapped—and invests its total resources equally in each to prepare him to achieve his personal goal to the full extent his talents and ambitions permit.

If one accepts the thesis that *de facto* segregated nonwhite schools are unrealistic social institutions that symbolize, in their way, the inevitability of the residential ghetto, then one must accept the integrated school as the public institution best able to prepare new generations to develop social mores compatible with the promises of a free and open society.

Those members of the professional staff of the Pittsburgh schools who have been deeply involved in the planning of the Great High Schools believe that the objectives previously stated can best be realized by building *five* high schools in Pittsburgh rather than a smaller or greater number. A high school, with enrollments at each of the four grades numbering 1,200 to 1,500 pupils, can provide a rich curriculum at several levels of pupil competence at dollar costs that are feasible. Enrollments of this size will sustain pupil membership in sequences of courses through the four years. School administrators are familiar with the improvisations that are typically used in small schools to provide a few pupils with four years of Latin or modern languages, and even four years of mathematics. A large high school provides the opportunity to support teaching and learning with such technological innovations as closed-circuit television, computer-assisted instruction, and electronic retrieval systems. Since we equate quality comprehensive education with the school's instructional potential to fulfill the needs of every high school pupil, we believe we have the best chance of providing it in a very large school plant, with many more pupils than one typically finds in schools across the country.

Pittsburgh, for years, had separate vocational high schools and so-called academic high schools. The vocational high schools, largely craft-oriented, had been losing enrollments for years. Two years ago, we began absorbing the pupils enrolled in them into the academic high schools. In some instances, the vocational schools and the academic schools were in close enough proximity to combine and share both facilities under one principal; in other instances, new spaces were created in the academic high school for vocational and technical programs. Every single high school in Pittsburgh today offers a rich curriculum of vocational and technical programs, with pupils commingled in classrooms, regardless of the program of studies they have selected. The Great High School will expand on this theme of comprehensiveness both philosophically and architecturally.

If a school system wants to provide the absolute in integration, it should operate but one school. Two schools, properly managed, would be an improvement on three. At some point in planning, a decision has to be made as to the number of schools that seems to have the best chance of achieving the stated objectives. After much study by staff and consultants, we in Pittsburgh have elected to build five.

It was also decided that our pupils would best be served in two-dimensional high schools. The first dimension would provide for the social-personal development of pupils. This function will be accommodated in a Student Center, with spaces designed to serve the out-of-classroom requirements of individual students, such as guidance and counseling, independent study, personal storage, and dining. The Student Center will be perhaps the most innovative feature of the Great High School. While physically separate, it will be related to the vast spaces provided for the second dimension—the classroom teaching-learning function. It was further decided that for the social-personal dimension, with its heavy overlay of guidance, the school would be organized into four separate houses. The teaching-learning dimension, on the other hand, would be organized into subject-area departments. In other words, all pupils, regardless of the house to which they belong, will report to a single Department of English, which will serve all four houses. The alternative to this plan would have been to provide separate instructional facilities and faculties for each of the four houses, which, in fact, would have meant building four complete schools on one campus.

It was our concern for the individual pupil that led us to the social-personal dimension and the house plan. Many of us who have worked for years with inner-city youth would agree that the social-personal development of such pupils may be even more important to their future fulfillment as adults than is their mastery of subject matter. We were also concerned with the effect of the size of school and the large numbers of teachers and pupils on certain individual pupils who, even in smaller schools, tend to become quite anonymous. The house plan is intended to minimize this probability.

Each house will be organized around an advisory unit of about thirty-five pupils, one-fourth of whom will be drawn from each grade level. As eight or nine seniors graduate, they will be replaced by an equal number of ninth-graders. Each advisory unit will be a microcosm of the total school population as to race, sex, ethnic background, abilities, etc. An advisory unit will be in the charge of a teacher-adviser, whose office will be located in his advisory group's space in the Student Center.

Ten advisory groups will compose a counseling group of approximately 350 pupils, to be served by a full-time counselor and supporting clerical staff. The counselor's office will be central to the location of the ten advisory groups he serves.

A house will comprise four counseling groups, one-fourth of the total school population. A dean will be the senior officer in charge. Each house will provide for a widening circle of group associations, from a one-to-one relationship with some thirty-five pupils in the advisory group, to 350 in the counseling group, to 1,400 in each house, and finally to the total school community.

Each house will provide its own social and political activities, such as production of a house newspaper, plays, musical events, intramural sports events in competition with other house teams, and election of student officers. Each house will become, in essence, a smaller high school concerned primarily with the social-personal development of 25 per cent of the Great High School enrollment.

The teaching-learning functions of the Great High School will be organized by departments into fifteen instruction centers. They are, alphabetically: Art, Business Education, English, Foreign Language, Mathematics, Music, Performing Arts, Personal Services, Physical Education, Resource Materials Center (Library), Science, Social Studies, Special Education for the Retarded, Technology, and Visual Communications.

The educational specifications provide for custom-designed spaces and equipment to serve the unique needs of each department. The Art Center, with its areas for sculpture, graphics, painting, ceramics, etc., will be quite different from the Social Studies Center, with its seminar rooms, movable walls for flexible spacing, and its rearscreen projection units. And both will be different from the Technology Center, with its 45,000 square-foot space to accommodate instruction in whatever courses are needed to supply trained personnel for the current demands of business and industry.

Each department will have its own satellite resource center, a teaching materials preparation room, a department head's office, and conference rooms.

The Resource Materials Center constitutes the academic nerve center of the entire school. It comprises the library and its modern complement—the multimedia section, with communications control and distribution station, television studio, listening area, previewing rooms, and recording booths.

In estimating the total enrollments of each of the Great High Schools, we have used a range of from 5,000–6,000 pupils. The 1,000 differential derives from an estimate of the use of the public high schools by the Catholic Diocesan School System. Firm commitments have been made by the Superintendent of the Catholic Schools to schedule approximately 1,000 pupils into each of the Great High Schools on a part-time basis. Some of these pupils will spend as much as a half day, every day, in the public school. Heavy enrollments are expected in foreign languages, advanced placement courses in science and mathematics, in physical education, the vocational-technical courses, and the arts. Parochial pupils will commingle with public school pupils. The problems of scheduling, even of the modular type, do not appear insurmountable, since each school will control the operation of its own computerized scheduling program. Part-time enrollment of parochial pupils is welcomed by the public schools as a significant opportunity to enhance the values of school-community integration and to maintain the racial balance in the public high schools.

The Great High Schools will be open day and night, all week, twelve months of the year. In the evenings, they will be open for adults to take credit and noncredit extension courses, for Manpower Development Training, for hobby groups, and recreation.

The performing arts center should attract amateur groups interested in music and drama. The auditorium and conference rooms will serve large and small community meetings.

If all goes well, the first high school will open in September, 1972. The others will follow at six-month intervals. Now that the educational specifications have been prepared and the architects are at work, we, on the educational staff, have four years to produce the teaching-learning specifications. These are the specifications that will describe in detail how administrators, teachers, and pupils will use the new buildings and facilities. A few task forces—which include principals, counselors, heads of departments, and teachers—are already at work on such assignments as describing the operations of teacher-advisory groups and the counselor in the Student Center, determining systems for individualized instruction and independent study, studying the implications of modular scheduling, establishing the curricular offerings of each department, and developing the uses of closed-circuit television and the electronic retrieval system. Ultimately, with the help of nationally recognized consultants and professors from Pennsylvania's universities and colleges, we will produce a series of handbooks that will give guidance to the professional and nonprofessional faculty and to the students, in order to facilitate the optimum use of new facilities. We also plan the involvement of the faculties in intensive training programs, beginning in the summer of 1969. In the fall of 1968, we will simulate in one high school a 350-pupil Student Center with ten teacher advisers and one counselor. Other simulations, if financially feasible, may be attempted during the next three years, if they are recommended by task force groups.

From the beginning of our planning, we visualized the Great High School as much more than a superb secondary school. We saw it as the nucleus of an education park, relating physically to its feeder middle schools, and they to their elementary and preprimary schools. We saw it as the hub of massive urban renewal efforts, and we saw it, most of all, as the symbol of the power of education to elevate the minds of men.

18. Toward the Education Park: Baltimore

by Cyril G. Sargent, John B. Ward, and Allan R. Talbot

For biographical information on the authors, see page 186.

In Baltimore, we had the opportunity to study the educational implications of the education park intensively. We had identified the major issues in previous studies in New York and Philadelphia, and were in a better position to investigate some of the specific advantages of the park. Moreover, the school system had taken the initiative in exploring the idea and there was no perceptible community pressure concerning the park, pro or con.

Dr. Laurence Paquin and his staff wanted us to direct our study toward the elementary and junior high school grades, where Baltimore has its greatest space and program needs. They wanted to know what educational programs and specialized instruction at prekindergarten-through-ninth-grade levels a park of approximately 6,000 students could offer beyond those planned in their smaller, scattered-site schools. The control group, for purposes of comparison, included a recently constructed elementary school and a junior high school.

The Baltimore superintendent and his staff were also interested in the feasibility of locating a park in the downtown area, closely allied in terms of planning with urban renewal activity projected for the vicinity of the Inner Harbor. They had two reasons: first, the need for new schools in and around downtown Baltimore; second, their desire for a visually prominent, strong physical role for the schools in the proposed revitalization of the downtown area. They also felt that new housing for mixed-income levels might have the potential to attract more middle-class families to the city and the public schools.

It was then agreed that the best way to test the education-park concept in light of these goals was to plan an actual park. This meant finding a satisfactory site, developing a park model, presenting ideas on the kinds of space allocations and programs it could provide, and then comparing the resulting plan, including its economic dimensions, to the control group.

Meetings with the school staff produced a list of six requirements to be met in the site-selection process. One was that the proposed park site had to be close to neighborhoods requiring elementary and junior high school space. Related to this objective was site accessibility—the location would have to be one to which a substantial number of children could walk, but adjacent to major street arteries for those who would need transportation. The third requirement was that the site had to be related to the Inner Harbor Project, a major urban renewal plan featuring new housing for mixed-income groups. The fourth was that the site had to be large enough to accommodate 6,000 students. Normally, this meant about 25 acres. (Generally, Baltimore site standards provide for 3 acres for an elementary school and 10 acres for a junior high school. A smaller site would do, assuming that we might create additional acreage through "made" land, such as structured parking, roof terraces, and covered play areas.) A fifth was that the location had to encourage school integration. The final requirement, which was really more of a hope, was that the site be highly visible so that, in combination with the park design, it could symbolize the importance of children and their education to the life of the city.

Requirements of this kind present obvious challenges, especially to those familiar with inner-city and downtown real estate. Such sites are difficult to find. They are usually expensive. They inevitably require substantial relocation of families, businesses, or both.

School sites appear to be premium-priced in Baltimore, regardless of location, and even with urban renewal write-downs. A 1965 school required an outlay of $4.00 a square foot. It was located in an urban-renewal project. City officials claim that the renewal write-down for school space in Baltimore is generally one-half the fair market value.

In the area under consideration, land costs were estimated at $8 a square foot, or roughly $360,000 per acre. This figure is based on one of the control-situation schools in a comparable location, for which land cost projected to 1968 was estimated at $8 a square foot. It was checked by estimating the density in the vicinity at forty to fifty dwelling units per acre, with average cost of acquiring and clearing at $7,000–$9,000 per dwelling unit.

The location of the park in the urban-renewal project could reduce the cost to $180,000 per acre, according to the current rule of thumb, but it was soon pointed out that local officials could provide no more than seven acres for a school in the project. At the outset, a significant economic hurdle stood in the way of an education park in central Baltimore.

The other site requirements led to a close examination of an area adjacent to Federal Hill, which overlooks the Inner Harbor from the south. This area was one of four possible downtown locations nominated by the City Planning Commission. Our studies showed that it met the basic social and educational requirements. It was adjacent to the Inner Harbor Project. Indeed, it joined the project area to the South Baltimore neighborhood, characterized by obsolete and overcrowded elementary and junior high schools, eight of which had been recommended for replacement in a school-facilities survey.

The 1980 population-projection and school-facilities survey for the area showed that the existing sound schools in South Baltimore and adjacent areas had a capacity of 800 students. An estimated 4,600 children would be enrolled in the elementary and junior high schools, resulting in a shortage of 3,800 spaces. Of the 3,800 students for whom new school space had to be provided, it was estimated that 3,200 would be white and 600 nonwhite. This projection was for South Baltimore and immediately adjacent neighborhoods. It took into account the net impact on the population of planned public improvements in the area, including highway construction and new moderate- and upper-middle-income housing in the Inner Harbor Project. The students would be within three-quarters of a mile of the site under construction. Therefore, most of them would be within walking distance.

Despite the deteriorated condition of its school plant, much of the housing in South Baltimore is sound. Much of its population is stable, and many of its families are white and have lived there for generations. It has a high percentage of blue-collar workers and a great deal of manufacturing employment in nearby plants.

While the park site could handle the school needs of South

Baltimore, it would by no means serve only that area. Its development into a park with a capacity of 6,000 students and its relationship to the Inner Harbor and the downtown area make it a neutral site related more to downtown as a whole than to any adjacent neighborhood. In other words, a park in this location could draw on the substantial white population of neighboring areas as a firm basis for school integration, but it would still have the capacity for an additional 2,200 students, giving it a city-wide role. School administrators could draw students from other areas where existing elementary and junior high schools are overcrowded or segregated.

The site is also highly visible and accessible. It has a commanding view of downtown Baltimore and the harbor. It is served by major arteries. Its accessibility is further enhanced, although its development potential is complicated, by the fact that three interstate routes—195, 170, and 183—converge along the borderline between the site and the Inner Harbor Project. Indeed, part of the site was included in the proposed land acquisition for the highways, presenting obvious complications. But it also offers some interesting planning opportunities.

The first of these stems from a growing concern in Baltimore about the impact of the interstate system on the city's landscape. As much as any other city in America, Baltimore has shown increasing sensitivity over the problems that can be caused by highway construction. This applies not only to displacement of families or businesses, disruption of local traffic patterns, and removal of valuable real estate from the tax rolls, but also to the visual quality of the new roads and how they relate to local planning objectives. In Baltimore, the convergence of the three interstate routes will take place at one of the most prominent points in the city. The roads will cut through the base of Federal Hill, a cherished local landmark, and then rise to bridge the harbor area. An account of the local controversy over how the bridge should be designed would by itself form a brisk chapter in any book on city planning.

The sensitivity and concern over these three routes is evidenced not only by local officials but also by the State Roads Commission, which has engaged design consultants to advise on road planning. These consultants have been given a relatively free hand to work with such devices as air-rights development over the highway to help the Commission relate its highway construction to local planning objectives. The result of this local and state government concern is a readiness to entertain ideas on how the road construction can be combined with other developments to maximize the public return on the expensive highway acquisition and alignment, and to minimize the disruptions—visual, social, and economic.

In the case of the Inner Harbor and Federal Hill area, we were encouraged to see what could be done with air-rights development to satisfy the school-site requirement set forth by the education staff, as well as to meet the physical and visual objectives of local planners. To many of the planners, this meant finding a feasible way in which the highways, as they went beneath Federal Hill, could be covered by an air-rights platform for an education park. Federal Hill is the culmination of a ridge rising 80 feet above the harbor and 50 feet above the surrounding land. Its geographical elevation affords the natural means of access to the elevated platform over the highway.

Most large American cities, including Baltimore, have examples of air-rights development. New York, the biggest city, has many. Park Avenue is one long, large air-rights development over the rail lines leading to Grand Central Station. The FDR Drive and the Brooklyn-Queens Expressway include a number of examples. In Baltimore, the New Charles Center Park and the school playground for P.S. 57, for example, are built on air rights. Air-rights development is not new or radical.

Traditionally, air rights have been most feasible in urban areas of high density where land is expensive. Increasingly, they have been used to reduce the offensive effects of major transportation corridors. As we studied Baltimore, air-rights development of an education park met these two broad tests of feasibility, as well as the site-selection requirements. The site that could be made available through air rights is close to areas of pressing school need, and highly accessible to others. It has significant integration potential. It could make possible a school that would not only be highly visible to the rest of the city but that could take children out of the back alleys and place them in attractive classrooms. The buildings, intimate and low-rise, would look out over the city—its harbor, its commerce, its housing, its people.

Among the significant technical problems of construction on air rights are those of ventilation, noise, and vibration. Analysis showed that the mass of concrete supports, as well as the platform, would cushion the structure against sound. Experience and other studies have shown that it would be necessary to eliminate openings between the highway and the park to remove undesirable effects of noise and unsound ventilation. Forced ventilation of the highway would have to carry fumes above the roof of the school. In planning, we assumed independent support of the park platform to avoid vibration. Environmental conditions could then be superior to those of a school next to a busy city street.

The actual cost of the site—largely a platform over the highway—proved similar to the site-acquisition cost of a comparable inner-city location. The exact comparison will come later in our economic analysis. The air-rights development would also enable the city to reap the benefits of multiple land use. The city would not have to take substantial acreage off the tax rolls, relocate thousands of families and businesses, and acquire approximately 20 acres of downtown property—just for an education park. Rather, it could build its park with most of these costs already absorbed by the highway.

Following our discussions with local and state officials concerning the highway, and as a result of preliminary economic analysis, we decided on a park site built largely with air rights next to Federal Hill. Specifically, the site was composed of 1.9 acres of private land, 4 acres of land in the Inner Harbor Project, and 5.5 acres of air-rights development. With this as a start, we sought to create an additional 10 acres through the use of terraces, decking, and covered play areas. To the degree that the park site had to fulfill the six requirements set forth by Dr. Paquin and his staff, and in view of the relationship we feel the education park must have to total city planning, this site assumption was inseparable from our work on the comparison of the park to six, scattered-site schools. To those who viewed our work mainly as a comparison between space allocations in a park as opposed to those in scattered-site schools, this site decision was separable from our findings on the educational implications of the park. Our study could then be divided into two parts—site selection, including the construction of a platform over the highways, and space allocations and design for the park above the platform.

To develop a useful comparison between a prekindergarten-through-ninth-grade park for 6,000 students and scattered-site schools with equal capacity required preliminary planning for the park. We had a firm benchmark as far as the scattered-site schools were concerned—the existing educational specifications for an 800-pupil elementary school and a 2,000-pupil junior high school. We had nothing for the park except some generalized claims.

The park design created for us by Peter Paul, a partner of The Associated Architects and Planners in Baltimore, was shaped by several key considerations. Some of these were suggested by the school staff, others dictated by the previous study findings. A major consideration was to exploit fully the advantages of consolidated facilities, while achieving intimacy in their scale and arrangement. This meant keeping the units small, creating small clusters within the over-all park, and developing separate park entrances and exits for the various age groups. It meant taking advantage of the economies of scale, not only to provide larger central facilities but to centralize functions as well. Another major goal in the design was to create ample recreation space and open areas.

A third consideration was to equip the park with facilities that could not only serve children during the day but could also be available for additional community use by parents after the regular school day, thereby increasing the public return on the financial investment. We also wished to achieve a flexible use of park space, with a minimum number of fixed-bearing walls and maximum opportunities for the school staff to rearrange space. Related to this need for flexibility was a desire to investigate the possibilities for quick and economical construction that a systems approach might offer in a project of this scale. Finally, the design had to exploit the location and prominence of the site.

The systems approach to construction entails the prefabrication of basic building blocks off-site, for on-site assembly. Developing some of the ideas suggested by the School Construction Systems Development project in California, we attempted to create a basic classroom module—that is, prestressed structural units that could serve as the basic building blocks for instructional areas in the Baltimore Park.

The basic module we developed is three stories high, although it can be lower or higher. Each tier measures 30 feet by 70 feet, and encompasses enclosed and covered instructional space, as well as a terraced, protected play area. Two blocks create six classroom units of 60 feet by 70 feet, four create twelve units of 120 feet by 70 feet, and so forth. The blocks can be stacked or spread out to create considerable variety, not just in interior dimensions but also in over-all appearance.

On the Baltimore site, we envisioned the blocks stacked in a steplike arrangement facing the harbor, giving each class unit a dramatic view of the harbor and downtown areas. Each unit would have its own recreation and play space.

The basic units of each module could be prefabricated. Columns could be erected on the school platform, and decks hung from the columns. The deck would provide the floor for the upper space and the ceiling for the lower space, and would serve as a conduit for utility lines. Space within the modules would be divided by movable partitions. The only permanent walls would be those erected to form a separate cluster of school units within the park, or those that, for design purposes, might create a staggering of the modules rather than long, straight rows.

In arranging the clusters within the park, we were guided by the need to keep the scale intimate, to provide for some separation among age groups, and to encourage a school organization in which the children could relate to a building and area within the park that would serve as their "home turf."

Because of its size—6,000 students—the prekindergarten-through-ninth-grade park in Baltimore offered the possibility of multigrading—the division of the children into three-year age levels, with each level located in a separate area of the park. One possibility would be to create five "houses" within the park, organized around the following age groups and enrollments and featuring nongrading, as the following table indicates:

House	*Age Level*	*Enrollment*
A	4-5-6	800
B	6-7-8	1,300
C	8-9-10	1,300
D	10-11-12	1,300
E	12-13-14	1,300
		6,000

As the table suggests, this age division should be flexible; children aged six, eight, ten, and twelve could be assigned to the next higher house if that should seem best for their individual needs. An eight-year-old in House B, for instance, could be assigned to House C.

Under the terms of this plan, each house can be subdivided into still smaller units with which the children can achieve their primary identity. House A contains 16 units of 50 children each; House B, 10 units of 130 children each; House C, 10 units of 130 children each; House D, 5 units of 260 students each; and House E, 5 units of 260 students each. This organization reflects the size and complexity of the child's environment as he advances from house to house.

This organization translates into space relationships. House A, designed for the four- to six-year-olds, receives more space per child than any of the other houses. Its buildings would be low density, with self-contained play areas and open space, a separate entranceway, and sixteen school units. House B, for the six- to eight-year-olds, overlooks the downtown area, and is more densely developed —ten units, each containing 130 children. It, too, is self-contained, with play terraces for each unit.

With the exception of some assembly functions and specialized service programs for individual students, the children in House B would spend most of their time, including their lunch period, in the house. It is assumed that food would be centrally prepared but delivered to each house. House C generally duplicates the density and downtown view of House B, although it is anticipated that at this age (eight to ten), the child would begin to leave the house under an individualized curriculum that would take him to some of the specialized facilities of the park. In houses D and E, the density increases to five units of 260 students each. Here the children would be from ten to fourteen years old and very mobile. These children would be too old to rely on play terraces for physical education, but would walk via a protected pedestrian mall to a nearby, four-acre playing field, made available in the Inner Harbor Project. They would also spend considerable time in specialized facilities, such as the library, shops, and language and science laboratories.

The generalized site plan translates the suggested organization and spatial relationships of the five houses into proposed buildings. The building module is reflected in decks and terraces along the outer perimeter of the park. The principal physical link uniting the various park elements is a school street, designed for pedestrians only and providing access to all facilities and houses. The park has five controllable entrances, which offer separate access for each grade grouping and for over-all park security. Parking for 500 cars is provided in a structure beneath one of the elevated highway lanes.

At the very heart of the proposed model are the consolidated facilities and services that have traditionally been among the biggest theoretical advantages of the park. One of our principal assignments in Baltimore was to determine how great these advantages are. Specifically, we were to contrast the park model with its equivalent in five scattered-site elementary schools and one junior high school, using as a control group current educational specifications for an 800-pupil elementary school and a 2,000-pupil junior high school.

We concluded that the park plan in Baltimore could achieve significant increases in space utilization, as well as subsequent space reductions in food-preparation and assembly areas. In the control group, 41,000 square feet were devoted to five 350-student auditoriums and one 1,000-student auditorium. In the park, because of increased utilization, we were able to reduce this by 19,000 square feet. Moreover, the assembly space in the park could include an 800-seat music center, a 500-seat theater, and a 250-seat, audio-visual center. For food services, the control group required 64,000 square feet—approximately 22,000 square feet for six kitchens and 42,000 square feet for cafeteria space. In the park, we were able to consolidate the kitchen space and decentralize some of the dining spaces into all-purpose rooms. This produced, at a conservative estimate, a saving of 10,000 square feet, after 2,000 square feet were devoted to a school snack bar. No change was provided in the basic space allocated for teacher planning, administration, or physical education areas, although we were able to provide for increased specialization in these areas. The following improvements are available in the park with no net space increases:

1. *Physical education:* A 1,800-square-foot training pool; a 25-yard, 6-lane swimming pool; 27,000 square feet of covered, private play areas; a field house; and an increase in physical education time and space to one hour per day at 100 square feet per student.
2. *Teacher planning and facilities:* A 2,000-square-foot staff library, a faculty seminar room, a central area for social and professional meetings, and reserved off-street parking.
3. *Administrative and health services:* An information storage and retrieval center, a health suite with public dental and medical facilities, and a school security office.

Increases were made in library and instructional areas. An additional 3,000 square feet in library space and a total of 18,000 square feet in additional instructional space were provided in the park. Instructional areas were increased from 28 square feet per child to 30 square feet per child.

The park also offered the opportunity to provide community-related facilities, such as the library, the recreation facilities, the swimming pool, the three auditoriums, and a small-scale community park at the southern end of the school.

Much has been written about extending the school plant for more efficient utilization. The park as developed in Baltimore offers great possibilities for putting these proposals into practice.

For more efficient utilization of special facilities—especially physical education facilities—some programing here has been extended over a nine-hour day from 8 to 5, rather than the six-hour (9 to 3) day. Staggered class starts at five half-hour intervals from 8 A.M. to 10 A.M., with staggered dismissal from 2 P.M. to 4 P.M., might be considered.

In addition to utilization advantages, this would reduce peak loads of students arriving or departing; an average of 1,200 would arrive for any given starting period. Distributed among four major pedestrian access streets, this would reduce average massing levels for the neighborhood school. It would also permit extended day programs to provide for children with working parents. It could provide study facilities for children who may not have them at home, and encourage the use of the school for after-hours academic or extracurricular activities.

A primary reason that the park can work for the extended day is that it places responsibility for maintaining school functions on staffs—library, maintenance, administrative, etc.—rather than on individuals, as does the neighborhood school. It also offers the possibility of nonconcurrent staff hours.

Having tried to show some of the advantages of the park, we then faced the problem of cost. How would the cost of such a facility compare with the costs of the scattered schools? One assumption at the outset was that the scattered schools would also be located in or close to the downtown area where the need is greatest, and their sites would reflect high land costs.

Site-cost analysis in this planning situation is filled with potential pitfalls because of the substantial use of air rights. As already explained, this is an effort to substitute technical problems for social and political ones. By incorporating 5.5 acres of air rights over a highway, one faces substantial engineering problems, while avoiding the problems of a significant degree of expensive land acquisition, displacement, and demolition. Preliminary engineering analysis indicates that air-rights development in this case—that is, for the construction of a school platform over the highway—would cost about $600,000 per acre, or $3.3 million for the 5.5 acres.* The 1.9 acres of private land that would be needed would cost approximately $350,000 per acre, or $660,000. The 4 acres of playfield space in the Inner Harbor Project would cost approximately $700,000, assuming a continuation of the present policy of offering renewal land at half the fair market value.

* In analyzing platform costs, it was assumed that supports would follow the most economical configuration without infringing on highway alignments, that all costs related to traffic would be borne by the highway, and that all costs of platform support and earth shoring for the school would be borne by the school.

This "made land" for the park—including decks, play terraces, and covered play areas—totals 7 acres. Assuming $3.00 per square foot of added building costs for increased structure, surface, and protection required by these areas, this would involve an outlay of $900,000. In addition, 1.6 acres of public right-of-way would be needed under the park-site proposal—for which we assumed there would be no charge. This makes a total park-site outlay of $5,560,000 for 20 acres.

The scattered-site schools would require a minimum of 24 acres, assuming current site standards and construction techniques. One should also, for purposes of comparison, assume that under the scattered-site plan at least 2 acres of public land could be included. It should be further assumed that the same 4 acres of urban-renewal land made available for the park could also be made available to the neighborhood schools at a cost of $700,000. The additional 14 acres would have to be acquired privately and at the same assumed rate as the private land incorporated into the park site—$350,000 per acre, or $5.4 million. This would make the total site cost for the scattered schools $6.1 million. Although no figure will be included in this comparative analysis, it should be noted that, under the scattered-site program, 19 acres of valuable downtown real estate would be taken off the tax rolls. Under the park plan, only 5.9 acres would be removed.

It is estimated that the building construction cost for the park and the scattered-site schools will be the same. If we are in error here, we err on the side of conservatism. The control group and the park are equal in space—560,000 square feet. It is possible, for reasons cited earlier, that the unit cost for park construction would be lower because of the scale of the project. Moreover, because the Baltimore park would feature modular construction, it is quite likely that further unit-cost reductions could be achieved.

The park would involve two major cost factors not present in the control group. One is the cost of a parking structure with spaces for 500 vehicles. At a unit cost of $2,000 per space, this would involve $1 million. The second is the cost of the added equipment required for the specialized facilities in the park, which we have computed at $1,620,000, compared to $1,350,000 for the control group. The following table summarizes the cost analysis:

	Park	Control Group
Building construction cost	$11,200,000[a]	$11,200,000
Site-acquisition cost	1,360,000	6,100,000
Platform and "made land" cost	4,200,000	—
Parking	1,000,000	—
Equipment	1,620,000	1,350,000
	$19,380,000	$18,650,000

[a] This does not reflect the savings we feel the modular construction might afford.

The cost per child is $3,230 for the park versus $3,110 for the control group. Assuming that the study is accurate to about ± 10 per cent, the cost difference is not significant.

Given the specific school situation in Baltimore and the goals of the education staff in that city, we recommended that the park concept be pursued as a means of meeting the school needs of the downtown and adjacent areas. To be sure, the short time and nature of this study left many gaps in this analysis, and many questions need more detailed answers. The full data and assumptions in our work, as well as a list of the major questions we feel should be pursued further, with the help of a full-time planning consultant, were turned over to the Baltimore staff. But, given our original mandate and the time limitations, we came to the strong conclusion that the park concept makes great sense in view of the local conditions in Baltimore.

19. Linear City: Brooklyn

by Allan R. Talbot

For biographical information on the author, see page 186.

Linear City is a plan for integrating a wide variety of educational, cultural, and commercial services along a primary transportation line in a heavily crowded urban setting. Some educators think the underlying concept is one of the few genuinely exciting ideas in recent urban planning. Others think it's no more than a wild gimmick.

To understand the Linear City idea, it helps to have a little background about the CORDE Corporation, an educational consulting organization that has played a significant role in education park planning. CORDE was formed under an Office of Education grant to evaluate the relevance of the education park to school needs in New York, Baltimore, and Philadelphia.

As one might expect, New York presented the most awesome problem. The area to be studied was East Central Brooklyn. With a population of 725,000, it was no mere neighborhood or community but a city within a city, larger than Boston. Its 1965 public-school population from kindergarten through eighth grade alone was a modest 95,742. They were housed in eighty-four buildings—an assortment of schools. Some ran from kindergarten through fifth grade, others through sixth, eighth, or ninth. Some were limited to only a few grades—sixth to eighth or seventh to ninth. Two of the five communities in East Central Brooklyn had predominantly nonwhite schools, two were predominantly white, and one was showing a dramatic rise in nonwhite population.

The area's school problems were typical of those found in most cities—segregation, overcrowding, obsolete schools, and a communication gap among education officials, teachers, and parents. The details of the gap are far too complex to explain here, but, at the time CORDE entered the picture, it centered mainly on the question of how and where new schools for the area were to be built. In 1966, parents in one of the communities had succeeded in getting an injunction from State Commissioner of Education James Allen to prevent the New York Board of Education from building seven neighborhood schools for the area.

The parents claimed that the new schools would do little to desegregate existing schools and would, in fact, lead to further school segregation. The parents proposed instead that the Board should concentrate its capital expenditures on the construction of a 15,000-pupil education park solely for the intermediate grades. The children attending such a park would be drawn from existing intermediate schools that were racially segregated. These schools would then be transformed into elementary schools. Under Commissioner Allen's injunction, the school board was to take a serious look at the parents' proposal, as well as any other steps that might lead to greater desegregation than could be reasonably expected under the Board's original idea of seven scattered schools. Enter the CORDE Corporation.

The first thing we learned was that the Board's staff and the parents were coming up with vastly different conclusions from the same raw demographic data on what was happening to population composition. The Board staff saw increasing nonwhite school enrollments mitigating against desegregation, regardless of how or where schools were built. The parents, with the help of a statistician, saw increasing racial stability in the trends. To make matters worse, CORDE's researcher, Marcia Feld, discovered that the school enrollment projections used by *both* groups underestimated the probable future school population, particularly the number of white students. This tended to confirm the parents' view on racial stability, but it also created more intermediate school students than their 15,000-student park would hold. More important, the locus of student increases was a newly developing community in East Central Brooklyn, at the farthest point from the parents' proposed education-park site.

The site chosen by the parents presented other problems, too. Unknown to them, it was destined to be decimated by the proposed Cross-Brooklyn Expressway. The school planners also seemed unaware of the highway. Its alignment also crashed through one of their proposed school sites. This bit of oversight might seem extraordinary to anyone not familiar with New York.

The biggest problem inherent in the proposed highway was the physical barrier it would present between the predominantly nonwhite northern areas and predominantly white southern sections of East Central Brooklyn. Given this obstacle and the other problems, it seemed to us that our role would be most productive if we avoided mediating between the parents' proposals and those of the Board of Education.

With this background, the Linear City concept began to develop. It was based on a number of simple premises. For example, schools should be an integral part of the community or communities they serve. This may seem a bit platitudinous, but this principle, for all its simplicity, is violated every time a new school is tucked away on a back street or its doors are closed to parents, as well as children, after 3 P.M.

One of the potential problems of the education park is that it can become an awesome monolith with no physical relationship to the community or other community improvements. Some park enthusiasts inadvertently demonstrate this danger. They produce sketches of 15,000–20,000–pupil parks containing a maze of schools walled off from the rest of the city, like City College of New York or Columbia University. I shudder to think what a large park might turn into in the hands of some education planners. I.S. 201 in Harlem—New York's first windowless school—multiplied by twenty.

In sketching out prototypes of urban education parks, we attempted to show how the park could be related to a community and serve as a stimulus for its over-all improvement. In some cases, the park became a nucleus of educational facilities and a community center joined to new or existing schools by walkways and an integrated education program. In others, we positioned schools along a major transportation corridor, with upper-grade-level schools placed next to the corridor and related, smaller schools placed back in the neighborhoods. In still others, we clustered schools near or adjacent to prominent landmarks, such as a museum or a university.

In every case, we called for the park to be related to other planning and improvements, such as housing, community centers, transportation, and recreation. This is particularly important if a school system takes its desegregation responsibilities seriously.

Clearly, the power to desegregate rests with more than one city agency. The man who plans and builds housing, for example, has just as much to say about who goes to which school as the fellow in charge of school boundaries. In East Central Brooklyn, we tried to find the key to blending education with housing, community facility, and transportation planning. We also tried to find some common denominator that could join the diverse communities of the area. We discovered both in a railroad cut.

Perhaps the best-known educational landmark in East Central Brooklyn is Brooklyn College. It was appropriate that our walking tours through the area should start there. At one end of the College, just beyond an athletic field behind some tall shrubbery and fencing, was a railroad cut, owned by the Pennsylvania Railroad. The rust on the track indicated that the cut was seldom used. We discovered later that this was a main New England freight line, which was being gradually phased out.

A look at a map and a continued tour by car and foot showed that the cut traversed each of the five communities in East Central Brooklyn. Aside from whatever lingering loyalties each community had to the Borough of Brooklyn, this railroad cut was about the only thing they had in common. Ironically, this railroad cut, slicing through Brooklyn, was also the preferred location for the same expressway that would obliterate the parents' education-park site and one of the sites selected by the Board's staff. The cut ran by both of them. The reason for this preference was understandable: Use of the railroad line as a right-of-way would minimize relocation and demolition.

Once this was known, we recognized (and then urged the appropriate city agencies to recognize) that the city was about to develop a major transportation spine through the heart of East Central Brooklyn. This, we thought, was an apt description of a highway running atop a rail line. We then did a rough inventory on the major land uses along the railroad cut. There was, of course, Brooklyn College. Then, after a mile or so of substantial single and multifamily housing, there followed about 2 miles of marginal wholesale and light industrial plants. Many were abandoned, and virtually all of them were eyesores with low levels of employment. Under any sensible renewal plan, they would be relocated to an area more useful to themselves, where they would constitute less of a blight on surrounding residential areas. There were also a number of vacant sites along the cut, including the two that had formed the basis for the controversy between the parents and school officials. At the far end of the cut, in Brownsville, we located a number of potential sites for a new community college that is scheduled for East Central Brooklyn.

This inventory showed us that there was an enormous potential for school, housing, and commercial development along the cut—development with a minimum of displacement. We, therefore, recommended that this take place as part of the transportation construction through a combination of renewal and air-rights development. In short, we called for joint school, housing, and commercial development along, over, and adjacent to the new highway and submerged railroad line. This was the basis of the Linear City proposal.

The key to this plan was the conversion of the old freight line into an East Brooklyn rapid transit line; or, as an alternative, the use of one of the highway lanes for a local transit service with stops at the major points, but most particularly at the major schools built into the Linear City.

As a piece of educational planning, this proposal is basically an education park—but one that is spread along a transportation spine traversing the communities it serves, rather than built in a single concentrated location. It is really a larger-scale version of a proposal we made in Philadelphia for a linear park stretching along Broad Street, from Temple University toward the downtown core. This idea is now being refined by planner David Crane and has been included in the Philadelphia capital budgeting program.

The Brooklyn schools are seen here as a part of total community planning. Their construction would be part of the new Linear City, along with shops, recreation centers, office buildings, and new housing. Linear City, itself, is anchored on one end by Brooklyn College and at the other by a new community college. In between, there are preschool centers and special facilities—including social science, fine arts, technical vocational, physical science, and community service centers. All these schools would be jointly administered under a total educational program. They would be linked together by the local transit service to be provided as part of the new transportation spine. Children from all parts of East Central Brooklyn would be in school as soon as they arrived at the transit stop nearest their home.

There were times when those of us who worked on this proposal thought it might just be a bit too far-fetched to be taken seriously. This was a reflection not on the enormity of the problems it was supposed to solve but, really, on the paucity of the efforts we generally mount to do something about the American city. Today the Linear City concept is taken seriously, but it still faces one overpowering obstacle—the usual inability of citizens, agencies, and planners to realize that the problems of a community like East Central Brooklyn are not just education, or housing, or jobs, or transportation, or physical decay. They are *all* of these, and they must be attacked jointly.

20. Programming Play

by M. Paul Friedberg

M. Paul Friedberg is head of the New York landscape architect firm bearing his name. A member of the National Action Council for Urban America and a member of the Advisory Board for the U.S. National Committee for Early Childhood Education, he has served as a consultant to the Washington, D.C., Public Housing Authority and a delegate to the 1965 White House Conference on Natural Beauty. He has won awards from the American Society of Landscape Architects and the New York State Council on the Arts.

It is a fact that a child's personality and intellectual capacity are formed within the first five years of his life. His personality can later be adjusted through an extensive treatment, but the intellect, once arrested in its development, will never attain its full potential. It is a fact that a child's environment has as much effect on his intellect and personality as do hereditary factors; therefore, we are, to a large extent, the product of our environment, and, if a child's intellect and personality take form before his fifth birthday, the home, the street, and the playground all have major roles to play in the composition of this all-important environment.

It is also a fact that children spend as much time in the playground as they do in the classroom. Psychologists have found that infants raised under environmental handicaps display deficient learning responses later in life. Therefore, emphasis must be placed on the development of an enriched play environment that will make possible or reinforce education. Contrast this with traditional play facilities. Most playgrounds in this country are sterile and devoid of interest, stimulation, excitement, or fantasy. They are cages, which are, by and large, enclosed by chain-linked fences. They are more closely related to prisons, compounds, or stockades than to educational facilities. Indeed, in full knowledge of these facts, educators, architects, landscape architects, and planners nonetheless continue to construct wastelands that are called playgrounds. It sounds almost elementary to say that those who take responsibility for designing playgrounds must have a profound, comprehensive knowledge of the requirements of children. Yet the design emphasis until now has been placed on management and maintenance.

A playground should make for a sensitive balance between physical activity—fun, games, action, and so forth—and a learning experience that increases awareness, perception, stimulation, and motivation. It should help develop physical, social, and educational skills. It should be an environment that is entertaining, stimulating, interesting, mysterious, creative, imaginative, sensuous, fanciful, and frivolous.

Physical skills can be acquired in such a world of fantasy, discovery, and exploration—a harmonious composition of masses, planes, and voids so juxtaposed as to open a variety of opportunities for jumping, hopping, skipping, swinging, crawling, and even sitting. This is a world easily achieved by patterning it after nature and the natural movements of children. The learning of social skills can be fostered by the creation of definable places and vantage points—gathering points where children can meet, sit, and relate. These can be provided by hilltops, tree houses, cubicles, elevated flat levels separated from the main stream of activity, and so forth.

The learning experiences—cognitive education and creativity—are based primarily on trial and error. Therefore, the enriched play environment should include a world of choice and discrimination. Traditional play elements reflect a one-dimensional concept. There is, for example, essentially only one method of using a slide, swing, or a see-saw. Its action is predetermined. Therefore, the experience is extremely restricted. Once having mastered the object, there is no further development. Furthermore, traditional facilities are isolated forms that do not fit into an over-all composition.

In contrast, the slide that is built into the hill offers unlimited possibilities for ascent and other uses. The rubber ball that hangs from a play structure can be used as a swing, a climbing rope, a pendulum, and so on. There are many objects that can be used to form positive play environments: construction objects (blocks, planks, tools, and other elements of building), plastic objects (clay, sand, plaster, and concrete), discovery items (prisms, magnifying glasses, mirrors, colors, and echo chambers), and cognition tools (abacus counters, graduated sticks, blocks, measuring objects, letters, and number murals). One can also use dynamic visual forms (hyperbolic parabolas, pyramids, spheres, cubes, cones, colors, banners, and sculptures) not merely as a series of isolated forms but grouped into total compositional entities. This should not create an artificial or bizarre experience but one rooted in reality and integrated into a world or area in which it is placed. For play is a preparation for the realities of life.

A sense of refinement and perception may be created through exposure to visual experience during a child's formative years. Is it not, then, improper to subject children to a tasteless, mediocre, inferior environment? We are just beginning to explore whole new areas: continuous play, which is the physical linkage of playforms that reinforce the programmatic content of the playground; vertical play, which permits higher densities in limited areas; adventure play; dramatic play; discovery play; construction play; and so forth. All these concepts reflect the need for an enriched play environment.

The middle- or upper-class child may glean enough from his home and his street to make up for the paucity of experience his playground offers. But the child from the disadvantaged home may not. In play, as in more formal education, we have been too long satisfied with the notion that the normal is the inevitable.

21. Beyond the Schoolhouse

by Frederick J. McDonald

Frederick J. McDonald is Professor of Educational Psychology at Stanford University and director of the Heuristic Teaching Program at the Stanford Center for Research and Development in Teaching. He has served as scientific director of the Terman Gifted Child Study Program and a consultant to the Project on Cognitive Processes and Teaching Strategies at San Francisco State College. He is the author of many technical papers on learning theory and behavioral science, as well as the book *Educational Psychology*.

The problems of the urban school can best be described by considering the kind of model on which both individual schools and school systems have been built, and by considering the consequences of this model for urban education.

First, let us recall a few obvious facts. Cities concentrate large populations of children, and, despite the high rate of American mobility, large numbers of these children stay in the same geographic area over a substantial portion of their lives—in many instances, over the complete span of time during which they are in school.

Second, the interests and attitudes of these children are most influenced by the immediate local environment, rather than by formal institutions. Despite the fact that urban centers provide relatively great mobility through rapid transit systems, a child growing up on the north side of Chicago may very well never see the Art Institute, the Shedd Aquarium, or the Adler Planetarium. If such children are also financially handicapped, the probability of their moving about the city easily to use its resources is extremely limited. Furthermore, the cultural environment of the ghetto is not likely to motivate them to avail themselves of such resources.

Clearly, one problem of urban education is to create a system in which the resources of the city are intimately integrated with the educational process, so that large numbers of children can utilize all the resources of the city for their education.

Now, let us return to the model that underlies the organization and development of the American school in the urban center. The essential organizational pattern of the school system follows the "mass production" model, which has been so effectively used in Western industrial civilization. In this conception, certain kinds of units are to be produced on a systematic and regular basis. In order to produce these units, resources are concentrated in strategic locations. Large numbers of units are assembled in these locales. A school assembles 600 or more children in one very restricted physical location. Such an arrangement facilitates the processing of these children, because the resources necessary to educate them are concentrated in these areas also.

Associated with these children is a group of teachers responsible for them. These teachers are organized by levels corresponding to the levels or strata into which the children are organized. Large groups of children are broken down into manageable units called classes. The teacher serves as an administrator who checks the attendance of the children, supervises, and directs their activities, and in general manages their daily lives. In the elementary schools, teachers do this for an entire class for the length of a school day; in the secondary school, the units are more finely divided, with teachers responsible for classes organized by the subject matter to be taught in these classes. But, in the latter case, a new invention was instituted to carry out the managerial functions ordinarily carried out by the elementary school teacher: The homeroom became the unit for accomplishing the management activities.

Given a number of these units, strategically located around the city in relation to the concentration of the population of children, resources can be funneled from a larger system to each of these subunits. Thus, in over 100 years, the American school system has evolved from a single school, servicing a wide variety of students in one classroom with one teacher, to schools headed by independent administrators, to a complex school system with a superordinate layer of administrators who funnel resources to these lower units.

All of this is familiar to us as the way in which the school is presently organized. What it is critical to perceive, in my opinion, is that this is a highly efficient way of processing large numbers of students—*if* we accept as unchangeable the assumption that pupils must remain relatively immobile. Yet, this factor is *not* unchangeable. The validity of this assumption depends, in large part, on the manner in which the total city is organized. It depends on the way in which we manage the distribution of the city's educational opportunities.

Although there are many obstacles to creating new forms of organization, and although many different arrangements tried on a sporadic basis have not been successful, it should be clear that, until a new way of conceptualizing social organization in the cities is developed, it is literally impossible to modify the present organization of school systems significantly. But until we do, the effects on learning will remain relatively unchanged.

What, then, are the consequences for learning of the present system?

First, children inevitably go to school with children from their immediate neighborhood. (It is surprising that a large number of Americans regard this arrangement as an absolute good!) There is also a widespread belief that moving the child from his immediate environment creates psychological difficulties for him. While this is not improbable, neither is there overwhelming evidence that the consequences are uniformly undesirable. So little mobility has been tried that it can be said we really do not know what the consequences would be. Our dire predictions are largely speculations about what *might* happen.

Second, children are inevitably exposed to a limited range of teachers—those who happen to be assigned to their particular schools. We know that these assignments are rarely made on the basis of the kinds of children that are in the schools, and that the system quite frequently operates to funnel inferior teachers into certain areas and schools. We also know that the learning that may be accomplished in a given school is, at least in part, a function of the kinds of teachers who happen to be assigned there.

Third, the resource system is particularly unwieldy. The means and materials for extending and enriching a person's education simply cannot be shifted around a large urban area with great facility. Keeping track of items and processing requests for them is an enormous task. Bussing is expensive and sporadic.

As noted previously, these consequences result, in large measure, from our thinking of the child as being relatively immobile. The child is thought to be immobile because he is a member of something called a "neighborhood." The concept of a neighborhood is particularly fuzzy. Usually, it is a conglomeration of physical boundaries and concentrations of social and ethnic groups. The weakness of the concept becomes apparent, however, when one looks at those urban areas that are composed mostly of large apartment buildings. Thousands of people live in these buildings. These people tend to be of roughly similar social and economic class, but usually they have few ties with one another. Frequently, they have highly divergent occupational interests. Rarely is there any social complex other than that imposed by the building in which they happen to live.

Despite this *lack* of social organization, people continue to think of the neighborhood as the basic unit of social organization in the city. Moving the child out of his neighborhood is regarded with horror because, it is thought, doing so removes him from a complex net of social ties—ties that are often simply nonexistent in the urban "neighborhood."

What about the mobility of his teachers? A teacher is assigned to a school, usually on an annual basis; midyear shifts of teachers from one school to another, or even from one class to another within the same school, are regarded as undesirable because they disrupt the life of the children in those classes affected by the move. However, since the system operates on a mass-production model, this difficulty is anticipated by mass-producing teacher units who are producing standard units of a standard curriculum. Even though moving teachers creates a "dislocation" in the system, it is one that is easily remedied by substituting a comparable unit.

Again, the consequences for learning are obvious. The child will be exposed to teachers who, although they do vary considerably among themselves, are essentially cast in the same mold. Similarly, the child is exposed to a largely standardized curriculum. Although teachers introduce some variations within a standard curriculum, the range is not great. The pressure on most teachers in most school systems is to follow the curriculum.

I do not wish to leave the impression that I am denouncing or decrying the administrative model that underlies the organization of the American school and school systems. I am simply pointing to its inevitable consequences. We must recognize that many of the learning problems that seem critical today are, in large part, the inevitable consequence of this form of administrative organization. No one can talk seriously about new learning arrangements without calling for new administrative arrangements.

Let me take some examples to illustrate this point. We are all aware that there are large numbers of children who enter school with what are euphemistically called "educational" and "cultural" deficits. Such a child is "processed" through the educational system in essentially the same way as the child who comes from a supposedly educationally advantaged environment. He is confronted with essentially the same curriculum, the same kinds of teachers, and is just as tightly bound to his neighborhood school as children in socially more-advantaged neighborhoods.

We ought not to overlook the fact that this system historically guaranteed that all American children would receive an equal education. I ignore here the fact that such education is not always equal, because I wish to emphasize that, in principle, it is designed to be equal. Many of the suggestions for improving ghetto schools simply ask us to upgrade these schools to make them equal in fact, as well as in principle. But, again, note that the mass-production model of school organization inevitably forces upon quite different people the same system of schooling.

We are thus led, as a necessary and even logical consequence, to programs of improvement that are essentially remedial. Programs for culturally disadvantaged children involve greater dosages of the standard curriculum, given earlier to compensate for what the home or neighborhood has not provided in its informal and incidental education. Such programs are packaged and administered in the same way as the standard curriculum. One rather sad example is the standard field trip, which appears regularly in these programs, to see the "bay," or the "country," or some other different environment that is supposed to convey to the child a concept of a larger and more significant way of living than that to which he may be exposed. I point to this example simply to note that it is a change made within the framework of the present system. Making such changes leaves unchallenged the whole conception of the curriculum to which the child is exposed, the sets of concepts and ideas that undergird it, the means by which it is communicated, and the very places in which learning is supposed to occur.

Underlying the whole system of administrative organization that characterizes the American school is a concept of uniformity in children. Such a concept, despite all disclaimers, presupposes a commonality or similarity among children, which simply does not exist and could never exist. Although we recognize that there are wide intellectual, cultural, and personality differences among children, we essentially mass-produce a curriculum for all children. Educators are not insensitive to differences among children. Indeed, they are probably more sensitive to the range of these differences than any other group. However, the model of school organization on which the school system has been built does not provide for this variety.

Many educators are bruised by any suggestion that the schools ignore cultural, social, and intellectual differences. They point to many instances in which the school has attempted to accommodate a wide range of differences. I do not wish to belabor this point but simply to call attention again to the fact that these arrangements always operate within the over-all assumption that pupils are there to be processed. We have tried off and on, over the last fifty years, a tracking system that funnels children into classroom groups in terms of some measure of aptitude. Such a system is simply a way of refining the classroom unit, essentially leaving its basic organization unchanged. Obviously, its locale has not been changed, nor has the method of teacher assignment been changed to any great degree. Similarly, systems of flexible scheduling make greater varieties or combinations of pupils possible, but again, even flexible scheduling systems operate within the present social organization of the school.

Thus, changes in learning in the American school system depend, in part, on the extent to which the concept of educational mass-production can be criticized, evaluated, modified, or even completely abandoned. This latter point, of course, raises all kinds of disturbing questions of an economic and social nature. Such questions would not be disturbing if the present system of organization were capable of meeting the challenges that face it. But it is hard to argue that the American school system, in its present form, can produce the social and cultural changes that are essential. It is also obvious that no large-scale change can occur so long as the change occurs solely within the boundaries of the educational system itself.

Let me suggest some concepts and principles that might underlie a radical shift in educational organization.

Let us begin by making some assumptions. First, the locale of education will be determined not by the location of the child's family but by such other factors as the ability to concentrate resources in a useful way. Let us also assume that the child is not attached to a particular locale but is highly mobile, in that he may move anywhere in the city for learning opportunities. Further, let us assume that the word "school" does not describe the institution we contemplate today. I propose that we abandon the word in describing a location of educational resources. But I have no better substitute for it, and I refuse to create a jargon to describe a new kind of environment in which learning occurs. At present, the only limitation that I will accept from the present system of organization is that education will occur within and around the boundaries of urban areas, although I think this limitation is not strictly necessary, and it is only a matter of years until larger geographic areas are regarded as potential sites for educational activities. Anyone, for example, who has seen the influx of students into the District of Columbia in the spring, can hardly regard this idea as revolutionary. However, today mobility is not a standard part of the educational system; it is a luxury, a special trip, an occasion, and even a "happening."

What I propose is that the notion of fixity be abandoned, and the notion of mobility become a central concern in organizing pupils in relation to learning opportunities. Moreover, the whole notion of fixed curricula must be abandoned. If one retains the idea of fixed curricula, he will create essentially the same kinds of learning environments that exist today.

If I may be somewhat contradictory, I will adopt momentarily the term "learning center"—meaning not a place in a schoolhouse but rather a creative learning environment, which may be located anywhere in a city, and in which we may assemble any size group, of any age, with the purpose of producing certain kinds of educational changes. In order to create such learning centers, it is necessary to have—as, in fact, I think we do have—a reasonably clear notion of what constitutes desired changes in children. What I am proposing is that learning centers be designed specifically to effect these changes, but that no one learning center attempt to produce all such changes.

Let me take a concrete example. One of the goals of our society is to teach children how to interact with one another in ways that are consistent with our democratic principles. This noble ideal, as we all recognize, is only partially achieved. We have for a long time assumed that it could be achieved in schools as they are presently constituted. However, anybody who has observed recent attempts at integration must be appalled by the fact that integration is largely a matter of moving people of different cultural or ethnic backgrounds into the same building. Once these groups are inside these buildings, however, they rarely interact in ways that are likely to lead to the development of social organizations or systems that, in fact, do integrate the various ethnic groups. Nor do the children in these groups, whatever their ethnic origin may be, learn to relate to each other in ways that will make them members of the kind of society that is clearly going to evolve in this country.

If such is to be our goal, why not place these children in environments where the curriculum does not stand between them? This means that, for large portions of the school day or even of the school year, these children must be grouped so that they work on significant tasks *together*. In order to achieve a genuine social organization within these groups, they may have to be separated for very large portions of the day—and even for extended periods of time, such as weeks—from their own families or neighborhoods. Or it may be necessary that a certain portion of each day be spent in activities that require close interaction among varieties of individuals.

I do not believe that simply grouping all students heterogeneously in social studies courses accomplishes this purpose. Nor do I believe that lining them up in rows in classrooms, or even occasionally moving desks into circles to discuss social problems, accomplishes this goal.

Although I can only dimly foresee what a learning center to foster these goals might be like, I can forecast what its essential characteristics must be. It must be a center in which the learner is far more active than passive. It is an environment in which social interactions are the major forms of student activity. It is an environment in which a variety of teaching methods are used, from role-playing to group-therapy sessions, from lectures and discussions to whatever method stimulates social interaction among the individuals involved.

What would be an example of such a learning center? Its primary requirement is that it create shared experiences—experiences that develop a communality of feeling and values and foster new forms of social organization that bring a variety of people into a closer social relationship. One way of creating shared experiences is by creating group productions.

All of us are familiar with the kind of total involvement associated with the production of a play, or the creation of choral or orchestral productions. Our urban centers have tremendous concentrations of musical, artistic, and dramatic talent. Suppose that we took a group of high school students—multi-ethnic in origin, diversified in ability—and placed them in a learning center where they were exposed to the best of music, art, and drama, and where they could create their own productions. Rather than having them passively read great works of literature that treat of fundamental problems of human existence, why not totally involve them in the production of such dramatic pieces? The production of a play or a musical event, with all its associated artistic activities, is a genuine group process, requiring a multiplicity of talents and a variety of individual roles.

Assume that large numbers of children lived in this kind of environment, in which the total curriculum consisted of producing the musical and dramatic literature that we usually associate with the humanities. We would be exposing these children, through active involvement, to the finest works of our intellectual heritage. They would be caught up in a rich life that would broaden their vision and teach them to live and learn with each other.

Suppose also that, in this particular center, we concentrate individuals who not only produce for the public but who actively work with these children. They become the teachers. The children in these centers participate in real ways in adult productions. (Obviously, the degree and extent of involvement will be a function of the age of the child and other factors with which we are all familiar.) In this way, the child will share in the cultural life of the community; it becomes his life also.

To create such an environment, one has to do more than assemble adults in the ways in which they are now concentrated in the great artistic and musical centers in urban areas. Such an environment must be open to the child for long periods of time, and it must be managed in such a way that the child becomes an integral part of this environment. Note, also, that the concept of a teacher in such an environment must of necessity be changed. Similarly, many of the activities of the traditional curriculum would have to be integrated into the activities of such a learning center.

In such an environment, the process of social development, which flows from sharing common goals and working cooperatively with other individuals, is more likely to be achieved. For those who are concerned about moving the child from his immediate environment, the educational relevance of the movement is clear. For those who are concerned about greater social integration in our society, again the relevance of this educational activity to the attainment of such goals is also clear.

What other kinds of learning centers might be created? Here I must abandon the word "center" and talk about those kinds of educational activities that are best conducted alone or, as we now use the term, in independent study. Certainly, among the purposes which we have set out for ourselves, there are many that are better accomplished by permitting the pupil to work for long periods of time by himself. To any practicing educator, at any level of education, it is obvious that the system of time-blocks, within which we all operate, inhibits some forms of educational growth.

We might take the great libraries of urban centers and create around them a complex of computer facilities for individual study. Similarly, we might use some of our industrial complexes or our university laboratories as centers for extended research. I recognize that, in describing these possibilities, I am assuming certain things about the maturity of students. As a psychologist, however, I also recognize that maturity is created by the kinds of environments in which we place people and the kinds of responsibilities we ask them to assume. An elementary school child might need to be more closely supervised in periods of individual study. It is conceivable that certain age groups will be supervised most of the time. It is also obvious that the very young child is not going to be able to participate in the same kinds of activities that the older child is. New centers, fitted to his age, might need to be created for him. Those centers, however, need not automatically be located closer to home.

Another way of organizing learning centers is around the media of instruction that would characterize them. The first type of learning center, described above, is one in which instruction is largely accomplished through imitation of adult models and by participation in common activities with adults and other children. It is a process that relies only secondarily on textbooks and similar materials.

Other centers might be created around the concept of visual communication. It is apparent that a great deal of instruction can be communicated through films and video tapes, developments which have only incidentally been exploited in school systems. Again, the reason for the failure to exploit these devices to their fullest probably lies in the type of organization that characterizes the school. Currently, the video-tape mechanism must be brought into the classroom, an environment peculiarly unsuited to visual instruction.

We need to determine—and here, hopefully, we psychologists can be of real help—those kinds of learning most efficiently transmitted by visual or audio-visual instruction. We need, then, to create the kinds of learning centers in which such visual instruction can be most fully exploited.

In the foregoing list of environments—a list that is obviously not exhaustive—two principles have been applied. One is that the purposes of instruction determine the kind of learning environment that is created. This concept is not foreign to people who have been involved in educational planning. However, I have broadened it so that these learning environments are not concentrated in conventional units called schools. I have also broadened this notion to involve other segments of the community; in fact, to reorganize a community, in part, around the creation of these centers. If one is willing to go even a step further—to recognize that education is not simply something that occurs between the ages of four and twenty-four but is something that the entire community needs—the notion of learning centers can be broadened still more.

The second principle applied in these ideas is that the mode of instruction also determines the nature of the center. Again, this idea is familiar to educational planners. I have simply taken it out of the context of the present system of school organization and created the center as an independent unit, designed to achieve a specific educational purpose.

Throughout this discussion, I have systematically avoided the term "remedial education." Although the urban schools face tremendous problems in this area, schools in their present form cannot solve these problems. Nor are these problems exclusively the domain of the schools. They are problems of the total environment. Therefore, the solution to these problems must be achieved by the community as a whole. I have suggested that learning centers be created as integral parts of a broader urban environment, and that the notion of the school as a building in a geographic location simply be abandoned. If this were done, many of the educational difficulties faced by all ethnic groups would, to a large extent, be remedied, simply because the system of education would be properly geared to the achievement of its objectives. At the same time, the notion of mass-producing comparable units of educated people would, in large part, have been abandoned once and for all.

I am well aware that an immense amount of research and development needs to be done to test what kinds of learning centers are required to achieve significant educational purposes. Nevertheless, I am hopeful that changes can be accomplished. For example, the Unified School District of the City of San Jose has developed a project, in conjunction with Lockheed Corporation (with the RAND group as evaluator), to change the nature of the educational process for disadvantaged children. One of the most unusual activities in this program involved taking a group of children to the Big Sur, on the California coast, for a week of educational activities. These children were transported from a lower socioeconomic section of the City of San Jose to one of the most beautiful environments in the United States. In this environment, they lived together for the week with their teachers and with special instructors.

This particular environment made it possible to create a land game that required these children to go out in teams to survey the surrounding terrain. First, the game created tremendous interest and motivation. In addition, the activity of working together as a survey team and making decisions in this situation created a genuine group atmosphere. It was also educationally significant, since the children were learning and using quantitative and other concepts. Needless to say, the activity was tremendously enjoyed by the children, by parents who were present, and by all of the instructors—some of whom were professional teachers, others of whom were Lockheed personnel who had invented this particular game.

Here was a small model of what a larger community learning experience could be, involving parents and teachers and children in an environment specifically related to the achievement of significant educational goals. Such activities have been tried in a variety of small-scale projects in many places throughout the country. They provide us with experience indicating that if we could create the larger social organizations to support such learning activities, many of our education problems in urban centers could be solved. This was urban education occurring over 100 miles from the actual urban center. This was the education of children who lived in urban environments. These children had their entire perspective on living and learning modified in a significant way. Given an entire educational system of this character, what was achieved in those few days could be enlarged, broadened, and deepened. Such are the kinds of models of school organization to which we must turn, if we are ever to accomplish the educational achievements that our society now demands.

Index

Conference Participants

JOSEPH AMISANO, Toombs, Amisano & Wells, Architects, Atlanta, Georgia

ADRIAN BLUMENFELD, Administrator, School Planning & Research Unit, New York City Board of Education

*DR. GEORGE B. BRAIN, Dean, College of Education, Washington State University, Pullman, Washington

*CHARLES WILLIAM BRUBAKER, Partner, The Perkins and Will Partnership, Architects, Chicago

HUGH CALKINS, Attorney, Member, Board of Education, Cleveland City School District

DR. JOHN CAMERON, Director, Division of Facilities Development, U.S. Office of Education

MARIO CIAMPI, Architect, Mario J. Ciampi and Associates, San Francisco

MARILYN CITRON, Deputy Special Assistant to the Secretary, U.S. Department of Housing and Urban Development

*DR. KENNETH B. CLARK, President, Metropolitan Applied Research Center, New York City

DR. DONALD D. DAUWALDER, Associate Superintendent for Business & Assistant Secretary, Pittsburgh Board of Public Education

ANTHONY DOWNS, Senior Vice President and Treasurer, Real Estate Research Corporation, Chicago

*GREGORY R. FARRELL, Assistant Commissioner, New Jersey Department of Community Affairs, Trenton, New Jersey

DR. WILLIAM D. FIRMAN, Assistant Commissioner, New York State Education Department, Albany, New York

*DR. JOHN H. FISCHER, President, Teachers College, Columbia University, New York City

*M. PAUL FRIEDBERG, Landscape Architect, New York City

RALPH GOGLIA, Director of Community Schools, New Haven Public Schools, Connecticut

* Indicates contributor to this book.

*Dr. Harold B. Gores, President, Educational Facilities Laboratories, New York City

Dr. Edward Gottlieb, Former Principal, Public School 165, New York City

*Ben E. Graves, Project Director, Great Cities Program for School Improvement, Chicago

*Dr. Robert J. Havighurst, Professor of Education and Human Development, University of Chicago

Robert Hazen, Deputy Administrator, New York City Housing & Redevelopment Authority

*Harold Howe II, Commissioner, U.S. Office of Education

Eugene Hult, New York City Commissioner of Public Works

*Dr. H. Thomas James, Dean, School of Education, Stanford University, Stanford, California

Norman Klein, Skidmore, Owings and Merrill, Architects, Washington, D.C.

Professor David Lewis, College of Fine Arts, Carnegie Institute of Technology, Pittsburgh

Dr. James D. MacConnell, Director, School Planning Laboratory, Stanford University, Stanford, California

*Bernard J. McCormick, Superintendent, Pittsburgh Board of Public Education

*Dr. Frederick J. McDonald, Professor of Educational Psychology, Stanford University, Stanford, California

*Daniel Z. Nelson, Executive Director, New York City Educational Construction Fund

Robert Royston, Royston, Hanamoto, Mayes & Beck, Architects, San Francisco

*Bayard Rustin, Executive Director, A. Philip Randolph Institute, New York City

*Dr. Cyril G. Sargent, Professor of Education, City College of New York

*Dr. Samuel Shepard, Jr., Assistant Superintendent, St. Louis Board of Education

Dr. Neil V. Sullivan, Superintendent of Schools, Berkeley Board of Education, Berkeley, California

*Allan R. Talbot, Director, Urban Policy Center of Urban America, Inc., Washington, D.C.

H. Ralph Taylor, Assistant Secretary, U.S. Department of Housing and Urban Development

Alan Temko, Center for Planning & Developmental Research, University of California, Berkeley, California

*Albert A. Walsh, Chairman, New York City Housing Authority

Other Contributors

Alvin Toffler, Author and Consultant, New York City

Dr. Mario D. Fantini, Program Officer, The Ford Foundation, New York City

Richard Magat, Director, Office of Reports, The Ford Foundation, New York City

John B. Ward, Vice President, CORDE Corporation, Wilton, Connecticut

Preston R. Wilcox, Staff Associate, Education Affiliate, Bedford-Stuyvesant Development and Services Corporation, New York City